Praise for *The Great Race*

"To explain the scramble for the next-generation auto—and the roles played in that race by governments, auto makers, venture capitalists, environmentalists and private inventors—comes Levi Tillemann's *The Great Race*. . . . Mr. Tillemann seems ideally cast to guide us through the big ideas percolating in the world's far-flung workshops and labs. He is an inventor himself: With his father and brothers, he conceived a gasoline engine, the IRIS, that is smaller and theoretically more efficient than standard designs of the same output, and over the past decade the design has won attaboys from NASA and ConocoPhillips."

—*The Wall Street Journal*

"*The Great Race* captures the drama of a global competition for markets and new technology that is changing the auto industry and indeed the world in which we all live. It is a gripping read that takes us inside critical decisions in China and Japan and the United States. Tillemann's experience as a tech entrepreneur focused on cars, his skill as a linguist (he is fluent in Chinese and Japanese), and his expertise on energy policy enable him to bring unique insights. The result is an epochal saga of leadership, money, power, global competition, and innovation; and Tillemann tells it all superbly. Whether your 'thing' is the clash of nations or the battle for global markets—or how fast you can get from zero to sixty—you'll like *The Great Race* a lot. Indeed, you will race through it!"

—Daniel Yergin, author of *The Quest* and *The Prize*

"It is simply the best book out there on not just electric vehicles, but the complicated nexus between innovation, energy security, and smart energy policy for the twenty-first century."

—Robbie Diamond, founder and CEO,
Securing America's Future Energy (SAFE)

"Mr Tillemann, an energy expert, writes about the car guys with the grasp of an insider. This seems to have been gained from founding a company which tried to bring a low-emission car engine to market and by the rigour of having led negotiations with Detroit. Fluent in Chinese and Japanese, he is able to take the adventure to the heart of the world's other automotive powers."

—*The Economist*

"If you like cars, you will love this book. If you care about climate change, you will love this book. And if you want to find out how the United States is retaining its competitive and innovative edge in the world, in a tale that reads like a spy novel, you will love this book!"

—Anne-Marie Slaughter, president and CEO,
New America

"No one is better positioned to write this book than Levi Tillemann. This book has much to say about how governments can succeed and also fail. Above all, *The Great Race* is a Great Read."

—Peter Bergen, author of *Manhunt: The Ten-Year Search for bin Laden from 9/11 to Abbottabad* and CNN's national security analyst

"[Levi Tillemann] is skilled, and sometimes relentless, at highlighting the ability of official industrial policy to work in the public interest."

—*The Washington Post*

THE GREAT RACE

The Global Quest for the Car of the Future

LEVI TILLEMANN

SIMON & SCHUSTER PAPERBACKS

New York London Toronto Sydney New Delhi

Simon & Schuster Paperbacks
An Imprint of Simon & Schuster, Inc.
1230 Avenue of the Americas
New York, NY 10020

First Simon & Schuster trade paperback edition January 2016

SIMON & SCHUSTER PAPERBACKS and colophon are registered trademarks of
Simon & Schuster, Inc.

For information about special discounts for bulk purchases,
please contact Simon & Schuster Special Sales at 1-866-506-1949 or
business@simonandschuster.com.

The Simon & Schuster Speakers Bureau can bring authors to your
live event. For more information or to book an event, contact the
Simon & Schuster Speakers Bureau at 1-866-248-3049 or
visit our website at www.simonspeakers.com.

Book design by Ellen R. Sasahara

Manufactured in the United States of America

1   3   5   7   9   10   8   6   4   2

Library of Congress Control Number: 2015410521

ISBN 978-1-4767-7349-0
ISBN 978-1-4767-7350-6 (pbk)
ISBN 978-1-4767-7351-3 (ebook)

For my father, Timber,
who taught me how to drive and dream;
my grandfather Tom,
who proved that a life lived for others is the only one worth living;
and my good friend Dan,
who taught me how to write a book.

CONTENTS

Part II   Leapfrog

Part III   Three Crises

INTRODUCTION

H E HAD gone forty-eight hours without sleep—fiddling with springs, checking control systems. Everything was shaping up nicely, but his friends and business associates—not to speak of his wife—were starting to worry. In fact, they had been worried about the obsessive young inventor for some time. For months, Henry Ford had been coming home from work and toiling late into the night. But the wait was almost over. It was now somewhere between 2 and 4 A.M. on a weekday and Ford was expected at work in a matter of hours. But he would not sleep. Ford was intent to finish the task before him.

Outside his 58 Bagley Avenue workshop, a hypnotic rain varnished the pebbled streets of Detroit. His spouse, Clara, and collaborator James W. Bishop helped where they could. But as the meticulous engineer wrapped up, it suddenly became clear that amidst all the springs and widgets Ford had omitted one highly significant variable: a brick wall. Henry Ford had built the equivalent of a ship in a bottle, for his Quadricycle could not fit through the workshop door.

At that point Ford could have retired to his bed and returned to his machine at a later date. But Ford decided it wasn't going to happen that way. Instead, he coolly grabbed an axe and began hacking at the door frame, and then the bricks. Blow by blow, Ford demolished a sizable swath of the rented garage. It was as if he was being propelled on by some invisible force immeasurably stronger than the physical barrier before him. In his gut Ford felt a fierce urgency that simply could not be bottled up one more day. He knew there were "barrels of money" to be made from this new invention, and time was wasting.

With the wall gone, Ford turned his attention back to the machine. He covered its air intake to "choke" the engine, James Bishop helped him turn over the crankshaft, and the Quadricycle's two pistons roared to life. The thirty-two-year-old electrical engineer braced himself in the driver's seat, shifted the clutch out of neutral, and bolted forward into the dawn of automotive history. While Detroit slept, Henry Ford charged into a race that would transform the city and change the course of mankind.[1] It was the first heat in a long series of contests that would relentlessly reform society, shift geopolitics, sow fortunes, and propel the global economy far into the next century and beyond; it was the race to build the car of the future.

At the time, the automotive industry was a speculative footnote in the vast global economy. But that would soon change. The industry was impelled forward by the genius, ambition, and relentless drive of insurgents like Ford. The prize was not just money, power, or glory: it was also a chance to control the fulcrum of innovation. It was a race that would soon be dominated by America's Ford Motor Company. That ascendency continued well into the decades past World War II. But eventually, contenders from Japan, Germany, and even China would challenge American dominance.

This book is the story of today's race to build the car of the future and of the heirs to Ford's legacy. It is about how a Japanese nuclear engineer, a former Audi executive, a South African visionary, and a Dutch chemist rocked the industrial landscape of the twenty-first century. Today automotive manufacturing accounts for almost $3 trillion of economic output—more than the economy of Brazil. And the automobile's importance to growth, trade, innovation, military technology, and the environment is, for practical purposes, immeasurable. The industry is a point of national pride, a center for manufacturing employment, and an instrument of state power for the world's most technologically advanced economies—much more so than most people realize.

Now, just as in Ford's time, the ether is tinged with implacable change. The question is not if, but who and how soon? Empires—both corporate and political—are in a Great Race to build the car of the future. Victory will be found in patents, assembly lines, laboratories, boardrooms, and battery plants. The prize will again be measured in "barrels of money," but also in mastery over a rapidly expanding share of the international economy—the global market for electric vehicles.

The Great Race

I first became aware of this race seven years ago as I worked with my father on our own invention. In some ways, the parallels to Henry Ford's early efforts were striking. Like Ford, my father was a lanky polymath with a keen eye for mechanical efficiency—and he always maintained a workshop to prototype his flights of fancy and ambition. Clean energy was his passion. So much so that when I was born, he announced my birth by inscribing LEVI on a Colorado license plate and proclaiming he had discovered a "mother lode" of energy that was characterized by "fully biodegradable wastes" and "short charge times."

Around 2005, we started work on a radical new internal combustion engine design. We called it the Internally Radiating Impulse Structure—the IRIS Engine. The IRIS Engine was designed to be smaller, more efficient, and more powerful than its competitors, and we dared to believe it presaged the future of the automobile. Within a few decades, we hoped, every automaker in the world would be licensing our super efficient design.

But product development rarely goes according to plan.

One spring day a brake malfunction sent my father's Dodge Caravan careening off a steep embankment near our home in Colorado. The car's fuel tank ruptured and before it had even come to rest, the vehicle was engulfed in flames. Doused in gasoline and fire, my father kicked out the windshield, pulled himself through, and rolled away from the wreckage. He had broken bones, but those were survivable. The gasoline burns over 90 percent of his body were another story—and the heat of the blaze had also seared his lungs. Ten days later he died in the burn unit of the University of Colorado Hospital.

My father was gone, but we wanted his dream to live, so at twenty-six years old I became CEO of IRIS Engines Inc. The company desperately needed cash, and I scoured Houston, Boston, New York, and Silicon Valley for investors. By early 2007, I had recruited a new advisory board and prototyped an early version of our design. A friend introduced me to FedEx CEO Fred Smith, who was willing to give us a chance. His conditions were simple: Smith would fund half of the engine's development if we could convince one of his friends in the auto industry to go along for the other half. It was an offer we couldn't refuse. Smith even made a personal introduction to Alan Mulally, then CEO of the Ford Motor Company.

One hundred and twelve years after Henry Ford first rode his Quadricycle, I walked into a dark room of Ford's global headquarters and gave the presentation of my life. When the lights came on, Derrick Kuzak, vice president for global product development, was sitting in front of me. He asked point-blank: "Why should I spend money on this? It's very clever, but the whole industry is moving toward batteries in the next ten to fifteen years." Kuzak had more than his share of battle scars from countless cycles of product design and development, and he knew how complex commercializing the IRIS Engine was bound to be. He asked again, "Why should I spend billions and billions developing an entirely new internal combustion engine?"

I rattled off the reasons. But Kuzak seemed unconvinced. In response, he calmly sketched out Ford's technology road map for the coming decades. It started right there in Dearborn with a turbo-charged engine technology called EcoBoost and ended up somewhere in batteryland.

I was stunned.

I had spent the last eighteen months telling people why batteries couldn't succeed. We thought the industry was in a race for a more ef-

ficient internal combustion engine, but now Ford Motor Company—
the same Ford Motor Company that had crushed Thomas Edison's
dream of an electric car a hundred years earlier—was telling me that
the future was in batteries.

As the going got tough for IRIS Engines, Kuzak's casual dismissal
rang in my ears. "The whole industry is moving toward batteries in
the next ten to fifteen years. . . ." Could that be true?

I began to wind down IRIS Engines and became determined to find
out for myself. I returned to Johns Hopkins University to write a Ph.D.
dissertation on the global auto industry. As I did, I discovered that the
science, technology, and policy necessary to create a new transportation system based around electric vehicles (EVs) were overwhelmingly concentrated in three countries—America, China, and Japan.
And Kuzak was right; there was indeed enormous momentum on the
side of batteries.

I taught myself Japanese, then learned Chinese, and spent years
traveling around the United States and Asia interviewing auto executives, scientists, and journalists, touring factories and schmoozing
bureaucrats—trying to figure out how much of the EV hype (especially from China) was sustainable.

Before long, I came to understand that the rules of the global automotive industry had changed. This was not merely a race of corporate titans, but of the world's industrial superpowers seeking to
control a pivotal emerging market. Their strategies and machinations
were driven by presidents and industrialists, but also by unexpected
characters—nuclear scientists, Silicon Valley moguls, and rogue executives. It was, I realized, a new and possibly final season of the
Great Race—a race to build the car of the future.

State and Market in the Age of Carbon

In this complex, multifaceted, and global race on the circuit of automotive innovation, the metrics for victory are more than market
share, technology, or state power. All these elements come into play,

but it is also about reconciling economic growth with social transformation and public goods. History has shown it is a contest in which companies and countries cannot rest on their laurels—for the field is fierce and it is easy to fall behind. While it is indisputable that Henry Ford won the early race for mass commercialization of the automobile, by the latter half of the twentieth century Toyota and Honda were trouncing Ford in successive heats for quality, then fuel efficiency and also emissions. In many senses Japanese cars also won the hearts and minds of the American people.

But today's race is fundamentally different than what came before, in that it marks a decisive shift away from Henry Ford's oil-fueled internal combustion engine to something else. The overwhelming odds are that the car of the future will drive on electricity in some form or another, and eventually it will be less car than robot. In other words, it will drive itself. It is a race that will unfold over the course of decades, but the early leaders are already clear. Ultimate victory will hinge on technology, but also a country's internal politics and its institutional understanding of policy tools and market design. Consistency of purpose and partnership between the public and private sectors will be a hallmark of success. But luck and, perhaps surprisingly, honesty will also have something to do with it.

Rules of the Road

We are on the frontier of an exciting new age. But for America to get there will require a recognition of the powerful potential for symbiosis between market and state. As a young entrepreneur, I had little appreciation for the pivotal role of government in driving innovation within large swaths of the economy. But I soon learned that angel investors, venture capitalists, and corporations are highly attuned to the policy priorities of city hall, the state house, and, not least, Washington, D.C. While entrepreneurs and corporations animate these sectors, governments not only provide the "rules of the road," they literally and figuratively build the "roads" to drive on.* Often, the process by which these priorities and rules are defined involves campaign promises, messy horse-trading, and well-intentioned (or not) public servants trying to discern the art of the possible. Regardless of how it is made, policy is critical to the success or failure of many—perhaps most—socially transformative innovations. America must embrace this truth if we are to compete in the twenty-first century.

In the nineteenth and twentieth centuries, state intervention was necessary to build infrastructure, secure the oil supply, enable new industries like the railroads, construct and expand the Interstate Highway System, launch satellites, and create and maintain the Internet—among many other things. In the 1940s, it was a massive surge in government spending (on war goods) that jolted the country out of the Great Depression and ushered in a new era of growth. After the war, the most remarkable economic transformations were not in comparatively laissez-faire countries like the United States, but in heavily interventionist countries like Japan, where bureaucrats sought to channel public and private resources toward specific "strategic" sectors. This practice of state intervention was called industrial policy.

Eventually, industrial policy would be treated with a great deal of skepticism, or downright contempt, in America—even as state investments in research, infrastructure, and technology fueled private sector growth. But America's burgeoning hostility to the concept of state-driven economic development was the exception. Other countries, such as Japan and Germany, embraced the role of the state and used industrial policy to great effect in developing sectors like high-end manufacturing.

This American wariness of industrial policy betrays a certain historical amnesia, but it is not totally irrational. Successfully executing industrial policy is not easy. Experience indicates that state economic planning programs are best overseen by technocrats with a strategic

---

*In fact, France was one of the first centers of automotive development precisely because of the quality of its state-sponsored roads and engineering schools.

view of the long-term drivers of global trade and economic growth.
It is hard to assemble such a cadre of public servants, and even the
smartest, most dedicated, and most incorruptible analysts can be surprised or make mistakes. On top of all that, many bureaucracies have
a stifling tendency toward conservatism. But in an age of tightening carbon constraints, strategic industrial policy will be critical to
America maintaining its innovative edge. Every nation has industrial
policy—either explicit or implied. And the real choice is whether to
ignore the critical role of the state in the modern economy or seek to
apply state power strategically.

Industrial policy can be sweeping or surgical. For instance, in
2008 the U.S. government made a specific policy decision to rescue
America's automotive industry because of its significance to the U.S.
employment, technological dynamism, and economic growth. Today,
many governments around the world are pursuing sweeping reforms
that recognize the inevitability of coping with issues such as water
scarcity, air pollution, acute dependence on foreign sources of energy,
and global warming in the twenty-first century.

Such strategic programs have an especially important place in sectors that are infrastructure- and regulation-intensive—where it is
foreordained that government will play a major role. This includes
the world of telecommunications and computing—which have fed
off government-funded innovations like touchscreens, GPS, and the
Internet. But strategic government support has also been critical in
high-tech, capital-intensive manufacturing sectors such as defense,
aerospace, energy, and transportation. Within these industries, long-
term, patient research and development (R&D), investment, and
regulation are critical. Countries that act as strategic practitioners of
industrial policy will give their economies an important advantage in
the twenty-first century.

In the past, America has been extraordinarily successful at this kind
of industrial policy in areas ranging from satellites to semiconductors.
For instance, America's boom in shale gas production, however con-
troversial, is at least partially the outgrowth of government-sponsored
research, development, and subsidies targeting the vast reserves of

energy locked in U.S. shale basins. Its continued success is the result of a policy consensus in Washington around the importance of maintaining secure access to cheap, abundant energy for American households and businesses.

Today we continue to reap the rewards of these public-private innovations in diverse forms ranging from iPods to cheap electricity. But these are the successes of decades past and America has fallen behind many of its international competitors in its ability to execute strategic economic planning. Our nation's economic future will be shaped by whether or not we can achieve a more honest political discourse—one that recognizes government's critical role in promoting growth and socially beneficial innovation. The United States cannot succeed in the Great Race—or myriad other contests—without the support of a strategic and proactive government.

Market Failure and the Man on a Horse

In addition to promoting growth and providing an infrastructure for innovation, government plays another important role in the modern economy: stopping practices that might benefit an individual or firm but harm society as a whole. Balancing this intersection of growth and other social goods is a difficult task.

In a Harvard lecture room, the Austrian economist Joseph Schumpeter once brashly stated that as a youth he "set out to become the greatest lover in Vienna, the greatest horseman in Austria, and the greatest economist in the world." During a subsequent moment of humility, he conceded that he never quite made it: "Alas," he lamented, "as a horseman, I was never really first-rate." There are no definitive reports on Schumpeter's romantic prowess, but as an economist he certainly left his mark.

One of Schumpeter's most famous arguments was that a capitalist system "incessantly revolutionizes the economic structure from within, incessantly destroying the old one, incessantly creating a new one." He wrote that *Creative Destruction* was "the essential fact about capitalism . . . what capitalism consists in and what every capitalist concern has got to live in."[2] In Schumpeter's view, the goal of each business concern is to win "entrepreneurial rent" (aka profit), and that process drives innovation.

But Schumpeter himself realized that there were problems with this model. In real markets, social needs are more complex than they are in economic textbooks. So while the market rewards certain forms of innovation, it does not necessarily reward other socially desirable innovations—even the most important ones.

Further, the market does not necessarily punish those who engage in socially destructive activities. Real markets often generate significant collateral damage in the pursuit of profit. When no one is required to pay for such collateral damage (aka "negative externalities"), incentives for innovation do not necessarily align with society's best interests.[3] This is called a market failure, and there are countless examples of such failures throughout history and the global economy. Carbon pollution has sometimes been called the "greatest market failure the world has ever seen." Today it is clear that carbon-intensive sectors of the modern economy will have to change. They will have to confront this market failure in the twenty-first century. For both corporations and countries that economic reckoning will be fraught with opportunity and peril.

Billions of Cars

Across the globe, electric vehicles will be part of a much larger economic transformation. But how to incentivize this transformation is a puzzle. For buying an electric vehicle does not appreciably reduce the negative externalities experienced by a single automobile purchaser or his family. It may give the driver some level of satisfaction, but an individual doesn't reap any personal climate dividend. Light-duty vehicles (cars, SUVs, and pickup trucks) account for around 10 percent of total greenhouse gas emissions.[4] There are about 1 billion cars in the world today, so each consumer purchasing an EV can theoretically eliminate about one-tenth of a billionth part of global greenhouse gas emissions through her altruistic decision—all while putting up with a shorter range and higher purchase price. In some senses, it's easy to see why the demand for EVs is limited.

Of course, there are other benefits to driving electric. EVs are much cheaper to fuel—about $1 a gallon equivalent.* They can also have great acceleration and performance. But after a hundred years of investment in Henry Ford's oil-fueled dream, EVs face high hurdles for consumer adoption.

Manufacturers also lack incentives. Car companies rarely capture the financial returns from socially desirable R&D, which leads to underinvestment in areas like emissions control and fuel economy. So although humanity as a whole would benefit from cleaner or more fuel-efficient vehicles—or a well-executed mass deployment of EVs— the very real social paybacks of clean cars can rarely be claimed by individual companies or consumers.

Like EVs, many socially desirable technologies have been stuck in suspended animation for decades. But these abstract ideas of social benefit and harm are becoming increasingly concrete as the effects of not only land, water, and air pollution, but also climate change begin to impact our daily lives and national economies. Fires are gaining destructive force and hurricanes are getting stronger and pushing farther north. Droughts are getting harsher and flooding more catastrophic. Dependence on the international oil market is costing developed nations trillions of dollars annually and all this is happening with a rising intensity. Because of this, the EV has become unstuck in history. This is what set off the Great Race among nations to build—and dominate the global market for—the electric car of the future.

---

*Based on mileage (see the U.S. Department of Energy's eGallon for additional information).

Organization of Contents

This book is organized into three sections. The first is, for all purposes, the prelude to the Great Race for electrification. It explains the automotive history of the United States, California, Japan, and China and the precursors to the return of the electric car. It starts with the epic story of California's battle against smog, Japan's drive to build its own automotive sector—which would eventually overtake Detroit as the world's leader in exports and technology—China's return to the global economy after decades of isolation, and the explosive growth in that country's market for passenger cars.

Part II focuses on the 2000s. It shows how Japan's industrial titans and economic planners struck out to develop a new market, China's politicians chased after them, and the United States struggled to maintain its standing amidst the galloping pace of innovation.

Part III covers the 2008–2012 crises that changed the rules of the global economy and could have spelled "game over" for EVs in Japan, China, and the United States. These included the Great Recession, a crisis of the U.S. auto sector, Japan's nuclear catastrophe, and China's crisis of competence. The conclusion and afterword describe the progress of the past few years and the emergence of the autonomous vehicle as the industry's inescapable future.

This is a story filled with surprises, and at the end of it all, there are clear winners, losers, and kingmakers. It speaks not only to the transformation of the auto industry, but to the fundamental nature of the global economy. It is about hard truths, tenacious visionaries, and unreasonable men (and women); it is about who we are as a people and why and how we seek to drive innovation. It is a breakneck rally through the hairpin turns of the social, political, scientific, and economic landscape of three countries that are desperately striving to harness the power of change and lead the industrial future.

PART I

Keeping Pace

I

The New Emperor and Wan
Gang's Eco-Wonderland

I T WAS something between a cotillion ball and a ritual war dance. Like
the Beijing Olympics two years earlier, the Shanghai World Expo was
a coming-out party for China's communist leadership. Over the summer
of 2010, 72 million visitors flooded the Expo. The government spent
more than $4 billion preparing for the fair—not including new rail lines,
roads, landscaping, and other improvements to the city.

China's pavilion was a massive crown-shaped pagoda, which cost
over $200 million to build and was packed with cultural treasures.
The building loomed like a sovereign over the Expo's international
guests, and countries from around the world paid tribute in diverse
currencies. The Swiss built a chairlift that suspended visitors on an
aerial journey over Shanghai's sprawling metropolis, and in the Expo's French quarter priceless Impressionist paintings hung on display.
Elsewhere, corporate sponsors showcased the future of clean energy
and "K-pop" megastars squealed, crooned, and gyrated for the new
emperor.

To anyone with the faintest sense of context, the Chinese government was sending a clear message: the Middle Kingdom was rising; it
was to be respected and shown deference; it was building a new world
order and a sustainable empire.

The Expo also represented a significant symbolic victory for one
man, an engineer named Wan Gang, China's enigmatic minister of sci-

ence and technology. The entire fairground was a canvas for his life's masterwork: securing Chinese dominance in the global auto industry. China was about to become the world's largest auto market, and Wan Gang's obsession was to make its national champions internationally competitive.

Over the preceding decade Wan had enjoyed an improbable rise to power. Rather than joining the Communist Youth League as a young man or ascending the ranks through family connections, Wan had left China to study engineering in Germany, and made a career as an executive with Audi. After returning he had penetrated China's highest circles on the strength of his conviction that one day soon China could lead the industrial future. China, said Wan, could dominate the twenty-first-century market for electric vehicles (EVs). All this would have been impressive in its own right, but the fact that Wan was not even a member of the Chinese Communist Party made it truly exceptional.

Behind Wan's enigmatic smile—and he almost always seemed to be smiling—was an iron determination to break a century of dependence on foreign oil and Western technology. The ultimate goal was to leapfrog over Japan and the United States so that the world's big markets for automobiles would import cars and factories from China rather than the other way around. To a nation just emerging from a self-declared "century of humiliation," the prospect was irresistible. The 2010 Expo was a powerful declaration of intent: China was in the race, and they intended to win.

Against this backdrop, the EV quickly became a national hero—and a focal point of China's technology ambitions. The Shanghai Expo was the culmination of a decade of engineering and imagineering under Wan's research program at Shanghai's Tongji University. Two years earlier, Tongji's Beijing rival, Qinghua, had led a similar effort for the Olympics. But the demonstration in Shanghai was more than twice as big and vastly more complex. There were electric cars, fuel cell–powered buggies, and buses that ran on fast-charging "ultracapacitors." Almost all of these were pre-commercial—meaning they were more science project than store shelf product. But for now, China did not need to work out the messy details of building the industry—the consumer technology, economics, and business plans that would help it grow. Wan Gang and the others seemed to believe that with enough money and political pressure, those would come. What China needed for the Expo was a declaration of its ultimate potential—a road map and a compelling story.

General Motors and the Shanghai Automotive Industrial Corporation (SAIC, GM's Chinese partner) were responsible for exploring the farthest reaches of this futuristic vision. As the country's largest automakers and prominent corporate citizens of the host city they were under intense pressure to perform. They delivered. The pair presented an ornate, dizzying, transformational spectacle. China's future cars would be smaller, smarter, faster, cleaner, safer, and sexier than anything that had previously existed.

Inside the SAIC-GM pavilion was the show to top all others. Visitors strapped into five-point harnesses as an IMAX-sized movie with computer-generated imagery flew them through a bright, crisp virtual reality. Electric pods raced through the streets at breakneck speeds. Stoplights, traffic jams, and even drivers were gone. By 2030, GM and SAIC promised, China would be animated by a living network of safe, efficient, zero-emission vehicles in constant communication with each other and the environment.

In this bold new world, a blind girl could race through the canyons of Shanghai in perfect comfort and safety, secure in her personal mobility pod. Rather than drive to work, the conductor of Shanghai's symphony reviewed his scores and made last-minute preparations for the day's performance. A pregnant mother made it to the hospital just in time thanks to a speedy autonomous ambulance. This was a machine as big as a city and intricate as a Swiss watch. After the ride, a curtain rose to reveal real-life EVs—which looked exactly like those onscreen—wheeling autonomously around the building. It was quite a spectacle.

For Expo attendees, this vision of 2030 was tantalizingly real—at least until they reemerged into the exhaust-laden smog swamps of Shanghai. Inside, skies were blue and the air was fresh. Futuristic ro-

bots rocketed silently down highways lined by space-age wind turbines. But outside, the air was chewy with soot and skies were gray.
The phalanx of electric cars and buses commissioned for the Expo
stopped at a chain-linked frontier demarcating the boundaries of Wan
Gang's eco-wonderland and China 2010. Real life meant navigating
manic waves of oil-burning SAICs, VWs, Audis, and Buicks. Indeed,
the 100 million automobiles on China's roads had become a distinctly
mixed blessing. China's megacities were stifled by putrid smog and
gridlocked.

No doubt, this is why in 2009 China's government announced
ambitious plans to leapfrog the West in developing and deploying
electric vehicles. In two short years, Wan Gang promised that China
would deploy 500,000 domestically produced EVs.

But even in 2010, there were signs that this vision was faltering.
Few analysts were ready to say that the emperor—or perhaps the
debutante—had no clothes. But half a decade later, the contours
of this failure were stark. Despite an intense government push to
electrify China's cars, the country's industrial giants had fallen far
short. China was the largest automobile market in the world, but its
domestic EVs were a blush-inducing afterthought. China, with its
double-digit economic growth rates, its 1.3 billion brains, and its
$3.4 trillion in U.S. foreign exchange reserves, had aimed to "leap-
frog" into the vanguard of automotive technology and dominate the
race to build the electric car of the future. Instead, it struggled to
keep pace.

Leapfrogging Leviathans

Part of the allure of leapfrogging was the difficulty of simply catching
up. The complexity of today's auto industry should not be underesti-
mated. The modern automobile is one of the most sophisticated pieces
of technology in the world. At the turn of the twentieth century, motorized cars were a novelty—they were finicky, dangerous, and there
was a reasonable argument that the horse was a better piece of hard-

ware. But within a decade or two this had changed. After World War II, the level of industrial specialization required to integrate ever more advanced automotive systems grew exponentially. The British futurist Arthur C. Clarke once famously wrote that "any sufficiently advanced technology is indistinguishable from magic." And by the beginning of the twenty-first century, the complexity of an automobile had far outstripped the understanding of the common man.

Making an automobile that was strong, safe, durable, clean, and efficient enough to be globally competitive required legions of engineers, physicists, specialists in areas like fluid dynamics, harmonics, kinematics, materials science, and an increasingly large number of electrical engineers and computer scientists. A typical car had around 30,000 individual parts, and computing specialists were involved in everything from writing the software for the car's new onboard computers, to building robots for factory automation, to honing the advanced computer-assisted design (CAD) tools that took the painstaking job of component design out of the physical hands of draftsmen and moved it onto digital screens. About 40 percent of the cost of a luxury vehicle was for electronics, computers, and software. A billion dollars might be spent on writing code before a single car left the factory floor.[1]

Building a modern automobile required ever-greater levels of precision. Sizing for pieces like fuel injectors and various control mechanisms had to be calibrated to the level of microns—about one-fiftieth the diameter of a human hair. What's more, all these precision elements had to be designed to withstand enormous abuse, and integrated seamlessly into a package that could be shaken, rattled, crashed, frozen, and scalded for decades at a time over hundreds of thousands of miles. If one of these systems failed, the result could be fatal.

Although China had sent millions of students to the United States and flooded the American academy with aspiring engineers, programmers, and scientists, the country's leadership knew it might take decades to reach global standards. Anyway, that race was already decided. Why try to redo the past? Why not instead spend that effort on the car of the future—an electric vehicle?

The "leapfrog narrative" was powerful, sensual, and compelling. But it was also hollow—like the futuristic concept cars often displayed at auto shows. Underneath a Ferrari exterior, it had no guts.

Today, China is the world's auto behemoth. But it still lacks the expertise to be an industrial superpower. It is losing the technology race to smaller, better-organized, and more nimble rivals. Japan and America lead the world in developing the cars of tomorrow—a new generation of electric and autonomous vehicles. But that is only half the story, because China is not really losing to Washington or Tokyo. It is losing to tiny groups of strategically minded technologists and regulators in Sacramento and Kanagawa. In California—a state whose entire population is smaller than commonly accepted rounding errors for China's citizenry—a clutch of indefatigable policy activists and techies have spent two decades grappling with Detroit, trying to force this revolution. And their efforts are finally paying off. In 2012, Tesla Motors' Model S—conceived and built in California by the pugnacious visionary Elon Musk—was anointed "car of the year" by *Motor Trend* magazine. *Consumer Reports* called the "S" the best car it had ever driven. The all-American Chevy Volt was similarly acclaimed as *Consumer Reports'* highest consumer satisfaction vehicle and repeatedly topped J. D. Power's consumer appeal survey.

On the other side of the world, in Japan, this revolution was sparked by a different sort of iconoclast: a nuclear engineer at the sprawling Tokyo Electric Power Company (TEPCO) named Takafumi Anegawa. It was Anegawa who laid plans for the world's first mass-produced consumer EVs. While Tesla has taken the crown for the world's coolest car, Japan has raced ahead in building and deploying a people's EV. In 2012 Japan manufactured almost three-quarters of the electric vehicles sold worldwide. By 2013, an American could lease a Japanese EV for less than $200 a month and fuel that car for a small fraction of the cost of a gasoline- or diesel-powered vehicle.

Today in Japan and America, the futuristic world of transportation portrayed by Shanghai's GM-SAIC Expo is actually much closer than most realize. Not only electric but "driverless" autonomous vehicles are within sight. The transition to electric and driverless cars will

usher forth a step change in both quality of life and economic pro-
ductivity and potentially be the most transformational social development since the World Wide Web. It will change the way we live and
many of the fundamentals of the global economy. That's why America, China, and Japan are in a white-hot race for the future of transportation. Indeed, the petroleum-free EV and what *Forbes* called the
"Trillion-Dollar Driverless Car"—those autonomous mobility pods
from the SAIC-GM Expo—are just around the proverbial corner.

Of course, there will be winners and losers. Some countries and
companies will inevitably move faster than others. And part of this will
depend on the sophistication of a country's car, battery, and technology companies—it certainly does not hurt to have a giant like Google
or Nissan as a national champion. The leadership of individual innovators, activists, inventors, and dreamers is also key—and a focus of this
story. But success also depends on the role that governments take in
strategic planning, and their competence in executing policies to encourage investors, banks, entrepreneurs, and businessmen to build the
economy of the future and invest in sunrise industries like EVs.

A Brief History of the Global Automobile

Few technologies have been as economically important and transformative as the automobile. Cars first appeared around the turn of the
twentieth century, assembled from extra bits of the bicycle and car-
riage industries. These wheels were mated with electric motors, tube
framing, and steam or spark ignition engines. For the first half decade
or so, electric vehicles were actually produced in larger numbers than
those powered by internal combustion engines. Electric taxi fleets
trolled the streets of major cities across the United States.[2] These taxi
companies witnessed speculative run-ups in valuation that looked like
something out of the dot-com bubble. Thomas Edison was also in on
the game. He—and many of his contemporaries—poured a decade's
effort and piles of money into developing a competitive EV. But by
1910 Ford had won. The advantages of liquid fuels had overwhelmed

the battery, and for a century the history of the automobile was the history of oil and internal combustion. Oil and its derivatives, such as gasoline or diesel, could hold much more energy for a given volume or weight than could any contemporary battery. Additionally, gasoline-powered cars could be refueled quickly, and that fuel was fairly easy to transport—though it was certainly dangerous.

By the 1910 model year, Ford was producing nearly 20,000 Model T's annually.[3] By 1927 that number had skyrocketed so that there was one car for every five Americans, and more than 50 percent of American families owned an automobile.[4] Even during the depths of the Great Depression, automotive sales fluctuated between about one and three million units a year.[5] With growth came consolidation, and by the 1930s the international auto industry was dominated by three giants: Ford, General Motors, and Chrysler.

Each of these companies ensured global ascendancy by harnessing the powers of oil, internal combustion, and economies of scale. Because their method of manufacturing was basically Henry Ford's concept, it was often called "Fordism." The strategy was to build one product in one color that was cheap, durable, and appealed to as wide an audience as possible. The momentum of this process came in the form of an "assembly line," which moved chassis along an escalating series of workstations—where employees would attach a fender or fasten a headlamp—until the final product was complete.

That approach allowed Ford to achieve what one scholar called "low prices, which kept falling"—in other words, economies of scale through mass production.[6] Ford's prices were so low that the company sold not only to poor rural American farmers, but to exotic markets like Tokyo and Shanghai, all at very competitive prices.

Ford's great rival, General Motors (GM), also practiced mass production. However, GM did not do so with the same single-minded zeal as Ford. GM was originally the amalgamation of many smaller automotive nameplates, which led it toward diversified mass production, product differentiation, and eventually planned obsolescence. This strategy was dubbed "Sloanism" after the company's managerial genius, Alfred P. Sloan Jr.[7]

Like oil, autos became militarily important. In World War I, new weapons like the "cistern" (eventually known as the tank), motorized troop transports, and other weaponized vehicles proved decisive to victory.[8] Three decades later, during World War II, America was clearly dominating the race for motorized wheels. Through this lens Japan and Germany's decision to declare war on the United States is almost unfathomable: the Allies industrial hegemony was absolute. Combined, Japan, Germany, and Italy produced about 437,000 vehicles in 1938, while the United Kingdom alone produced 445,000. At the same time, the United States was producing 3.5 million automobiles.[9]

After Pearl Harbor, the U.S. automotive industry became the beating heart of the "arsenal of democracy." So vital were the auto companies to the war effort that federal agents occupied their headquarters—leading the aging and, by this point, slightly deranged Henry Ford to believe they were trying to kill him.

Chrysler was the largest tank producer of the war, and together Ford and Willys-Overland produced 2.5 million military trucks and 660,000 of their iconic "jeeps." In total, the auto industry built some 4,131,000 engines (including 450,000 aircraft engines and 170,000 marine engines), 5.9 million guns, and 27,000 aircraft for the war effort—crushing the Axis against the anvil of U.S. industrial might and establishing the military prerequisites for a new Pax Americana during the latter half of the twentieth century.

After World War II, the market for automobiles roared and it fueled the astounding growth of America's suburbs. But in 1965, Ralph Nader put the brakes on this unfettered expansion when he published the book *Unsafe at Any Speed*, which caused a sensation in its treatment of the dangers of modern cars. This as much as anything symbolized the beginning of an arms race between auto producers and regulators—in safety, efficiency, emissions, and quality—that continues to this day. Fixing the problems outlined in Nader's book would not be easy.

From an environmental perspective, the most serious problem was emissions. For a long time, engineers did not really understand the alchemy of internal combustion that dictated how emissions were formed. Since it was impossible to see—or even measure—certain aspects of internal combustion, the process was two parts science, one part artistry, and a dash of luck. From the 1970s on, government regulations forced carmakers to apply new rigor to this issue of emissions. Enormous progress was made in controlling toxic exhausts, dramatically improving air quality and human health across America and much of the industrialized world. New standards set by the Environmental Protection Agency (EPA) were so strict that engine specialists said EPA stood for the "Employment Protection Agency"—their work would never end. In California, the effects of pollution were particularly severe. In fact they were so severe that the state set a goal to end this incremental tweaking of the internal combustion engine by eliminating it completely. The heart of their strategy was electrification. In other words, California wanted to reexamine the battery and its potential.

Over the past eighty years, batteries had changed. But most were still based on the same chemistry Edison's competitors used in electric cars before World War I—lead acid. The first electric vehicles from California were almost entirely powered by a new generation of lead acid batteries. However, by the mid-1990s, a more power-dense chemistry called nickel metal hydride (NiMH) came to market. This chemistry had a relatively long history, but from a commercialization standpoint, its fundamental breakthrough came in the 1990s from a Michigan-based entrepreneur named Stanford Ovshinsky and his company, ECD Ovonics.

Born in Ohio to immigrant Jewish parents in 1922, Ovshinsky was a consummate outsider. His father was a Lithuanian-born scrap metal dealer, and as a young man Ovshinsky himself had started his career as a lathe operator. Ovshinsky's formal education went only as far as high school, but the public libraries were a fitful schoolroom for such a subversive genius. His self-directed study nurtured a deep streak of intellectual independence.

Long before the oil shocks of the 1970s, Ovshinsky understood the environmental and geopolitical dangers of relying too much on oil to fuel an economy and set out to find alternatives. Together with his wife, Iris, he set up a "storefront lab" that eventually grew into the publicly traded company ECD Ovonics. At Ovonics, Ovshinsky invented a new family of semiconductors, hydrogen fuel cells, and thin-film solar cells. The *Economist* magazine called him the "Edison of our age."

In the automotive space, his most lasting contribution was in batteries.[10] Ovshinsky received funding from the U.S. Department of Energy (DOE) to develop his company's NiMH technology. The Ovonics battery held significantly more energy than its competitors—it was "power dense"—and could dispense that energy quickly. In other words, it was "high power." In many ways, it was a game changer and served as the basis for every hybrid electric of the late 1990s and early 2000s.

At the same time, a few manufacturers (such as Mitsubishi) were also beginning to experiment with lithium-ion batteries—which were originally developed in Exxon's labs, and first commercialized in portable electronics by Sony. But that chemistry still had safety and performance issues to work out. It was subject to what one industry executive called "the old 80/20 rule, the last 20 percent of the progress takes 80 percent of the work."[11] They did not come to dominate the EV market until the mid- to late 2000s. By that point lithium-ion batteries had already become integral to laptop computers, cell phones, recorders, and other electrified mobile devices.

This new generation of batteries was a game changer for EVs. There were diverse lithium chemistries: lithium magnese–oxide, lithium cobalt–oxide, lithium iron phosphate, etc. While these were expensive and still lacked the energy density of petroleum, with a strong policy boost, some additional research, and mass production they held out the prospect of servicing 90 percent of the day-to-day transportation needs of the global public. With mass production, these batteries might also be economical in the future—especially if costly petroleum was pitted against cheap electricity.

Another boost to EVs came from the hybrid electric vehicle. The concept of a superefficient hybrid electric vehicle—a car that recap-

tured energy, stored it in a battery, and recycled it to the drive train—
had been around since at least the 1890s. In 1977, Earth Day founder
Denis Hayes wrote that "[t]he physicist's conception of the efficient
vehicle is one that operates without friction. At a steady speed on a
level road, it would consume no energy. Energy used for acceleration
would be recovered during braking; energy used for climbing hills
would be recovered when descending . . . car manufacturers could
approximate the physicist's ideal much more closely than they do."[12]

However, it took a politician, not a scientist, to get the hybrid car
off the blackboard and into the labs of the major automotive manufacturers. A Clinton administration effort sought to marry cutting-edge
research from the Department of Energy's National Labs system with
the practical needs of Detroit. The Partnership for a New Generation
of Vehicles (PNGV) aimed to build an 80-mpg family sedan by combining high-efficiency diesel engines with hybrid systems.[13] Spooked,
Japanese automakers took a leap of faith over the hybrid abyss.

Toyota's Prius and Honda's hybridized Insight both provided
valuable technological learnings. But it was the Prius that truly took
flight.[14] In addition to technical knowledge, the cars also generated a
potent "halo effect"—convincing American consumers that Japanese
automakers cared more about the environment than America's domestic manufacturers. In Japan, the effect was no less pronounced. For the
first time, new college graduates ranked Toyota as Japan's most desirable company to work for.[15] By 2010, the Prius was Japan's bestselling car, and by 2012 Toyota had introduced an entire line of hybrids
branded under the Prius nameplate. The car's success familiarized
Toyota with the basic elements of EV drive systems and normalized
the idea of battery electric vehicles for the international consumer. For
Toyota's competitors—American, European, and Japanese—the Prius
became the "big green monster." It was an industry standard against
which they could not hope to compete and it nurtured an inescapable
inferiority complex. By the mid-2000s Toyota's dominance had com-
pelled others toward a strategy of aggressive innovation to bypass the
era of hybrid vehicles—and the internal combustion engine.

Henry Ford built his first "Quadricycle" in a tiny garage. But by the end of the twentieth century, the days of garage bench manufacturing were long gone. Building a world-class automobile was now among the most complex industrial endeavors of the global economy; building just an engine manufacturing line might cost $2 billion. Sophisticated automotive companies had two armies of engineers: one devoted to designing the cars themselves, and another entirely focused on optimizing the thousand-legged manufacturing machine synonymous with automotive production. For new pretenders to the field, such as China, breaking in would be a challenge. For all car companies, the technology leap toward electrification was daunting.

Winning the Race

The world is building a new energy economy. In the future, much of the investment and capital that would have gone to fossil fuels extraction and imports will be redirected toward manufacturing and services. It is not too much to say we are running a race for the future.

Today America confronts serious challenges in securing its place among a fiercely competitive field—one that will likely be dominated by rising Asian giants. But too much of America's private sector rises and falls on the basis of quarterly profit reports, and many companies have abandoned the basic R&D that begets long-term innovations. The U.S. government is not doing much better. It is hamstrung by slow-moving institutions and contentious politics.

To dominate a twenty-first-century economy, to win this race, America will have to change—and to some significant degree that change will have to be political. America must learn to be goal-oriented, tactically flexible, and driven by long-term macroeconomic trends rather than short-term political or financial interests. In many ways such a philosophy is nothing new, but represents a return to the mode of operation that supported America's economic greatness over

most of the twentieth century. With smart, strategic leadership, the
United States can again tap into unparalleled forces of entrepreneur-
ship, innovation, and creativity. In spite of recent challenges, America
is not out. It still has the potential to lead the world today and for
decades to come—and it sometimes draws strength from unexpected
places.

2

California Rules

How One State Began a Global Technology Revolution

I N 1990, somewhere near Astoria, Oregon, fifty identical military vehicles snaked their way up a misty coastline. The all-terrain beasts had a unique profile. They were squat, wide, and spectacularly muscular—the bulldog of the automotive world. Not far off, a steely-eyed observer spied the parade and silently closed in for a better look. "Look at those deltoids; look at those calves," he declared in a thick Austrian accent. He inspected the vehicles at close range and was soon infatuated. Arnold Schwarzenegger, a former Mr. Universe bodybuilder, undoubtedly saw something of himself in the brawny HMMWV—or Humvee. He had come to Astoria to shoot the movie *Kindergarten Cop,* but Arnold now had another mission: he wanted a Hummer.[1]

Years earlier, the HMMWV—or High Mobility Multipurpose Wheeled Vehicle—had been designed for the U.S. Army by a division of the American Motors Corporation (AMC). But the all-terrain vehicle truly exploded into the public consciousness during the successful Persian Gulf War campaign of 1990–91. Its place in the American psyche was about to get much bigger.

After an extended negotiation, Schwarzenegger succeeded in procuring the object of his desires. But for a variety of reasons the world's first nonmilitary HMMWV was not street legal—for one, it came fitted with a machine gun turret. So the muscleman spent $100,000 transforming his new HMMWV into a battle tank fit for the streets of Los Angeles. By 1993, he had helped drive development for a new commercial model and anyone with $43,000 to spare could get in on the game.[2] Arnold's Hummer came to epitomize the gas-glugging America of the 1990s.

But six hundred miles south of Astoria, a group of West Coast bureaucrats was laying plans that would eventually help sink the Humvee and drag an unwilling automotive industry in precisely the opposite direction. Over the previous decades, beating back air pollution had become one of California's top political priorities. And because California was the largest auto market in the country—and one of the biggest economies in the world—the state's air quality problems quickly became a central focus for the global auto industry, whether the industry liked it or not.

The California Air Resources Board (CARB), which was responsible for clearing California's sullied skies, spent decades forcing automakers to design, build, and deploy technology that Detroit and others said was "impossible." CARB often did this by coaxing and cudgeling American automakers into compliance. And they frequently encouraged Detroit's Japanese rivals—who were eager to please California's emissions bosses—to outflank America's industrial giants.

But ironically it was GM, scions of the Hummer franchise, and not Toyota or Nissan, that eventually convinced California a zero emissions vehicle was a real possibility and set America on the road to electrification. When GM showcased a sexy electric concept car called the Impact at the Los Angeles Auto Show in the early 1990s, they gave CARB its perfect weapon against atmospheric grime. Almost two decades later, Arnold Schwarzenegger would become an almost menacingly aggressive champion for EVs.

It all started on a scorching summer day in 1949 with another European transplant—a chemist at the California Institute of Technology named Arie Haagen-Smit.

The Desolation of Smog

It had been a busy morning. Professor Arie Haagen-Smit was extracting the juices of six thousand pounds of pineapple and perhaps he was beginning to feel a bit overwhelmed. It wasn't quite lunchtime, but Haagen-Smit had earned a break. He wanted to get out of the lab.

As a chemist, Haagen-Smit was world class. In the 1930s he had taught at Harvard, but he was lured to Caltech in 1940. His passion was analyzing the chemical composition of plants: their smells, tastes, and healing powers. Haagen-Smit was something of a fixture on campus. He was ruggedly handsome and well liked, with a scientifically conservative bent. Perhaps his foremost quality was a piercing integrity and evenhandedness. It was a temperament that likely helped him in his scientific pursuits. Haagen-Smit had a long list of discoveries to his name—including the flavor components of wine, garlic, and even THC, the active compound in marijuana.[3] But now it was pineapples, and Smit was obsessed to know just what produced the fruit's distinctive flavor.

But as Haagen-Smit stepped out for a breath of fresh air he smelled—even tasted—something repulsive. His mouth and lungs were filled with searing, chemical-laced smog.[4] The man was revolted, but the chemist's curiosity was piqued.

This kind of weather had become commonplace in Southern California, and the phenomenon was intensifying—it was even destroying some of his plants. But the source remained a mystery. Haagen-Smit brought the problem to his colleague Arnold Beckman, and they started discussing various explanations. Some people said the smoke was produced by backyard incinerators or the manufacture of women's pantyhose—a relatively new phenomenon that had coincided with the onset of the unsightly haze. But neither scientist accepted these explanations. Researchers at Stanford and across California had spent half a decade trying to track down the secrets of smog, but all had failed. For his part, Beckman thought Haagen-Smit could do better.[5]

One of Beckman's other associates was Louis C. McCabe. Two years earlier, McCabe had been made the first director of the Los Angeles Pollution Control District. Theoretically, McCabe bore responsibility for dealing with Los Angeles's air quality. But despite the fact that he had a strong background in the sciences, a staff of almost fifty people, and a significant budget dedicated to addressing the problem, neither McCabe, nor anyone else, knew how to control the smog. For no one really *knew* where it came from—though McCabe himself suspected the city's oil refineries played a role. But the politics of smog were already compelling. It wasn't long before McCabe's honeymoon as director was over and he was being pilloried by the local media for his inefficacy. McCabe could not find the smoking gun. But figuring out the source, and ideally a solution, would make him a hero.

McCabe now wanted action. What he did not want was to fund some long, plodding, inconclusive academic study on the possible explanations for Los Angeles's atmospheric soup. So when Beckman asked McCabe to fund Haagen-Smit's investigation, he rejected the idea outright. The process might drag out for months, or even years. Yet after a few months of spinning his own wheels, McCabe changed course.[6] His methods weren't working and although McCabe's erudite speeches on the problem of smog could draw an audience, they weren't getting the job done.

For his own entirely nonpolitical reasons—mostly intellectual curiosity and the damage being done to his plants—Haagen-Smit was just as keen to get started. There was no handbook for where to begin, but the canny scientist devised a plan.

On a pea soup day, he set up a massive fan to draw "30,000 cubic feet of Pasadena air" through an industrial freezer. The frigid air shed its moisture and Smit distilled this synthetic dew into a few tablespoons of vile brown sludge. He subdivided those elements, analyzed the components, and discovered that the California air was suffused with "organic peroxides."[7]

The source couldn't have been more obvious if the finger of God had etched the word *cars* into Haagen-Smit's microscope. These "peroxides" were known eye irritants and they were responsible for the stinging sensation that smog brought along with it. The "hydrocarbons" were not the product of pantyhose or rubber plants, but the unburned gasoline being dumped into the atmosphere by the exhaust pipes of millions of internal combustion engines. The sun was baking these compounds, oxidizing and transforming them.[8]

The evidence was right there, and it was irrefutable.

As far as Haagen-Smit was concerned, he had done his job. He would have likely closed his books, returned to the lab, and refocused on pineapples. But fate intervened. A large group of oil and gas companies decided that Haagen-Smit's results ought to be refuted—they were too damaging. When McCabe's successor, the new head of the Los Angeles Pollution Control District, announced Haagen-Smit's results to the media, it created quite a stir. So the anti-Haagen-Smit consortium funded a Bay Area group called the Stanford Research Institute (its connection to Stanford University is unclear) to do its own study. It also did a hatchet job on Haagen-Smit's research and reputation. They accused Haagen-Smit of sloppiness. They said his results were not replicable and that he had no definitive proof. His conclusions were a leap of faith—or worse, merely a guess.

The usually unflappable Dutchman was enraged. Although he had little interest in cars and no desire to remake the automotive industry, this slander could not go unanswered—nor unpunished.

He responded with a fusillade of evidence that demolished the credibility of opponents. As Haagen-Smit churned out a growing mountain of research, he also developed a bit of PR flair. He produced smog in a bottle and built smog chambers that would wilt plants and suffocate any who dared enter—all in a familiar, stinging, peroxide haze.[9]

Through it all, Haagen-Smit became progressively more identified with the state's efforts to fight smog. He was even called the "father of smog," and under successive governors he built an unrivaled set of labs and research institutions dedicated to understanding and fixing the problem. When the state centralized its balkanized community of pollution control agencies into the California Air Resource Board (CARB), Haagen-Smit was the obvious choice to lead the effort.

Yet Haagen-Smit was not temperamentally suited for the political rough-and-tumble of CARB. It wasn't that he was disliked. Haagen-Smit was not an effusive man, but people certainly liked him. Politicians liked him. Even the automakers—the subject of his criticism—liked him. They thought he was fair and reasonable— someone with whom they could do business. But before long, some observers started to criticize CARB's first chairman for being too soft on industry. So it came as a shock when Governor Ronald Reagan— who had originally appointed him as chairman of the board—sacked Haagen-Smit for ordering Californians to install a thirty-five-dollar retrofit on their cars to reduce emissions.

By this time, Haagen-Smit was an institution unto himself. He had practically created the new science of air pollution. Even the federal government recognized that California's air quality research establishment was probably the best in the world. But in the end, Haagen-Smit's transformative term as California's air-scientist-in-chief was unceremoniously cut short for a surprisingly small infraction against Reagan's free-market ideology. Despite the fact that he had approached his tenure with a notably light touch—perhaps too light given the severity of the health crisis facing California—he was axed for what were basically ideological reasons. In Reagan's mind, the retrofit represented too much regulation—big government—and he simply could not abide too much regulation.

But Reagan's victory against big government in California was short-lived. When he stepped down from the state's governorship in 1974, his successor brought a radically different vision to Sacramento. The new governor was actually the son of Reagan's predecessor, Pat Brown. The younger Brown was a meditating, pot-smoking Yale Law School grad—kind of a political hippie. Jerry Brown had few of Reagan's antiregulatory compunctions. Indeed, under Jerry Brown, the industry would remember Haagen-Smit's tenure at the California Air Resources Board as a golden age of lenience.

The Reformation: CARB's New Doctrine of Principled Extremism

Sitting in his office not long after a successful election, Jerry Brown asked his campaign manager Tom Quinn which position he would like in the new administration. Without hesitation, Quinn responded that he wanted to lead CARB. It was 1974. Brown was thirty-six and Quinn was thirty-one. They were both high on victory and intent to change the world.

Quinn was not experienced in the science or policy of pollution control, but he had grown up in Los Angeles and hated smog with a white-hot passion. He also worried about his children's health. And there was something else: "He knew there was power in that position," remembered one of his contemporary board members.[10] His request to Brown wasn't a simple "plug and play." Up until that point, the chairmanship of CARB had not been a full-time position—or even paid. It took quite a bit of footwork to engineer it into a suitable perch for Quinn. Nonetheless, Quinn's wish was granted.[11]

Once Quinn assumed the chairmanship, he got to work repopulating CARB's staff with a strong team of legal and technical experts—all of them aggressive environmentalists. None of these was more important than a twenty-eight-year-old Yale Law grad named Mary Nichols. Despite her age, Nichols had already accomplished some remarkable feats. Most notably, she was hot off suing the EPA for its failure to enforce portions of the 1970 Clean Air Act. Nichols's lawsuit against the Nixon administration provided a template for principled extremism that would define much of Quinn's tenure at CARB.

It was a philosophy in keeping with the national mood. Even President Nixon's environmental agenda had been remarkably aggressive. In fact, on a crisp New Year's Day in 1970, the president had signed the National Environmental Policy Act, laying the groundwork for the EPA. With great conviction, he declared that the 1970s "absolutely must be the years when America pays its debt to the past by reclaiming the purity of its air, its waters, and our living environment. It is, literally now or never."

There was a striking, national, bipartisan consensus that these issues needed to be addressed, and a flurry of legislative activity ensued. On a popular level, the country's political commitment to the environment was symbolized by the first Earth Day—celebrated on April 22, 1970. All around the United States, environmental organizations, community groups, and high school and college students organized cleanups of parks, ponds, and rivers, while politicians gave speeches on the importance of the global environment and sometimes lent a hand in the trenches.[12]

In many ways, California was clearly the leader. But despite this, the state had surprising difficulty complying with EPA regulations. In many parts of the state, the topography and atmospheric conditions simply made it harder to achieve the national clean air standards than elsewhere in the country. This was especially true in Los Angeles.

The city of Los Angeles was named "The Angels," but its microclimate was defined by five mountain ranges named after saints (Santa Ana, San Bernardino, San Emigdio, San Gabriel, and San Jacinto), which formed an expansive atmospheric basin. The effect of this geography was that sea breezes could trap large bodies of air in this cul-de-sac. Even before the age of hydrocarbons, this had sometimes given the area a slightly smoky feel. But as humans put more and more chemicals into the sky, things got much worse. The sun baked these into a cocktail of truly noxious vapors. The result was a pall that plagued Los Angeles for much of the 1950s through the 1980s.

All this meant that Los Angeles was frequently far out of compliance with the Clean Air Act of 1970. Environmentalists like Mary Nichols knew this, and they used the new federal legislation to their advantage. "Being a clean air activist requires that you be able to think more than one thing at the same time," she remembered some years later. "You have to be able to hold in your head, and in your heart, the belief that—even though it may seem impossible—we really can achieve clean, healthy air. This law, prescriptive and outrageous as it seemed, was a good tool for getting there."

The EPA administrator, William Ruckelshaus, was declining to enforce some of the more "outrageous" elements of the new Clean Air Act in California. He thought the standards were simply too strict, and in California it was clear that they would be enormously expensive to implement—requiring draconian restrictions on growth and severely curtailing the amount that Angelenos could drive. But Nichols and her employer, the Center for Law in the Public Interest, were absolutely intent on cleaning up the skies. So they sued. When they won, the federal courts ordered Ruckelshaus to get with the program.[13]

With Mary Nichols's victory, Ruckelshaus risked going to jail on contempt charges if he did not act. And so, he dryly told Angelenos, "faced with a choice between my freedom and your mobility, my freedom wins."[14]

The Ruckelshaus EPA responded by proposing that the federal government should curtail development and ration gasoline shipments to California by 25 percent in summer months, with most of the cuts targeted toward the Los Angeles basin.[15]

Obviously, this would not be good for California's economy—or for the automakers, or oil companies. So many in the business-minded community quickly learned to despise the EPA. Automakers in particular felt as if they were under siege: they were being required to both reduce emissions *and* increase fuel economy—in response to the oil shocks—at the same time. The technological burden was staggering.

Technology Forcing—"Impossible" Standards

All of this was very much in line with the new thinking at CARB. Tom Quinn's attitude did not endear him to the automakers—not one bit. And under Quinn's leadership CARB forced manufacturers out of their comfort zones—mining them for data about what was possible and pushing them precariously close to the technology frontier. Quinn expected them to adhere to his regulations, and he punished failure. Unlike Haagen-Smit, the evenhanded scientist, Quinn had no particular sympathy for Detroit. According to one former colleague, Quinn could "look you straight in the eye and tell you to go to hell with a smile and without animosity."[16]

Indeed, Quinn seemed to enjoy this confrontational mode—and perhaps he thought that others should, too. "The more pressure you put on (companies), the better citizens they become," he told one reporter. "I don't think government friendship has accomplished much over the years."[17]

Quinn cross-examined automotive lobbyists and advocates to discern what might be possible. He played them off each other and pilloried them for inconsistencies. He liked to throw automakers off balance, and he did this in a number of ways. Sometimes he would write press releases during the automakers' testimony in order to beat industry execs to the media punch.[18] Other times he would just leave a hearing for hours, return, call for a vote mid-testimony, and adjourn.[19] He had little patience for Detroit's carefully crafted lobbying campaigns and public relations stagecraft.

Some would argue that Quinn went too far. The new CARB chairman carried out policy irrespective of economic conditions and seemed impervious to the difficulties faced by Detroit. Japanese imports were surging, and the first oil shock had tremendously weakened the appeal of America's biggest, most profitable cars. And the industry's problems did not stop there. Quality was starting to sag. By the early 1970s, the average American-made car went to market with more than two dozen defects.[20]

But despite these tough times, Quinn was intent on making California into America's pressure cooker for new environmental technologies.

When it was discovered that a shaky Chrysler had sold 21,000 vehicles that transgressed California's standards in 1975, Quinn forced an expensive recall.[21] In another incident, the American Motors Corporation (AMC)—maker of Jeep, and later the Humvee—presented data that showed its emissions were the best in the industry. State tests disproved these claims, showing cars to be starkly out of compliance. In fact, they were among the very worst. So Quinn accused the automaker of "gross negligence" and fined AMC $4.2 million—though he offered to spend 75 percent of that amount to help AMC improve its testing protocols. AMC was in no position to take such a hit. And while there were many other contributing factors to the automaker's demise, it didn't survive long. The company was eventually absorbed into Chrysler.

But Quinn's aggression was remarkably effective. By 1980, Chrysler's emissions had fallen 93 percent, Ford's 46 percent, and General Motors' 29 percent, compared to where they sat in the last year of Reagan's governorship. Across the fleet, a 1986 model produced roughly 89 percent less pollution than a 1974 model.[22] CARB's new doctrine of technology-forcing mandates appeared to be working.

Competing Goods

EPA and CARB regulators succeeded in forcing automakers to clear the air with greater speed and economy than the industry had said was possible.[23] They forced adoption of technologies like the catalytic converter—which reorganized toxic nitrous oxides, carbon monoxide, and hydrocarbons into much less problematic carbon dioxide and dihydrogen oxide (otherwise known as water).

The postwar president and CEO of GM, Charlie E. Wilson, had been frequently quoted as saying that "what is good for GM is good for America." It was a misquote, but it was a misquote that lodged stubbornly in the American mind—probably because it represented something essential about the character of the company. But with California's clean air crisis that construct was beginning to fray. When American carmakers couldn't or wouldn't meet new emissions regulations, California decided it could not outsource its judgment to GM any longer. CARB would look elsewhere for an industry partner to validate its technology goals—across the Pacific Ocean, to Japan if need be. For that country's auto sector—which just a few decades earlier had sought protection from Detroit's manufacturing giants—was now a force to be reckoned with.

Along the Japanese archipelago, a clutch of voracious industry rivals were eager to devour Detroit's lunch. With Sacramento's encouragement, they were soon doing just that—and obliterating engineering obstacles that American manufacturers had said were insurmountable.[24] At the same time, California's regulators were learning that what was good for GM wasn't always good for their state; and GM's competition could be harnessed for California's own provincial economic and environmental goals.

3

Japan's Strategic Capitalism

B Y THE 1970s, American automakers were playing defense against surging Japanese imports. Not only were Japan's cars cheap, but their quality, and even technology, was increasingly superior to American models. And Japan's automakers were hungry. When California, or Tokyo, set a new bar for safety or auto emissions, the Big Three would fight back. But one or two Japanese rivals would step up and solve the problem.

How had this happened? In 1950, Japan's industry was not even an "also ran"—it was a pathetic afterthought. But by 1975 it was a mortal threat. Again, Japanese cars were not only of better quality than their U.S. counterparts, but they were $750–$1,500 cheaper—for by the 1970s Japanese automakers were 40–50 percent more productive than counterparts in America.[1] By 1980, only one of the top eleven small cars in the U.S. market was American.[2] This represented the success of a strategic decision not only to protect Japan's manufacturers from international predation, but also to force them into the global market—and into a Darwinian struggle with one another. Government planners were bent on driving domestic manufacturing to attain international standards.

MITI and the Japanese Miracle

To truly appreciate just how outclassed Japan once was—and its eventual success in promoting domestic automakers—one must return to the cradle of Fordism, the United States of America. Nowhere did the American Century dawn brighter and more glorious than on the assembly lines of Detroit. For the individual worker, the line could mean percussive drudgery, but as an instrument of industrialization it was magnificent. Henry Ford's masterpiece was the modern American assembly line, and its momentum was irresistible. Fordism, also known as "mass production," utilized specialized labor and parts, and it modularized fabrication in such a way as to meld workers and capital into a seamless, high-volume symphony. Taken as a whole, it was the process innovation of the century.

But as Ford's charcoal-colored carriages spread across America, in Japan cars were still quite rare. That is, until the country was rocked by a national calamity.

On Saturday, September 1, 1923, Tokyoites were going about their routines—cooking midday meals and lunching at noodle shops—when suddenly, the ground shook violently beneath them. Lit stoves and fires were tossed about, igniting houses made of wood and paper. Petroleum storage tanks ruptured above the port of Yokosuka, sending a black and burning torrent toward the harbor and transforming the city's bay into a "sea of blazing oil."[3] All told, 5 million were made homeless and almost 150,000 died amid the flames and rubble.[4]

The Great Kanto Earthquake of 1923 left an indelible mark on Japanese society and culture. Tokyo was redesigned. It was filled with parks that could serve as refuges from future quakes and public buildings were rebuilt to be stronger and more resilient against natural disasters. In a very real sense, the tragedy was also the origin of Japan's auto manufacturing sector.

Just as in the San Francisco earthquake of 1906, the automobile played a critical role in rescue and reconstruction. Unlike horses, cars could work around the clock. After the earthquake, an enormous number of Ford Model T's were imported. And as the immediate demands of recovery eased, many of these trucks were converted into public buses.[5] They were excellent at navigating the ruins of the city, durable and cheap. From the standpoint of both economics and utility these vehicles held a commanding advantage over the alternatives—mostly pack animals or domestically produced cars and trucks.

Japan Outclassed

To survive the swarm of American imports, Japan's native automakers needed an unfair advantage. At first this came in the form of subsidies for domestic trucks. These handouts were not, in any short-term sense, economically rational. But that didn't matter much since the government was inclined to take a long view. But even with subsidies, companies like Kaishinsha, the predecessor of Nissan, were on the verge of ruin.

Kaishinsha produced a competitor to American imports at a time when Ford trucks were selling as cheaply as $290 in the United States.[6] In Japan, Ford's Model Y sold for about 2,200 yen during the 1920s (~$850). This, combined with its comparatively high quality, made the Ford truck a bargain. Just the subsidy for a Japanese truck dwarfed Ford's selling price. The Subsidy Act for Military Use Automobiles gave a 1,000-yen production incentive to Kaishinsha for each vehicle built, an additional 1,500 yen to the buyer, and a 400-yen annual stipend for maintenance.[7] So while the Ford Model Y sold for 2,200 yen unsubsidized, the subsidy alone for Kaishinsha's domestic truck stood at 2,900—with annual sweeteners to follow.

But subsidizing Japan's domestic trucks would be essential if the country wished to someday develop an automotive sector of its own. This was especially important to Japan's military, which did not want to rely on foreign imports during its buildup and eventual invasion of the Asian mainland.

As Japan's economy continued to develop, so did its appetite for cars. Ford and GM thrived in this emerging market and both established plants in Japan to assemble "knock-down kits"—cars built from components that were manufactured in America, but assembled elsewhere. In 1934 they built and sold more than 35,000 units in Japan. In comparison, all of the heavily subsidized Japanese manufacturers combined were selling scarcely 1,000 cars and trucks a year.[8]

But the country was on a collision course with the Pacific's emerging superpower—the United States. Just as the West was being forced to abandon its foreign colonies, Japan's thirst for conquest was reaching a crescendo. Its brutal Pacific offensive started in September of 1931 with the invasion of Manchuria and for more than a decade thereafter, pushed into China, Russia, Southeast Asia, and the Pacific islands. Japan's militarists used both politics and violence to promote their expansionist agenda at home and abroad.

The decision to develop Japan's own domestic auto sector was, ultimately, political and strategic. As Japan's military clawed its way deeper into the mainland, it was no longer tenable to rely on the United States for automotive imports.

Picking Winners

Three companies typify the story of the Japanese auto sector: Toyota, Nissan, and Honda. The oldest of these are Nissan and Toyota, both of which owe their survival directly to Japan's industrial policy of the 1930s. As tensions between the United States and Japan rose, the country's military government rooted out foreign automakers and handpicked their successors. Toyota, Nissan, and Japan's other early automakers knew that their immediate fates did not depend nearly as much on whether they could compete with Ford or GM as on whether they could impress the imperial bureaucracy and become one of its chosen sons.

Toyota

In December 1935, Risaburo Toyoda rode along a bumpy highway on the way to the Hinode Motors dealership in Nagoya. Suddenly, without warning, his company's newest truck ground to a halt. "Will our trucks ever run?!" he screamed in exasperation. Risaburo was close to despair. Ford and GM were selling tens of thousands of units a year in Japan—millions around the world—but Toyoda Automatic Loom Works survived on government largesse and the equivalent of corporate charity. Toyoda knew that the only customers who bought Toyoda cars were "sympathetic to the idea of fostering a domestic auto industry." Everyone also knew that anyone who drove a Toyoda should live close by a repair shop.[9]

Risaburo was president of Toyoda Automatic Loom Works, which was in the process of attempting a bold transformation from loom builder into automobile manufacturer. The loom company had been founded by Sakichi Toyoda and his son Kiichiro, and Risaburo had married into the enterprise. Risaburo's father-in-law was a graduate of Tokyo University, an indefatigable inventor and scrappy entrepreneur. His loom company had been in and out of business over the decades. But in the process of building it, Sakichi and Kiichiro had made some powerful friends, especially in the Mitsui trading house, which repeatedly funded the Toyoda clan.[10] Risaburo was the son of one of these Mitsui friends. He had married Sakichi's daughter and taken the Toyoda family name—a not-uncommon practice in Japan.

Although this path had landed Risaburo at the side of the road next to a broken-down truck, the marriage was nonetheless a shrewd move. Toyoda's fortunes as a loom maker had turned decisively for the better after World War I. Through trial and error, the Toyodas learned the importance of controlling for quality on every single rivet of their machines—down to the threads they wove. When local thread was found to be unsatisfactory, Toyoda set up a factory to manufacture his own. By the 1930s, Toyoda looms were not only among the best in the world, but much cheaper than British and German competitors. Because of this, on December 29, 1929, Toyoda was able to license his patents to the British company Platt Brothers for the princely sum of 100,000 pounds.[11] It was this windfall that funded the company's transformation into the Toyota Motor Company.

Like Japan's bureaucrats, the Toyoda clan also took a long view of progress and innovation. Before his death, Sakichi left his successors with five principles to live by. In addition to encouraging his employees to "be kind" and "create a warm homelike atmosphere," he also urged them to "be at the vanguard of the times through endless creativity, inquisitiveness and pursuit of improvement."[12] It was in this spirit that Risaburo's brother-in-law, Kiichiro, had established the company's automotive division.

Unlike looms, cars really were at the "vanguard of the times." And they were also something of a hobby. The Toyoda men harbored a well-known obsession with cars—and had for some time. They wanted to buy them, drive them, and build them. But in order to sell them, they would have to compete with the likes of Ford. Though the Toyodas had been to the United States on numerous occasions and meticulously studied the art of mass production—walking the assembly lines of Ford's River Rouge plant and spending long nights imagining how they might be re-created at home—the issue of scale was insuperable. Even for Japan's largest, most powerful concerns, it would have been madness to challenge America's industrial titans.[13]

For Toyota, times were getting desperate. Because of this the company was trying to establish a tie-up with GM or Ford. This appeared to be the only reasonable prospect for survival.[14]

Nissan

The other major firm trying to sell passenger vehicles was Nissan, and its immediate prospects did not look much brighter. Nissan's history with cars extended farther back than Toyota's, and was basically a series of ambitious failures. Like Sakichi Toyoda, the founder Masujiro Hashimoto had also gone to college, but then joined the army. He was eventually sent to America on a scholarship from the Japan Ministry of Agriculture and Commerce. There he became convinced that automobiles were the thing of the future. After he returned home to Japan, Hashimoto designed guns for the Japanese military, but resigned in 1911 to pursue his real passion and build an automobile company—Kaishinsha.[15]

The company was not equipped to manufacture its own cars, so it imported and repaired British knock-down vehicles. When Kaishinsha did begin manufacturing its own cars, they were called DAT—an acronym for Hashimoto's funders (Den, Aoyama, and Takeuchi) but also for the English words Durable, Attractive, and Trustworthy. [16] At the beginning, they built and sold only about two units a year. Much like Toyoda, these early models were sold to the "benevolent" or "curious."[17]

Kaishinsha was in and out of solvency for a decade and a half, which led to a number of mergers and name changes. However, again and again the company's business model returned to subsidies offered by the Japanese military for domestic production of trucks.[18] By the late 1920s, its cars were no longer called DAT, but "son of DAT"—Datsun. (The word "sun" was swapped for "son" in order to avoid using the Japanese homophone for "loss.")

Then in 1934, Kaishinsha was acquired by the Nippon Industries Joint Stock Company zaibatsu (Nippon Sangyo Kabushiki Kaisha), and it became simply Nissan.[19] Zaibatsus were massive conglomerates that provided the backbone of Japan's industrial growth during the interwar period, but capital requirements of the auto industry were such that soon Nissan too was in severe financial straits. It aggressively pursued GM to make a joint venture of the Japanese market. Even with zaibatsu backing, Nissan's position against American imports was untenable—it was outclassed.

Sonno Joi: Kicking Out the Barbarians

Almost a century earlier, Japanese nationalists had responded to Western encroachment with the slogan "sonno joi"—revere the emperor, expel the barbarians. In the 1930s such chauvinism was once again on display. Amid heightening tensions with the United States over Japan's military adventures in Asia, the government declared what amounted to a ban on foreign automobiles. This meant salvation for both Toyota and Nissan. The ban was codified on August 9, 1935, by the Ministry of Commerce and Industry in the uncreatively named Automobile Industry Law.[20] "Entrusting such an important industry pure and simply to the complete control of foreigners is an extremely unsatisfactory situation," the law said. Auto production should be "placed in the hands of Japanese both in name and reality, now and in the future."[21]

The law's author was Nobusuke Kishi, who later served as minister of commerce, as minister of munitions in Hideki Tojo's war cabinet, and finally as prime minister after the occupation.[22] Kishi was also the grandfather of Japan's later prime minister, Shinzo Abe. Kishi, Japan's foremost technocrat, designed heavy import tariffs (50 percent) on knock-down kits for foreign automobiles and a ban on foreign tie-ups with Japanese manufacturers. The ministry's "designated" manufacturers would inherit Japan's market from the spurned Americans.

Kishi's plan was for only two automakers to be selected as "designated" producers.[23] The rest would be squeezed out of business. And this meant that no one could rest easy.

To better its chances, Toyoda frantically organized a series of exhibitions to showcase its latest models. It must have come as a great relief when, on September 14, 1936, in the midst of one of these events, notice arrived from the Ministry of Commerce and Industry: Toyoda had made the cut—together with Nissan.[24]

Previously, the company had been called "Toyoda," but now its name was modernized to Toyota—spelled in katakana script generally reserved for foreign words. The new Toyota quickly set about cementing its bonds with the government.[25] Despite Kishi's original intentions, Isuzu was also allowed to continue its operations building trucks for the military throughout the war.[26]

On a quiet Sunday morning, on December 7, 1941, the scope of Japan's war expanded considerably. Japan launched an audacious sneak attack against the U.S. Pacific Fleet in Pearl Harbor, slaughtering thousands and destroying or incapacitating eighteen warships as well as hundreds of planes. The attack was, in large part, an attempt to remove America's military as an obstacle to Japan's quest for resources in Asia and the Pacific. For months, America had been throttling Japan's access to raw materials—especially oil.

This pervasive wartime scarcity had a profound impact on the country's economic structure. During the war, industrial production was managed by the Ministry of Munitions and Industry. Japan's dearth of materials pushed manufacturers away from the traditional Fordist system of mass production—which required large amounts of inventory to be maintained—and encouraged the beginnings of a massively synchronized and integrated method called "just in time," which required much less inventory.[27] Japan's auto companies were building military necessities like trucks and planes, and passenger cars were largely ignored. By the war's end, the vehicles industry was thoroughly militarized and running ragged from overutilization and neglect.

A "Bulwark" in the East

In August 1945 the United States bombed Hiroshima and Nagasaki and put an end to the war with Japan. The combination of nuclear weapons and the Soviet Union's declaration of war from the north meant that Japan's military situation rapidly deteriorated from hopeless to suicidal. On August 15, Japan's Emperor Hirohito offered his unconditional surrender to the Allies and broadcast it to the Japanese people over the airwaves. "The enemy has begun to employ a new and most cruel bomb," he said. Resistance, he declared, would "lead to the total extinction of human civilization." A dramatic coup d'état was launched to prevent the emperor's capitulation, but it was snuffed out by senior officers. The war was over.

The trauma of nuclear defeat seared into the *kokutai,* as the Japanese called their body politic, like a hot knife. But it was also the beginning of a new political and economic era—one that would make the Japanese people among the richest in the world and give them a true democracy.

In the beginning, the void of authority left by Japan's brutal military was filled by the imposing, bombastic, but basically benevolent General Douglas MacArthur. He received the title Supreme Commander of the Allied Powers (SCAP) in Japan and exercised complete control over the country's military, civil, and economic future from the Allies' General Headquarters (GHQ). MacArthur's immediate plans for the occupation included a massive deindustrialization of the country, one that would leave it with little ability to make war—or cars—for the foreseeable future. But this soon changed. A mere three weeks after the war was declared over, GHQ realized that trucks would be necessary to achieve even basic recovery. Toyota, Isuzu, and Nissan were all allowed to resume production.[28]

Unbearable Retreat

Japan would need a strategy for reconstruction, so on March 13, 1949, its Ministry of Commerce and Industry, Trade Agency, Small and Medium Enterprise Agency, and Industrial Technology Agency were all reorganized into the Ministry of International Trade and Industry (MITI).[29] The new bureaucracy was the heart of Japan's postwar economic planning apparatus.

One of its many functional divisions was dedicated to autos, but immediately after the war this section was considered a dreary backwater. After all, Japan was not even allowed to produce cars—just trucks. The bureau labored assiduously to right this situation. It sought to curry favor with the Americans at GHQ to regain the right to manufacture domestic automobiles.

Industrial conglomerates, such as Toyota and Nissan, were itching to reenter the market, but their American overlords had other priorities. Even if GHQ relented, Japan's return to the automotive world was not a foregone conclusion. Among the Japanese elites a furious debate erupted as to whether investing in the industry was a good idea. There was a strong argument that Japan should not. GHQ and many Japanese leaders felt that cars were a luxury item most could not afford. For those who could afford them—and for things like taxi cabs—

they could be imported. One influential voice was Hisato Ichimada, the governor of the board of the Bank of Japan. He argued that automobiles were not the country's comparative advantage.[30] The market would guide them, he said. "We have to follow the principle of the international division of industry. For instance, developing an automobile industry in Japan does not make much sense," he wrote in an editorial for the *Nihon Keizai Shimbun*—the country's most respected financial daily.[31] Adding weight to his argument was the fact that Toyota, Nissan, and Isuzu were all bleeding cash—none of them seemed like a viable business.

But Japan's bureaucrats were mortified by the prospect of abandoning the sector. It would be "unbearable," they said, "for Japanese . . . to return to international society as a nation of culture" without an auto industry.[32]

In the end, MITI's emotional appeal carried the day, and soon Japan was ready to kick out the foreigners once again and develop their own indigenous champions.

Sayonara, Uncle Sam: Ejecting the Americans, Again

On October 5, 1949, SCAP removed the prohibition on Japanese manufacturers building passenger cars. Almost immediately the industry was in dire straits. But salvation came unexpectedly—from Korea.

On January 12, 1950, at the National Press Club in Washington, D.C., Secretary of State Dean Acheson delivered a high profile, and ultimately fateful, speech on the United States' military disposition in East Asia. As the dean of U.S. foreign policy, Acheson explained that the defense perimeter that "must and shall be maintained" against Soviet expansion ran "along the Aleutians to Japan and then goes to the Ryukyus." This invisible and unbreachable line continued "to the Philippine Islands."[33] It was taken as a definitive statement of U.S. foreign policy and, critically, it excluded the Korean peninsula. Acheson's remarks set in motion a series of machinations by North Korea's leader Kim Il-sung to gain support from China and the USSR for a surprise attack on the government of the South. And although the Soviet Union's leader Joseph Stalin opposed the move, North Korea struck anyway. On June 25, 1950, North Korea attacked and a desperate effort by the United States to ensure the survival of the southern regime followed. Before long, all-out war ensued.

Japan's carmakers were rescued by an influx of orders for trucks to support the Korean War. One MITI official called these Allied orders "manna from heaven." By 1951 Japan's automakers were, once again, profitable, and this was almost completely thanks to truck sales to the U.S. military.

But America's presence in East Asia was not an unmitigated boon. For so long as the Americans occupied Japan, so did GM, Ford, and Chrysler. It was not an uncommon sight to see an American GI, in a big American car with a Japanese girlfriend in the front seat, cruising through the streets of Tokyo or Osaka.[34] In general, those who could afford it bought a new American car. For those who couldn't afford a new GM or Ford, a used one would do. Usually these were purchased from an American soldier.

To rebuild its auto sector, Japan would have to—once again—remake the rules of competition. "Orthodox policy tools are not always too reliable," wrote one Japanese scholar. Time lags required to achieve equilibrium under neoliberal approaches had the "potential to destroy the stability of postwar Japanese society."[35] In other words, the Japanese did not trust markets. Better to give the industry a forceful nudge.

When MITI regained control over the auto sector it quickly instituted "the virtual equivalent of an import ban."[36] Severe tariffs were levied on foreign imports in 1951, and the heaviest taxes focused on larger vehicles—most of which happened to be American. This pushed Japanese consumers toward smaller cars, as did a series of foreign exchange controls that dictated what technologies Japan's companies could import.[37] The clear aim was to protect the Japanese auto market from American imports.

Go West

At the same time as MITI was busy kicking out American automakers from its domestic market, it was also eyeing U.S. markets—with a particular focus on California.[38] Japan wanted to export, but to do this, Japanese manufacturers would need to meet global standards. Part of MITI's plan to promote exports was to richly reward Japanese manufacturers who sold goods abroad by giving them preferential access to foreign exchange and technology.

The Toyopet S. Crown was Toyota's first U.S. export. Introduced in 1957, it was remembered as an extraordinary "lemon" and the vehicle soured Toyota's reputation in the United States for decades. Even the company's own executives disdained the car. When one Toyopet broke down on a test drive through Arizona, two Toyota executives spent a night shivering in the desert—where they were eventually rescued by a state trooper.[39] But the Japanese were intent on closing the gap in quality and performance and only by exporting could they be sure that their cars were, indeed, world class.

And while Japan did not want to import U.S. cars, they were more than happy to import American industrial knowledge, employ it, and even improve on it. In fact, this ended up being one of Japan's defining advantages over U.S. manufacturers over the coming decades. The ardor with which the Japanese embraced the techniques of American quality control guru W. Edwards Deming stood in sharp contrast to the snub Deming received from carmakers in Detroit. During the war Deming had helped design and implement statistical process control methods for the U.S. military. Thereafter, he had desperately wanted to teach American automakers the intricacies of statistical quality control, but they paid him little mind.[40] In 1947 the Allied Occupation brought Deming to Japan to assist with a host of tasks—which ranged from assessing Japan's nutritional needs to preparing for the country's upcoming census. Deming and Japan were a good fit and before the year was out, he was inducted as the first honorary member of the Japanese Statistical Society.[41] It was the start of a long, fruitful relationship.

At the same time as they soaked up Deming's wisdom, Japanese were also pioneering their own set of process innovations focused on quality, and even more so efficiency.

In this Toyota rushed to be an early leader for two reasons. First, there was the self-evident competitive advantage of having more efficient workers. The second reason was that Toyota was terrified by the prospect of labor radicalization and wanted to exercise strict control over new hires.[42]

In the 1950s a major labor dispute had resulted from pay cuts and layoffs and leftists had almost brought the company to its knees. So rather than risk hiring communists, Taiichi Ohno, Toyota's production manager from 1945 to 1953, streamlined production with ruthless intensity. In years past, each worker used to operate one machine. But Ohno crisscrossed assembly lines so that workers could operate two at once.[43] As production ramped up and labor became tight, Ohno added another perfectly synchronized assembly line—boxing in workers on three sides. Through increasing automation, and giving individual workers ever greater responsibility, Ohno kept adding lines. Eventually Toyota got to the point where one worker might operate as many as seventeen machines simultaneously. An average worker was operating somewhere between five and ten. The results were astounding. Between 1950 and 1956, Toyota quintupled its output without hiring a single factory floor worker.[44] At the same time, quality was improving—and markedly so.

Toyota and other Japanese manufacturers were using Deming's statistical methods—constantly measuring outputs to reduce variation in components and eliminate waste. They produced parts in small batches to minimize inventory costs, and also to keep tabs on any defect that might have crept into the process. Individually packed boxes filled with just the right number of pieces were assembled for each car—to ensure nothing was omitted. Americans eventually dubbed these techniques "lean production" and the *kanban* system. Cumulatively, they were called "the Machine That Changed the World."[45] The efficiency of this new "machine" was extraordinary—it was a marked improvement on Ford's techniques. It gained steam like a freight train and chased down global rivals; for four decades its momentum seemed unstoppable.

Japan had come a long way.

MITI's Strategic Retreat

The progress was not limited to Japan's auto sector. Its entire economy was soaring. They called Japan's first economic blast the "Jimmu Boom"—or the greatest period of economic growth since Japan's mythical founder, Jimmu.[46] That hyperbolically named growth spurt was followed by the Iwato Boom—or the biggest boom since the ancient gathering of the gods.[47] From 1953 through 1971, Japan's economic growth rate was astounding—over 9 percent. It was by far the highest in the industrialized world.[48] Demand for domestic vehicles soared higher and higher and by blocking foreign imports, MITI ensured that Japanese, not Americans or Europeans, benefited from skyrocketing sales.

When both tariffs and restrictions on domestic investment were lifted in 1973, one might have expected Japan to be inundated with foreign cars. But instead a torrential outflow of Japanese autos ensued. They were better, cheaper, and more efficient than their foreign competitors. By 1980, the Japanese had steamrolled Germany to become America's largest source for automotive imports. Japan now accounted for 80 percent of foreign autos sold in America.[49] In fact, it was now Detroit that needed protection.

4

The Audacity of Honda

S JAPANESE autos poured into U.S. ports, and spilled into American driveways, more and more Japanese themselves were buying and owning cars. Japanese could work and travel like never before. But just like in California, where cars multiplied, smog followed. Residents of Tokyo were horrified by the veil that descended over the city in the early 1970s and they knew exactly what it was. California had already done the heavy scientific lifting to figure out where smog came from. But California had not yet succeeded in resolving the thorny environmental issue. Part of the reason for this was the magnitude of the technology challenge. Another part was that American automakers lacked any competitive incentive to deal with the problem. The automakers had closed ranks against regulators, and in Detroit there was a firm belief that consumers bought cars on the basis of style, luxury, and horsepower, not emissions.

In Japan, things were different. For one, the competitive landscape of their auto industry was more crowded. Toyota and Nissan were Japan's equivalent of America's Big Three. They were the dominant market players. Like the Big Three, they were basically content to do the bare minimum necessary to satisfy California's environmental standards so they could export. But on the fringes of Japan's industrial landscape lurked other contenders. These included a fierce underdog that would rattle the industry's status quo. The name was Honda.

"The Fighting Spirit Is My Nature"

Soichiro Honda grew up in the shadow of Mount Fuji. From his childhood he had never been content to play by others' rules. His father was a blacksmith and his mother was a weaver. Honda himself had little formal schooling, but he always demonstrated a subversive ingenuity. One story dates back to Honda's time in grade school. Japanese children were supposed to have their grade reports regularly stamped by parents with a signature seal called a *hanko*. But Honda decided that this was unnecessary. He manufactured his own *hanko*—and stamped his own reports. His *hanko* was flawless and teachers had no reason to suspect it was forged. So soon Honda began to manufacture parental *hanko* for his classmates as well. But eventually the young counterfeiter's luck ran out. The quality was still impeccable, but unlike his own name, in which both characters were symmetrical (本田), most other names were not (for example, Suzuki, 鈴木). Parental oversight was restored when Honda accidentally carved a character from one of these names backward.[*1]

Without doubt, Honda was a firebrand, but he was also a meticulous tactician with an insatiable appetite for victory. "I am filled with an abundant, unshakable confidence that I can win," said Honda. "The fighting spirit . . . is my nature."[2] By the 1970s the rebellious Honda reveled in his plans to destroy the auto industry's comfy equilibrium.

Honda started small. His first company began as a supplier of piston rings to Toyota. But by the early 1950s, he had graduated to small motorcycles. One MITI official recalled walking into the Honda Motor Company workshop and seeing the company's founder dressed in coveralls tinkering away at a fiberglass scooter. It was a decidedly low-tech machine, but he was absolutely fixated on improving its performance. Even as he remained firmly grounded in the present, Honda

---

*This particular story about Honda's childhood may or may not be apocryphal. Its source is Aditya Sharma, *"Honda—It Ain't a Dream Without Everyone Being a Part of It,"* Autospace, October 31, 2012, http://autospace.co/honda/http://world.honda.com/MotoGP/history/Man-TT-Declaration/.

made clear that his goals were much bigger: to build a world-class automobile like a Jaguar or Porsche—both of which he had owned.[3] Start with an audacious dream, and then realize it incrementally—that was the Honda way.

The epic journey of the Honda Motor Company, which started with piston rings, would eventually produce the finest racing machines in the world.

The Isle of Man TT

In 1954, Honda made a bold declaration to his team. The Honda Motor Company, said Soichiro, was bigger than Japan. It was going to prove, once and for all, that a Japanese manufacturer could define the global standard. They would do this on a stage that no lover of automotive technology could possibly ignore: the Isle of Man TT.

The Isle of Man TT was the Super Bowl of motorcycle racing; no Japanese contestant had ever entered—not to speak of winning. It was not for the faint of heart. Cyclists tore through hairpin turns, launched off hillsides, and drew almost perfect lines over the British country-side. Honda was undeterred. "We are equipped with a production system in which I have absolute confidence," he said. It was, he believed, the best in the world. "The scrupulous care that is required when tightening a single screw, and the commitment that refuses to waste a single sheet of paper . . . will open the way before you."

So, starting in 1959, Honda began entering his bikes into this grand challenge. From the very beginning, they were a force to be reckoned with. But by 1961 they were *the* force to be reckoned with. That year tension was thick along the sidelines as a file of Hondas screamed across Isle's grassy dells. At the finish line, flabbergasted Brits looked on as one sleek 250cc Honda blew past, then another, then another. Japan had not only won, it had swept the podium—in both the 125cc and 250cc divisions.[4]

Soichiro Honda's prophecy was fulfilled.

Muskie and the "Market Defect"

Honda was perpetually confident that the Honda Motor Company could win. Because of this, the chance to compete was always a blessing, never a burden. Winning the emissions race was just another chance at victory—and on a grand stage.

Japan's reaction to smog was much more violent than California's. By the 1970s Japan was becoming a wealthy country and many believed it could afford to sacrifice some level of economic development for cleaner air. Pollution, stated one government report, was a "market defect."[5] It had to be addressed by nonmarket means. Even the labor unions—which in America focused on improving their own pay and labor conditions to the exclusion of much else—agreed. They stated that an "industrial policy that places top priority on production and subordinates environmental and other concerns should be basically changed."[6] The race was on.

In 1971, a year after Nixon established the EPA in the United States, Japan also set up a new environmental agency. It was responsible for designing and implementing Japan's new emissions standards. In its search for appropriate policy, the agency reviewed the U.S. Clean Air Act amendments and decided to follow America's lead.[7]

Beyond Japan's new regulations, the country's automakers also had another incentive to clean up their cars: doing so would make it easier to export to the United States—and especially California. In Japan, the U.S. Clean Air Act of 1970 was known as the "Muskie Act," after Senator Edmund Muskie, who had played a critical role in drafting the legislation. The United States was already an important export destination, and Japanese manufacturers would have to meet Muskie standards in order to maintain the market.[8]

The sheer magnitude of the business opportunity in the United States was awesome. And there was another reason why exports loomed large: Japan's economy was starting to slow. The first oil shock led to inflation and Japan's first postwar decline in economic activity. After two decades of screaming growth, the Japanese economy grew at "only" 5.2 percent from 1970 through 1977—less than half the average of the previous decade.[9] Japan's economy was no longer the engine of prosperity it had been for the last twenty years, so new opportunities would have to come from abroad. Buoyed by these synergistic environmental and economic goals and broad social consensus, Japan quickly enacted some of the strictest pollution standards in the world.[10] Initially, Japanese standards were not simply inspired by those set in Washington; they were essentially one and the same.

The Race to Clean

For Honda, it was a complicated but counterintuitively auspicious moment. Only a few years earlier, one of MITI's top priorities had been to stamp out automotive upstarts like Honda. From MITI's perspective, competition was good, but fragmentation of the auto industry was bad.[11] Honda would have been forced to stick to motorcycles, or perhaps merge with another Japanese auto manufacturer. The bill failed in 1963 and again in 1964, and Honda avoided the administrative axe. In 1968, it broke into the passenger car market with an elegantly engineered sedan called the 1300.[12] Honda was now a legitimate car company. Racing had always been Soichiro Honda's passion and from 1964 through 1968 Honda was obsessed with competing on the F1 circuit. But after the death of his F1 team's American driver in 1968, Old Man Honda shut it down. That left Honda's racing team, which included some of the finest engineers in the world, in need of a challenge. What better than an impossible engineering feat?

One of Honda's most promising engineers was the twenty-seven-year-old prodigy Yoshitoshi Sakurai. In the 1980s Sakurai would build a crushingly dominant F1 racing team by pioneering the use of advanced telemetric and computer controls and forever change the sport of racing. He explained the value of his new system through an analogy to another prodigy: F1 racing legend Ayrton Senna. "His brain," said Sakurai, "could simulate . . . RPM of [the] engine, gear position, braking point [and] steering." According to Sakurai, Senna could compute the complex dynamics of a racing machine so perfectly and so efficiently that he would calibrate his racing times to the hundredth of a second. If he said he was able to run 0.6 seconds faster, he would run 0.6 seconds faster.[13] Since Senna was *the* singular exception in this regard, Sakurai developed a computer monitoring system to accomplish these tasks for mere mortals. But all that was a decade into the future. In the 1970s, with the racing team mothballed, Sakurai was put to work on the emissions challenge.[14]

Automakers had been expecting emissions controls for some time. Toyota, for one, created an emissions study group as early as 1964 and by 1968 it built an entire laboratory for studying and developing emissions control technology.[15] In 1965, Honda founded its Air Pollution Research Group with an eye toward meeting emissions regulations in the United States.[16] However, the standards of the 1970s were much more aggressive than anyone had expected and the infusion of talent from its racing team gave Honda a huge leg up.[17]

Under the rally cry of "blue skies for our children!" Soichiro Honda led the charge himself. "Every day, every day he came to the lab," remembered Sakurai. "There were three designers, and three test engineers, it was a very small team." At first Old Man Honda let their creative instincts run wild. The engineers explored dozens of possibilities for cleaning up exhaust. They researched exotic designs ranging from gas turbines—which spin like a pinwheel—to Stirling engines. Honda even jettisoned petroleum to experiment with hydrogen and alcohol as low-emission fuels.

But eventually Mr. Honda brought the venture back down to earth. He declared that alternative engine architectures and fuels were impractical and uneconomical. The obstacles to deploying these new technologies were too high, and the scale of Honda's investments in manufacturing facilities was significant. So he ordered his researchers to focus back in on the conventional piston-in-cylinder, gasoline-fueled designs.[18]

Trial and Terror

Virtually every other manufacturer assumed that the eventual solution—if there was a solution—would involve some sort of filtration system for a car's exhaust. But Honda told his engineers he wanted to achieve his goals through manipulating the combustion event inside the cylinder. Sakurai and the team zeroed in on an approach they believed could satisfy the stringent requirements of America's new emissions laws. It was called "lean combustion." It allowed the fuel in the cylinder to burn much more thoroughly than in the carburetors they—and everyone else in the industry—had previously used to mix gasoline and air into a rich, explosive mist.*

To make Honda's lean combustion work, a small external chamber was attached to each cylinder. There a superrich mixture of air and gasoline (high fuel-to-air ratio) was ignited in order to catalyze the lean mixture (low fuel-to-air ratio) in the main cylinder.[19] They had not yet crossed the finish line, but victory was tantalizingly close. It was like licking honey through glass.

Honda's founder had a disconcerting habit of announcing his victories to the public first and only later informing the engineering team what they would have to accomplish to make good on his boasts. "Many people didn't like this habit of his," remembered Sakurai. But the impish Honda thought it was great fun.

And so, on February 12, 1971, Soichiro Honda called a bold press conference—held in the grandiose Federation of Economic Organizations Hall in Tokyo's Ote-machi district. "Old Man Honda" announced that his company had unlocked the riddle of emissions. And then he made the assembled audience an audacious promise: Honda would start producing cars to meet the 1975 standard by 1973.[20] Honda did not release any technical details, and in order to confuse competitors, he named the system Compound Vortex Controlled Combustion (CVCC)—which meant almost nothing to anyone.

---

*Engine enthusiasts might note that what happens inside an internal combustion engine is not technically an explosion, but more of a deflagration.

After his triumphal "mission accomplished," Soichiro basked in the limelight. He had done it again. He had turned the tables on Japanese regulators—who less than a decade earlier had wanted to stamp out his ambition to build cars—and vanquished Toyota and Nissan, not to speak of Ford and GM. But his engineering team was not nearly so confident.

In fact, many of Honda's engineers were furious—and terrified. They had not been consulted, and the technology was not ready, not fully tested, and certainly not set for commercialization. In fact, Honda's research was so much ahead of its production capabilities that the CVCC technology was prototyped and tested using a Nissan engine and in a Nissan body.

Honda was unrepentant. He told them, "If I asked you guys when it would be completed, you'd never tell me. . . . The company would go bankrupt before you'd say that."[21]

The team redoubled its efforts and, in the end, Honda succeeded in its gambit to leapfrog Toyota and Nissan—which, along with American companies, were forced to license Honda's pollution control technology. Honda earned princely sums off these royalties.

Yet even then, American companies did not like to admit they were behind the engineering curve. When the young Sakurai was farmed out to Ford to help them implement CVCC in its own engines he remembered how hard it was to be heard within Ford's research edifice. "I tried to get them to redesign the entire engine," remembered Sakurai. "But they didn't want to learn from a 30-year-old Japanese guy." Ford's first implementation of the CVCC design sacrificed 20 horsepower off a 100-horsepower system. So in a group meeting of Ford's Advanced Engineering Department, Sakurai challenged his colleagues to a contest: he would spend a month redesigning the Ford engine, and the forty engineers on Ford's advanced engineering team should do the same. At the end, they would see which engine produced more horsepower—without sacrificing emissions.

Sakurai spent long nights at the drafting table, and so did his forty American colleagues. After two months the new engines were prototyped and ready for the dynamometer. The Ford team registered an impressive 95 horsepower—just short of their original target. Surely they had won. But when Sakurai's engine went onto the test bed, it registered 125 horsepower. "The next morning I came to my desk at 7 A.M. and there were 10 people waiting to talk to me," he recalled years later with evident glee.

And Honda wasn't the only Japanese upstart to solve the emissions problem. Mazda also succeeded. But Mazda's emissions fix was for a completely different engine design—a rotary engine. Almost all engines in the world used a "piston in cylinder" architecture—which operated much in the same way as a bullet being forced from a gun. The piston was the bullet, and the cylinder the gun. The bullet was married to a crankshaft to provide rotary force. It was the same design Honda had forced his engineers to work with, and that almost all automobiles use today. But Mazda's engine rolled around like a triangle wheel inside a hollow casing. Despite this, Mazda also met Japan's tough new standards. Yet more proof that small innovative companies could sometimes achieve standards the big boys had said were impossible.[22] Japan's state-brokered competition was pushing the industry to a new technological plane. In other words, it was succeeding brilliantly. As a direct consequence, the Japanese Environmental Agency ordered all automotive companies to comply with the tough 1975 emissions requirements.

Blood in the Water: The Battle of 1976

Japan's 1976 standards were significantly more stringent, especially with regard to a toxic emission called NOx (oxides of nitrogen). Again, the standards were based on U.S. goals. Japanese regulators believed they would have to reach the goals to export and that America's standards were rooted in science and must be within reach.[23] But in reality the U.S. process had been largely political and there was no guarantee of success. Because of this, the standards caused an uproar in Detroit, and in America the federal government eventually backed down—abandoning the aggressive requirements to reduce NOx emissions. The 1976 standards were not, it seemed, good science. Even California's aggressive technology forcers relented—convinced that it was, indeed, a bridge too far. It appeared that the automakers had won this particular point of the technology argument.

But in Japan, the debate raged on. Japan's tough regulations—based on the now-defunct U.S. standards—led to a pitched battle within the Japanese industry, and indeed Japanese society. Since they were no longer necessary for exporting, Toyota and Nissan wanted the 1976 standards suspended indefinitely. MITI warned that they would lead to unemployment and further damage Japan's already slowing economy. And initially MITI won. Unlike the United States, Japan's political establishment was highly attuned to the counsel of its powerful meritocracy—and when it came to economic matters, MITI's priorities and proposals more often than not carried the day. And so the 1976 standards were postponed for two years.[24]

But Japan was changing. To a new generation of environmentally conscious Japanese politicians and citizens' groups, MITI's interference in this issue of public health was wholly unacceptable. Because of this, MITI's attempt to forestall the clean air regulations met with a lightning response from an "ad hoc" environmental committee in Japan's national Diet—as the country's legislative body is called—and a coalition of mayors from Kawasaki, Tokyo, Yokohama, Nagoya, Kyoto, Osaka, and Kobe.[25] In some quarters of Japanese society, MITI's chronic corporate apologism had led to suspicion and resentment.

MITI and Japan's industrial complex had a dubious record when it came to protecting the environment and public health. In the 1950s a strange syndrome called Minamata disease emerged in the areas around a chemical complex in Kumamoto Prefecture. Eventually, it was discovered that Minamata disease was, in fact, mercury poisoning. But MITI, along with a number of other government agencies, was complicit in denying or ignoring overwhelming scientific evidence that residents of Minamata were being poisoned and debilitated or killed by mercury-tainted seafood.[26] Around the same time, itai-itai disease, a horrendous case of cadmium poisoning, emerged in Toyama Prefecture as a result of the activities of the Mitsui Mining & Smelting Company. Although MITI was not directly complicit, the incident confirmed the suspicions of many environmentalists that industrialists were perfectly willing to profit over the dead bodies of Japanese citizens.[27]

The emissions fracas was seen as more of the same: MITI was protecting the interests of Nissan and Toyota, at the expense of Japanese health, *even though Honda and Mazda believed that there was still room for improvement.*

Soon it became clear MITI and its allies had committed a spectacular blunder; Nissan and Toyota had won the battle but lost the war. The conflict came to a head in September 1975, when Eiji Toyoda was called to testify in front of the Diet as head of the Japan Automobile Manufacturers Association. The regulators, he said, should slow down. Toyoda explained that standards achieved by Honda or Mazda in a laboratory setting might not be feasible in the real world. It did not go over well. In response, the celebrated industrialist was pilloried by the media, politicians, and environmental groups. It was a public relations fiasco.[28]

Eiji Toyoda's misstep was Soichiro Honda's golden opportunity. Honda again smelled blood in the water. He realized that the stricter environmental regulations might allow him to broaden his beachhead in the war against Toyota and Nissan and he pushed furiously forward with emissions research—eventually achieving the 1976 standards as well.[29] It was a painful lesson for Nissan and Toyota at the hands of a rival they had considered their inferior. Old Man Honda had beaten them again.

"Protectionist Trickery"?

By the late 1970s, Japan's emission requirements were so strict that one report from the Organisation for Economic Co-operation and Development posited whether they might be a form of "protectionist trickery." The report answered that question decisively: no.[30] Part of their evidence was that the standards were actively opposed by Toyota and Nissan. But in the end these rules had huge benefits for both companies. Japan's strict regulations laid the foundation for decades of environmental dominance by its automakers—including those opposed to the 1976 rules.

These "unreasonably" strict regulations forced the country's entire industry onto a circuit that was more than a decade ahead of other advanced economies. The Japanese dramatically improved their understanding of emissions control technology, and Eiji Toyoda's thrashing at the hands of environmentalists also taught Japan's automakers that while short-term gains could be extracted through stalling environmental policies, long-term damage could also be done.

Yes, Toyota and Nissan had been schooled by Old Man Honda, but they learned their lesson: keeping ahead of the regulatory curve in fuel efficiency and emissions could be a comparative advantage. In the next decade, Toyota and Nissan would push boldly into new frontiers like hybrid vehicles and electrification—moving far beyond what regulators required.

In 1990, when California decided to push a new global emissions standard, Japan's automakers were ready to go.

5

Sudden Impact

Toyota was gobbling up the market for small cars and would soon move upmarket with Lexus. Honda was chewing away at GM's and Ford's reputations and also sales—with technologically advanced, high-quality, affordable, efficient vehicles. America's automakers were under siege. So when GM acquired Hughes Aircraft in 1985, the automaker immediately dangled the idea that it would vault back into contention by integrating aerospace technology into its cars. To many, GM's boast sounded like a hollow promise—a marketing ploy. But Howard Wilson, a vice president at Hughes, had a plan that might actually make it happen. Wilson's somewhat fanciful quest proved to be the starting gun in a race that would ultimately require hundreds of billions of dollars in research and investment from corporate titans and governments around the world.

The Hughes executive had received an envelope from Australia. Inside that envelope was an invitation—no letter, no explanation, just an invitation—to compete in a race. Just like at Honda, grand races were, in some senses, part of Hughes's genetic code. For thirty years, Hughes had been a critical part of the space race against the Soviet Union—building warplanes, satellites, and guided missiles for the U.S. government. But this was a race for cars. It was for a very specific type of car—a car powered by the sun. A silent armada of solar-powered vehicles was supposed to sun-sail across the Australian Outback under the blazing austral sky, bisecting the continent from top to bottom, from Darwin to Adelaide. Like the space race, glory was the ultimate prize.

Wilson wanted that prize for Hughes and GM. He had approximately zero experience designing automobiles, but lightweight materials, electronics, and solar panels were all specialties of Hughes Aircraft. Because of that, he thought, they had a chance.

From Darwin to Adelaide

What could be a better symbol of GM and Hughes's new partnership than winning a race filled with cars of the future? With the right team Wilson reckoned they could build a winner. But there was one catch: Wilson didn't actually want to use any engineers from GM—at least not GM proper. To build the solar-powered racer, Wilson wanted his own automotive skunkworks. That term derived from the famously innovative, nimble, secretive, and independent division of the Lockheed Aircraft Corporation responsible for some of the company's most advanced projects. Wilson was an aerospace guy and he wanted to work with that kind of team—innovative Californians, not a bunch of Rust Belt "gearheads." He asked around town and kept hearing the same name: AeroVironment. The company was a clutch of eccentric technology buffs who thrived on "off-the-wall" engineering challenges. Persuaded he had found his team, Wilson jumped on a plane and headed for Detroit to make his case.

But when Wilson pitched his plan to GM's head of North American operations, he was firmly rebuffed. What did solar-powered cars in Australia have to do with selling Chevys in the United States? they asked. It looked like the end. But on his way out the door, the Hughes VP made one last, desperate appeal. He ducked into the executive office of GM's Truck and Bus division—its head also happened to be in charge of international business. Inside that room, Wilson's luck changed, and he emerged with a $75,000 commitment for a feasibility study. That study eventually morphed into a full-blown solar racing program.

Back in California, AeroVironment was bubbling over with creativity. The team leader, Paul MacCready, had been hailed as the "Engineer of the Century" by the American Society of Mechanical Engineers. And MacCready was not only a visionary; he could implement. He was most famous for building the Gossamer Condor, a featherweight contraption that took the world record for longest man-powered flight. MacCready followed that up with the Gossamer Albatross, which crossed the English Channel on human power. He had built solar-powered planes and boats that stretched the limits of imagination. This gave his team ample experience in the kind of lightweight integration that would be necessary to win the solar race. Still, there was one particular engineering brain MacCready wanted for the GM-Hughes venture that was not part of his trust. That brain belonged to Al Cocconi.

Cocconi was an electronics whiz, but this whiz had zero intention of joining AeroVironment. As one observer put it, he was "not a team player." Yet after some negotiation, he agreed to work as a contractor—from his own house, keeping his own hours and on his own terms.

It was a compromise well worth making. Soon Cocconi was spinning out a stunning series of innovations. Where other electric cars were using DC power, Cocconi built a slender AC–DC converter that would allow his car to run on AC power and reach much higher speeds. The converter also cut down on weight. Cocconi had other tricks up his sleeve as well. By reversing his high-speed AC motor, Cocconi could generate electricity. This meant that as the car braked, he could capture energy that would otherwise be lost. That energy went straight back into the car's high-tech battery for future use—regenerative braking.

By fall of 1987, the solar-powered car was ready and it was christened the Sunraycer. As its sleek, PV-coated, teardrop figure slid away from the starting line in Darwin, the Sunraycer silently accelerated past two dozen rivals—never to be overtaken. It reached a stunning top speed of 60 mph, and averaged well above 40 mph throughout the race. The car was 100 percent American, 100 percent solar-powered, and crushingly dominant. It demolished the competition, crossing the finish line in Adelaide in just five days—two days ahead of its nearest competitor. For the first time in a long time, GM basked in the warm glow of complete American adulation.

AeroVironment sensed an opportunity and with Howard Wilson as their sponsor, they proposed that GM keep going and develop the Sunraycer into a full-fledged electric concept car.

Getting the Impact Out of the Chute

The Sunraycer generated a media lovefest, and GM's then CEO, Roger Smith, was hooked on the feeling. Despite internal opposition Smith pushed ahead with the team at AeroVironment. To follow up the Sunraycer they built an all-electric, two-seater sports car.

On January 3, 1990, Smith rolled into the showroom of Hughes in his newest toy—the Impact. The car's creators at AeroVironment had wanted to call it the "Santana" after California's famous Santa Ana winds, but GM's president exercised his veto power. To some the name Impact portended catastrophe, but for Smith it signaled a revolution— a new era for Detroit. "Most engineers would still be working on the 1971 Chevrolet if somebody hadn't grabbed it away from them," Smith explained of his decision to showcase the car. "I just figured it was time to get this thing out of the chute."[1]

The car was publicly unveiled at the Los Angeles Auto Show. As it entered, the Impact was completely silent and had no noxious fumes—it had no tailpipe at all. Smith touted the car's ability to go "further and faster than any previous production-oriented electric vehicle." According to its designers, its range was 124 miles at 55 mph.[2] Smith confidently announced that GM was considering commercialization. "We're looking to our customers," he concluded, "to tell us what they really want."[3]

But GM's bold foray into battery- and solar-powered vehicles was about to take an unexpected turn. It was not GM's customers who latched on to the AeroVironment masterpiece. Instead, the all-electric Impact was like catnip for California's tech-happy regulators.

Proof of Concept

The California Air Resource Board (CARB) had been considering the possibility of a "zero emission vehicle" (ZEV) for some time and Smith's announcement looked like proof of concept. Given the proper incentives, CARB thought, the auto industry was ready to move past the internal combustion engine into the future.

GM proudly showcased the Impact to CARB staff—even letting them drive it. And CARB was impressed. The two-seater clearly couldn't replace a minivan or a truck, but it could replace your average commuter vehicle. They thought automotive technology was poised to enter a new era, if regulators could only nudge them in the right direction. Ironically, the policy path toward implementing CARB's electric vision was paved not with batteries or solar cells, but instead methanol. For in California, the zeitgeist of clean air policy was coalescing around a sweeping and costly transition from gasoline and diesel to methanol-fueled vehicles.

Methanol was a liquid fuel that, unlike gasoline, could be produced from almost any feedstock with sufficient amounts of carbon—natural gas, coal, wood, or even municipal waste. Whereas gasoline and diesel produced a suite of toxic emissions, methanol produced only two: methanol and formaldehyde, both believed to be more environmentally benign than other gasoline emissions. One study at the NASA Jet Propulsion Laboratory suggested that a transition to methanol could reduce smog by 58 percent.[4] For CARB—the guardians of California's clean air—this was certainly worth fighting for.

But automakers and most oil companies hated the idea. Methanol mixed with water, and water could rust automotive components and pipelines. Car and oil companies would have to significantly redesign fuel systems to ensure compatibility and durability.

When oil companies realized the seriousness of this methanol-switching regulation, they went all out to oppose the state, but also to find a solution. Before long, they discovered that a much cleaner-burning gasoline—and also diesel—could be produced. In August

1989, the Atlantic Richfield Company (ARCO) unveiled a "reformulated" gasoline chemically engineered to create less pollution. This largely undermined the case for methanol, but surprisingly, regulators pushed on.

Nobody Paid Any Attention: Methanol, Natural Gas, and ZEVs

It was another battle royal, with CARB and clean air groups on one side and the car and oil companies on the other. In the midst of this fracas, California's regulators quietly slipped a new provision into the forthcoming regulations: a timeline for automakers to deploy progressively cleaner cars. Transitional low-emissions vehicles would give way to low-emissions vehicles, which would lead to ultra-low-emissions vehicles. Buried deep down inside the new rules was a requirement for automakers to produce something that would challenge the very nature of the modern automobile: ZEVs, or zero-emissions vehicles.

This was a very big deal. The "low-emissions vehicles" would require advances in the quality of fuel chemistry and engines. But ZEVs would demand an entirely new set of products—ones based on technologies demonstrated by the Sunraycer and Impact. For all intents and purposes, they would need to be powered by batteries—and that meant no oil.

"How could this be a problem?" thought the California regulators. After all, they had seen GM's electric car on the showroom floor. They had driven it! GM's sell job on the Impact prototype had been too good. CARB had not understood that the technology to commercialize EVs did not yet exist. Virtually every piece of the Impact had been handcrafted by its talented designers at AeroVironment—not manufactured. Transforming it into a production vehicle would require the car to be reinvented or, indeed, invented from the ground up.

CARB's rule declared that by 1998, 2 percent of new vehicles would be required to be ZEVs, and 10 percent of new vehicles would be ZEVs in 2003. This was a daunting mountain to climb. But in comparison to the methanol dustup, the car companies seemed completely unperturbed. "Auto companies are big, they're thoughtful, they're technically oriented. They don't freak out," said Clay Phillips, director of technology and energy intelligence at GM.[5] And this was certainly the initial reaction. In fact, according to one auto executive involved in negotiating the regulations, "nobody paid any attention to it."[6]

A Matter of Perspective

California's program was extremely aggressive. It was certainly "technology forcing"—meaning it required automakers to deploy technology that did not, at the time, actually exist. But, at the same time, its fundamental design was subtle and clever. The policy borrowed a number of sophisticated tools from Washington—devised for everything from improving fuel economy to eliminating acid rain. For instance, it used "credits" as a mode of compliance. When an auto company sold a ZEV in California, it would earn a specified number of ZEV credits depending on the characteristics of the car. CARB did not care which companies sold EVs: They could all be sold by one company, or be sold by many companies. However, if a company did not produce EVs, it was required to purchase credits from a company that did produce zero emissions vehicles. ZEV sales minimums depended on an auto company's market size, but companies were allowed to "over-comply" in early years of the mandate and bank those credits for later years. Finally, the ZEV mandate did not affect all manufacturers, only those with yearly sales of 35,000 or more in the state of California. At the time, this included Chrysler, Ford, General Motors, Honda, Mazda, Nissan, and Toyota.

In theory, the mandate was technology neutral, but CARB knew exactly what kind of cars it wanted and expected from the ZEV rule. It wanted cars like the Impact—electric cars. As far as CARB was concerned, these were the only true "zero emissions vehicles." Of course, some people disagreed with that assessment. Even battery-powered vehicles, they argued, were not truly "zero emissions" because EVs pull electricity from a coal- or gas-burning power plant. One energy expert called them EEVs, or Emissions Elsewhere Vehicles.

But there were two reasons the EEV argument didn't quite hold up. First, in addition to coal and gas, EVs would also draw upon nuclear power, hydro, and renewables like wind and solar. This meant that they had the potential to be much cleaner in terms of both air pollution and carbon emissions than gasoline-powered cars. The second reason is what happened to electric vehicles as they aged—or rather what didn't happen. Internal combustion engines became "detuned" as they got older—and they still do. In California, this meant that despite the fact that the state required regular smog checks, engine emissions from any particular car would likely deteriorate over the years. Batteries, on the other hand, had no such problem. In fact, a growing proportion of natural gas, nuclear, and renewable energy in California's generation fleet meant that EVs would become cleaner over time.

There were other problems as well. For instance, lead-acid batteries were toxic. But California anticipated this and planned for a major battery recycling program to address the issue.

Perhaps the cleverest element of the LEV and Clean Fuels Program is that it anticipated its own imperfection. In other words, it didn't expect to get things right the first time. Every two years regulators planned to come back to reexamine their assumptions, ensure that goals remained reasonable, and correct course where they might be off. One reason they could do this is that the program was politically uncontroversial—no politician was going to try to kill it, at least not in California. "Air quality was bipartisan—or at least until recently was bipartisan—and the political constituency for it was so powerful that there was no need to bother with other motivations or social goals," said University of California, Davis professor and CARB board member Dan Sperling. Rather than jamming policy through, as legislators frequently must in Washington, California had the luxury of actually getting the policy right. This did not mean, however, that the process was going to be pretty, nor that the mandate would make CARB any friends in Detroit.

GM CEO Roger Smith had wanted his electric Impact to change the world, and it was about to have an undeniably transformational impact on the global auto industry. But whether it signified a revolution or catastrophe was really a matter of perspective—and Detroit inclined toward the latter view.

6

CARB's Long Reach

D ETROIT HATED the mandate, but it had no real option but to comply. CARB, remembered one embittered auto executive, could "pretty much do whatever they want[ed]." Automakers said the mandate was overambitious, punitively expensive, and that compliance was infeasible. But some degree of acrimony was inevitable. Since Tom Quinn's tenure as chairman, CARB's entire strategy had been based on squeezing new technology out of the automakers. Over the ensuing decades there was rancor in abundance. But CARB's reach was now international, and it leveraged its advantages to the fullest. In the battle between Sacramento and Detroit, it was CARB that held the upper hand.

Detroit Was King

In Detroit the automakers were king. But in California, they felt more like a whipping boy for the state's environmental sins. Most American auto executives look back on the battles with varying degrees of resentment. One was Eric Ridenour—who started his career at GM before shifting to Chrysler, where he skyrocketed to the C-suite. Ridenour was a consummate Detroit man. Raised in Michigan, he was the first person in his family to attend college—with a BSME and, eventually, an MBA from the University of Michigan. He had a massive Germanic build, a keen engineering mind, and he spoke in tense, clipped, executive clauses. "They were totally focused on how to minimize different pollutions in California and the L.A. basin—which certainly was a very important and good thing to do," he remembered. Unfortunately for the likes of Ridenour, that often meant a drubbing for Detroit.

If clean air policy had been made in Michigan, the power dynamics would have been completely different—the auto industry would have had much more clout. But in California, the industry was incidental to CARB's central goal: clean air. "They didn't care what the cost was to the auto industry," Ridenour recalled with some acidity. "They didn't really care because the tax base was mainly outside of California."[1] Ridenour eventually made a remarkable transition: he became a convert to electric vehicles and CEO of the electric motors company UQM Technologies. But he still cringed at the memory of battles with CARB—quite.

According to one analysis, "virtually no automotive executive thought that the mandate was good policy, [but] the internal—not necessarily public—reaction to it varied across and within companies." Some American auto execs surely thought the mandate to be a case of government overreach, and a generally bad idea. But others thought it might be an opportunity to bounce back after decades of losing out to their Japanese competition—to leapfrog. Nowhere did these embers of reform burn brighter than at General Motors. The company was "trying to 'reinvent itself' by changing its image and rethinking the way engineering was done."[2]

But that was merely one strain of thought within a gigantic corporate empire—and it was by no means the dominant one. And before long, it became clear that fulfilling the mandate was going to pose a significant technical challenge and budgetary commitment. As costs mounted, so too did GM's resentment. Worse, as GM struggled with CARB it could not escape the fact that the company had—in some sense—created the mandate. At very least, they had inspired it. This irony hung thick throughout the 1990s as GM fought California and struggled to bring its electric Impact to market as the EV1.[3]

"No Plan B": Commercializing Electric Vehicles

Reengineering the EV that GM's CEO Roger Smith had delivered at the Los Angeles Auto Show was not a straightforward task. The Impact had not really been built by GM, but by AeroVironment. As a result, it had no radio, no AC, and little safety equipment. The new car had to be sturdy and comfortable enough for the GM customer and the radical custom-built componentry had to be redesigned for mass production.

As the car moved from concept to production, it became heavier, safer, and slower. Its range got shorter and its cost went up. It became clear that the Impact's mileage numbers were dramatically inflated— not because of misrepresentation but because they were generated during a highly optimized cruise around a racecourse at GM's proving grounds in Mesa, Arizona, instead of under real-world driving conditions. The vehicle had been so thoroughly preened during testing that mirrors had been removed, seams were duct taped over to reduce aerodynamic drag, and electrical auxiliary components were disconnected to prevent any drain on the battery.[4] Not only would performance need to improve, but the car's price and the price of the battery would have to plummet if the EV was to succeed commercially.

Roger Smith retired from GM on July 31, 1990, and it would fall to others to fulfill his pledge.[5] The idea of commercializing the Impact was radical, and from a business perspective perhaps radically irresponsible.

But it wasn't all bad. Auto companies learned early on that EVs could generate a media extravaganza. In 1996, six years after the original commitment to turn the Impact into a commercial vehicle, GM's EV1 was launched, again at the Los Angeles Auto Show. Public interest in the car was extreme. The event was broadcast to more viewers than that year's Super Bowl.[6]

Just like the EV1, the initial results of the ZEV mandate were, in many senses, spectacular. But they came at a high price to carmakers. And so, Detroit tried all sorts of methods to attack the regulations, from casting doubts on the environmental benefits to bluntly arguing—in exasperated language—that one could not simply mandate innovation. "One of the wonderful things about people in government is this: All they have to do to make something happen is make a wish, pass a law, and—lo and behold—they think it happens," read one biting editorial. "I wish that, instead of zero-pollution vehicles, CARB had mandated a cure for cancer," complained *Automotive Weekly.* "Maybe next time."[7]

But by 1994, the mandate was no longer a joking matter. The industry press had transitioned from analysis, to sarcasm, to mourning. "The zero-emissions rule hangs heavily over automakers," lamented one writer. A GM spokesman complained, "we're not being pessimistic, we're being realistic." Mazda explained that they would appreciate some "flexibility."

It was the opposite of regulatory capture—a situation in which the industry effectively controls regulation. For the automakers, it was a regulatory reign of terror. California was a market in which car companies simply *had* to compete. But it seemed auto execs, lobbyists, and lawyers could not convince California's dauntless leaders that producing competitive, profitable electric vehicles was simply beyond their technological capacity. Eric Ridenour remembered it this way: "I don't think they had a balanced view. They didn't have a crazy view—they weren't incapable of rational thought—but it took a lot of work."[8]

But California's regulators didn't *want* to sound reasonable. "There is no Plan B," said Jacqueline Schafer, the incoming CARB chairman.[9] The automakers, she said, would have to produce electric vehicles for the 1998 deadline, come hell or high water.

California and Japan

Though GM had set this entire process in motion, it would also lead the charge against the ZEV mandate—even as it worked to commercialize the EV1. In contrast, the Japanese automakers largely accepted California's regulations as a fait accompli and dove headlong into the technological crosscurrents.

There were a number reasons for this. First of all, Japan had just gone through a nasty bout of "Japan bashing" in the United States and it wasn't about to stick its head up. In the 1980s, its companies were attacked on Capitol Hill and its cars were literally smashed to bits by union sledgehammers. American factory workers accused Japan's carmakers of destroying their jobs and unfairly undermining U.S. competitiveness. By the 1990s, the Japanese had already started to invest in U.S. manufacturing facilities and things had subsided somewhat. But America was still Japan's largest export market for automobiles and the Japanese knew they were "guests" in this critical domain. Their best strategy was to play the model citizen. The emissions battles of the 1970s in Japan had also taught the country's automakers that fighting environmental regulation was not without peril—consumer backlash was a very real possibility.

In sharp contrast, GM, Ford, and Chrysler were not guests. They had "built this country." They had as much right as anyone, by their argument more than anyone, to push back. They were in no hurry to appease CARB.

But there were other reasons that the Japanese auto companies suddenly became more technologically aggressive. For its part, Toyota had been spooked by the Clinton administration's Partnership for a New Generation of Vehicles (PNGV). Clinton had promised to work with American manufacturers to build an 80-mpg "supercar" with all the luxuries of a modern sedan, and a fraction of the energy use. Facing a truly efficient and competitive American car was a chilling prospect for Japan's auto giant. Honda, on the other hand, was just a bit manic—never one to shy away from a challenge. It was almost as if Honda believed that any engineering challenge was possible—so long as an internal combustion engine was involved.

Toyota's Moon Shot

The Prius was part moon shot, part defensive bulwark. After the Japanese onslaught of the 1970s and 1980s, the Clinton administration took a much more aggressive stance in promoting the U.S. auto manufacturing industry. Clinton had a plan that was driven by both technology and policy.

Like GM and Hughes, Clinton thought that marrying America's cutting-edge research centers with its auto companies could revive Detroit's glory days. Clinton—and even more so Al Gore—sat down with automakers to lay the groundwork for the industry's resurgence. By 1993 they had settled on an effort to mine America's multibillion-dollar network of national labs for technologies that would enable American manufacturers to build a full-sized sedan that achieved 80 mpg. They called this effort the "Partnership for a New Generation of Vehicles" (PNGV). It appeared that the tables had turned. Now it was America that was carrying out an aggressive industrial policy in its automotive sector.

Reports of Clinton's PNGV program penetrated directly into the boardroom of Toyota. At the time, Japan's companies were the best in the world at combining price, quality, and fuel economy. But how could they compete against this government-sponsored monster? It was like a nightmare from the dark recesses of some Toyota exec's twisted imagination.

Toyota's aggressive response to this strategic threat ended up being much more material to the global auto industry than the dreaded PNGV. In early 1994, Eiji Toyoda challenged his team to build a monster of their own. He told them to start thinking about the "car of the future"—a vehicle that would survive an era of resource scarcity and reduced carbon emissions. The project was meant to produce a global car for the twenty-first century, and so it was called G21.

Eventually Takeshi Uchiyamada would serve as Toyota's chairman, but in the early 1990s he had never led a development team. In fact, he was something of an odd choice for the G21 lead. He was a specialist in harmonics and vibration. Nonetheless, Uchiyamada was charged with the task of creating a reasonably priced family sedan with gas mileage that was approximately 50 percent better than Toyota's already oil-sipping fleet.

After scrutinizing the technical hurdles and energy saving potential of more than eighty designs, they offered management the slightly cheeky hybrid design. "Sometimes when you get a very extreme piece of homework from your boss, the best solution is to respond with an extreme technology," remembered Katsuhiko Hirose, a former nuclear engineer and one of Uchiyamada's team members.[10] Surprisingly, management told them to build it. "We said, 'this is crazy,'" remembered Hirose.[11]

Uchiyamada's team was given absolute freedom in their design choices—they did not have to share components or platforms with other Toyota models. Their contraption yoked an electric drive train to an internal combustion engine and used each power source (battery, engine, or both) only when it was most efficient. Uchiyamada also slipped in a seldom-used but highly efficient engine design. It ran on a thermal dynamic cycle called the "Atkinson cycle"—with a compression stroke that was shorter than its expansion stroke. A properly executed Atkinson cycle allowed the engine to extract more useful energy out of the hot expanding gases inside the cylinder than the traditional Otto Cycle—where the expansion stroke was equal to the compression stroke. (The drawback was that the more efficient cycle sacrificed power for efficiency.) In addition to this, the car also used the same regenerative braking found in the Sunraycer to recapture some of the energy lost from slowing down and stored this energy in an onboard battery. This worked especially well in stop-and-go city traffic.

Building such a complex system was going to be a challenge on any timeline, but it looked feasible by the projected launch date of 1999—just in time for the new millennium. But in the spring of 1996 the company's chairman, Shoichiro Toyoda, and its president, Hiroshi Okuda, decided that they wanted to accelerate the car of the future, and told the team to have it ready by 1997. It was only afterward that Uchiyamada understood his company's mad dash to achieve its G21 goals: they wanted the launch of the Prius to coincide with the United Nations Framework Conference on Climate Change in Kyoto, Japan. The conference was intended to secure a landmark environmental agreement to place international limits on the emissions of carbon dioxide, and thus slow the rate of global climate change. Toyota's new commit-

ment to low-carbon transportation would be an important symbol of
Japan's industrial leadership. They had just two and a half years—as
opposed to the five or six usually allowed for developing and designing a new model.

The 1997 deadline almost set off a revolt within Toyota's engineering ranks, but management did not retreat. Project G21 was moved to
a war footing, even though Toyota's engineers were still having trouble getting the engine and battery computers to communicate. Sometimes the car would just sit on the tarmac, refusing to move. Other
times, it would burst into flames.[12]

At the same time, development was helped by the fact that Toyota's
engineers found the entire project engrossing. Hirose recalled that he
would go home at night and he couldn't get his mind off creative solutions for whatever obstacle stood in his way.[13]

By October 1997 the snub-nosed Prius was complete. Like the Sunraycer, Impact, and EV1, it was part car and part marketing campaign.
And in the end, both components functioned beautifully. Together
with its other fuel-efficient vehicles, the Prius burnished Toyota's reputation as a "car company that cared" about the environment. It also
established Toyota as the industry's undisputed technology leader.

On the other hand, Toyota's electric vehicle—designed to fulfill
the California mandate—was a classic example of a "compliance car":
built to regulatory specifications along the path of least resistance.
For the Prius, Toyota engineers had laboriously crammed two separate
powertrains into a subcompact vehicle. They did this because putting
the hybrid system into an SUV would have sent the wrong environmental message—even if the fuel economy savings were even more
impressive.[14] But for the California EV mandate, Toyota took no such
care. Instead, they simply bought a bunch of batteries and engineered
them into a RAV4 SUV—which had lots of space for energy storage
devices. The all-electric RAV4 went on sale just in time to meet CARB's
ZEV requirement.

By the standards of the day, Toyota's RAV4 was a completely respectable electric vehicle, but it wasn't a moon shot and it certainly
wasn't a game changer.

The Curious Case of Honda

Toyota's reticence on electric vehicles was largely lost on the general public, and its Prius made it the darling of environmentalists. On the other hand, Honda's intense focus on engineering solutions once again endeared it to CARB. As always, the regulators wanted to push the industry to its technical limits, but not beyond. To do so, they required an auto company that was willing to probe those limits. "The general posture was that you needed to find at least one car company that would go with it," said CARB board member Dan Sperling. "Honda was usually that company."

Honda developed close relationships with NGOs, regulators, academics, and other local interest groups. It sought out their technical, political, and ideological input. The company was shrewd, intensely focused on California's market and dedicated to delivering technology solutions. Honda's leadership believed it made more sense to engineer answers than fight city hall. For all these reasons, CARB loved Honda.

But initially when the ZEV mandate came out, Honda's engineers were as perturbed as anyone else. It was sure to be expensive—and challenging. After all, they were an engine company, not a battery maker. Nonetheless, the company's labs soon got to work and "went all out." If they were going to do this, they would do it right. So Honda built the first "advanced battery" electric car, with a nickel metal hydride power pack, and worked overtime to improve performance and bring down cost. Honda's management also made sure to signal to its employees that their work on the EV project was just as important as anything else going on within the company.

At GM, many of the EV1's enthusiasts were railroaded, demoted, and left with a bitter taste in their mouth. At Honda, they were "respected and promoted," remembered Honda North America's vice president for R&D, Ben Knight. He recalled that Honda "appreciated the challenges, we appreciated the learnings, we appreciated the technologies . . . versus some other companies where people kind of dead-ended."[15]

CARB had assigned the automakers some challenging homework,

and Honda played the typical teacher's pet. It didn't simply meet the minimum requirements, it went all in to satisfy the professor's neurosis. It built a battery-powered vehicle, but it also did something else. It started to research the feasibility of constructing a zero-emission engine.

Trees Emit More Pollution than Hondas

When CARB announced its low-emissions vehicle (LEV) rule, it demanded a vehicle that produced zero "criteria emissions"—this meant no NOx, no carbon monoxide, and no unburned hydrocarbons. Every other car company assumed that this meant no combustion engine. But Honda rejected this logic. Two decades earlier, when Honda was just getting into automotive production, it had audaciously leapfrogged Toyota and GM and achieved emissions standards those companies said were impossible. Similarly, after California set its LEV rule, the company set an internal goal to completely eliminate criteria emissions from its exhaust. Other auto companies were saying "customers don't care about this." But CARB did care, so Honda did, too.[16]

As a result, one by one, CARB's "impossible" emissions standards fell conquest to Honda's engineers. In 1996, Honda's compact Civic became the first gasoline-powered vehicle to achieve California's LEV standard. That year, Honda also "stepped out and said we can achieve a ULEV [ultra-low-emissions vehicle] standard in two years."[17] Less ambitious manufacturers were livid—they knew that they would have to follow in Honda's footsteps. But still, Honda did not rest. It pushed ahead to SULEV (super ultra-low-emissions vehicles) and upper management egged them on. "Keep going," they said.

Eventually, criteria emissions from Honda vehicles got so low that they couldn't even be measured by CARB's cutting-edge emissions labs. A decade and a half earlier, Ronald Reagan had been quoted as saying that "trees emit more pollution than automobiles do." In the past, that was certainly untrue. But now, unbelievably, it was. California had to build new instrumentation to detect the tiny amounts of criteria emissions from Honda's most advanced engines. Some of Honda's engines were running so clean that the air coming out of the tailpipe was *cleaner* than the ambient levels in the lab and natural environment. Of course, CO_2 was still a problem, but Honda had achieved what others had thought impossible, a zero (criteria) emissions internal combustion engine.

Like any teacher's pet turned valedictorian, Honda took a good amount of pride in its accomplishments. "Others snapped back," remembered Ben Knight. "We solved it elegantly and beautifully."[18]

Old Man Honda had passed away in 1991. But surely he would have been proud. His company had become one of the greatest engineering empires the world had ever known. It was building cars that were better in every way than the Jaguar he had once bragged on as a young man. Honda's zero-emissions engine was another notch on the belt for the engineering culture its founder had so assiduously cultivated. The company called it "the power of dreams."

Defending the Mandate

But even Honda could not, at that point, make an electric car that was truly competitive with its gasoline-fueled counterparts.

As companies began to actually build and deploy electric vehicles, the technical hurdles came more sharply into focus. What also became clear was that some of the tough talk from CARB—that there was "no Plan B"—was posturing. There had to be a Plan B, because CARB had demanded too much. When regulators realized that automakers were not going to meet the 1998 mandates, they backed down. In 1996, CARB agreed to postpone the rules until 2003. But CARB also wanted to extract some concessions in exchange for this temporary reprieve. So it decided that in 2003 automakers would have to make 10 percent of their California fleet emissions-free and there would be no ramp-up period. They would also have to meet the new EPA clean air guidelines, so called "49-state car" standards, three years earlier than the federal government required.[19]

The mandate had lost its innocence. After 1996, what began as a simple, unequivocal directive started to evolve into a much more complex set of rules. These allowed automakers different amounts of ZEV "credits" for different kinds of vehicles with different technology and emissions characteristics.

On the one hand, the relaxation of the EV requirement was a boon to manufacturers, as it gave them additional time to prepare their cars for the California market. But it also undercut the certainty of the new rules.[20] The temptation for the automakers to probe the limits of CARB's resolve was overwhelming. For if CARB was willing to change the mandate, this intimated something else: they might also be persuaded to kill it entirely.

7

The Electric Car Is Dead,
Long Live the Electric Car

With all this technology-forcing regulation, California had become ground zero in the auto industry's internecine innovation wars. The results were a curiosity to regulators, drivers, and technology buffs around the world. They inspired widely divergent passions.

On a hot day in 1997, Quentin Willson, host of the BBC television series *Top Gear*, slid behind the wheel of something that looked less like a car he might normally drive than an outsize metallic Tylenol with a glass pod on top. It was GM's response to the California rules—the EV1. The British automotive connoisseur was about to get a taste of California's new electric coupe.

With about twenty miles of range left on the battery, Willson decided to put on a bit of a show. He clicked off the air-conditioning—presumably to save batteries—and began to worry out loud that he might not make it back. Stranded in the mean streets of Los Angeles, he would be left at the mercy of axe murderers and serial killers. Pulling into the Saturn parking lot with just four miles left in his battery pack, the sweaty TV host pronounced his final verdict: "probably the most stressful ride of my life . . . The batteries suck, the range is appalling and if you had to buy one it would cost you a whopping 35,000 pounds."

Wilson's brush with death was playacting—*Top Gear* would pull a

similar stunt with the Tesla Model S some years later. But he wanted to
send a message: the EV1 had a long way to go before it would be ready
for a broader audience.

But to a clutch of Californians, the EV1 was much more than the
sum of its parts. Certainly the EV1 was quiet. Its range was respectable.
And its handling and acceleration—zero to 60 in about 8 seconds—
were both up to par for the day. But all of this paled in comparison to
the coupe's raw symbolic power. For its supporters the EV1 was more
than just a car, it was an idea. It symbolized a commitment to ending
America's dependence on foreign oil, society's reliance on fossil fuels,
and to building a new American auto industry that could innovate its
way to the front of the pack in a rapidly globalizing economy. And so,
when California started to loosen its regulations and GM decided to
remove its cars from the streets, the result was a media firestorm.

Who Killed the Electric Car?

Under the hot Los Angeles sun, a lifeless body lay draped in a midnight satin shroud. But the grim, glassy death stare was mechanical,
not human. A few minutes earlier, a parade of EV1s had filed into a
parking lot behind a bagpipe player droning "Amazing Grace." The
cars were charged and ready for the open road, but none would drive
again. Each of these EVs would be loaded onto trucks, sent to the
GM proving ground in Mesa, Arizona—just yards away from where
their forerunner, the Impact, was road tested—and unceremoniously
crushed.

Dozens of sullen, well-heeled Californians assembled in black suits
and funeral dresses to mourn the death of the electric car. The activists had offered to buy GM's herd of electric horses for $1.9 million,
but the company had rejected their proposition. The funeral, their last
act of protest, was seared into the American consciousness by the cult
documentary hit *Who Killed the Electric Car?*

In fact, it wasn't just the EV1. A long parade of electric Toyotas,
Hondas, and Ford EVs were also sent to the crushers in the early 2000s.

The facts behind why automakers were literally shredding their most advanced consumer vehicles were in sharp dispute. One side of that argument was represented by a petite young redhead who whimpered as she lay a bouquet of flowers on the hood of a doomed EV1. Her name was Chelsea Sexton.

At the age of seventeen, Sexton had walked into a Saturn dealership in Southern California to buy a car. The strawberry blonde was smart, vivacious, passionate, and very pretty. By the time she left, she had both a new set of car keys and a job offer. Sexton became the youngest salesperson at Saturn and, as such, she worked overtime to prove herself to the dealership's patrons. "As a seventeen-year-old girl in the car business, you have to know twice as much to be thought half as good," remembered Sexton. By the age of twenty, Sexton was already a three-year veteran of the sales force, and she had taken an interest in GM's EV experiment. She inquired about joining the EV1 sales team. After an *"American Idol*–style" set of interviews, Chelsea was drafted.

It was a heady time. Many on the EV1 team believed that they were the vanguard of a transportation revolution, and Chelsea fell passionately in love with her mission. The young team trained, traveled, and played together, all with the goal of promoting the EV1. When GM decided to retire the car, Chelsea just wasn't ready to let go.

Together with a small group of EV1 enthusiasts, Sexton spearheaded the campaign to save GM's electric car from destruction. She had lost her job with the closure of the electric car program, but she was still working for the EV1. Now her goal was to shame her former employer into preserving the doomed effort—or at least the cars themselves.

A surprising coalition grew up around her crusade. It included national security buffs like former head of the CIA James Woolsey, actors like Mel Gibson and Danny DeVito, scientists, policy makers, conspiracy theorists, environmental groups, and everyday EV enthusiasts.[1]

The Culprits

For her part, Sexton accused the car companies of sabotaging the EV effort from the start. Others proposed additional villains—some real and some imagined. The oil industry was one. As soon as California's ZEV mandate began to take hold, the oil industry began to push back with a variety of arguments—many of them tenuous—against the commercialization of electric vehicles. For instance, groups supported by the oil industry argued that EVs were not "socially equitable" because poor people couldn't afford them. This line of attack raised eyebrows among those who had not hitherto seen the oil industry as a champion for social equity.

At a national level, Republicans were increasingly positioning themselves as opponents of new environmental technologies and alternatives to oil in transportation. In Congress they beat back repeated Democratic efforts to eliminate rich tax incentives for Americans who purchased gas-thirsty sport utility vehicles like the Hummer.[2] The incentive offered up to $100,000 in tax credits for the heaviest, least efficient vehicles. It had initially been conceived to help small businesspeople who served as limo drivers or needed to buy farming equipment, but now it was enabling an entire generation to buy Hummers and other large SUVs almost for free. At the same time, the George W. Bush administration was using its authorities to stymie California's ZEV regulations.[3]

Some EV activists also attacked the California Air Resource Board, and particularly Alan Lloyd, who chaired the board from 1999 to 2003. Lloyd had spent much of his career working on fuel cell technologies and was very open to the industry's argument that the future would be more about hydrogen fuel cells than EVs. And so Lloyd blessed a shift in the mandate's focus from battery electric vehicles to a much smaller number of hydrogen fuel cell vehicles. For this, Lloyd was roundly vilified.

But it was hard to believe that CARB, which had served as the midwife to commercializing consumer EVs, had now switched sides. It was more accurate to say that CARB was recalibrating in the face of a significant body of evidence that the mandate was not working out. Costs were still high and range remained a problem. While batteries appeared to have stalled out, there was a great deal of industry optimism surrounding fuel cells. It's also possible that CARB didn't want to be left behind in the fuel cell revolution that Washington was trumpeting with such grandiosity. There were disagreements and divisions within CARB, but these were transparent to the media and public. After ten years, some at CARB felt justified in tweaking the mandate's focus.

At the same time, it is undeniable that the board made some mistakes, both technological and also in terms of communications with the growing community of EV enthusiasts. First, in the early 1990s CARB had gone too far, too fast on EVs. Then, just as lithium-ion batteries were gaining force in the market, CARB began to ease pressure on automakers. "You think that you understand the technology and that you're right on the science and that people will just understand that," said CARB's chairman Mary Nichols some years later. "That leaves out the emotional element of people's relationship with these issues and you can't do that." Fundamentally, said Nichols, there was no murder conspiracy against the EV. It was a technology-driven decision. But in the end, that didn't matter—CARB seemed implicated. "Boy was crushing those cars a horrible thing to do."[4]

8

Catching China's Eye

AFTER CARB's RETREAT, the EV was not dead in America, but it was certainly not in rude health. Yet despite the uncertainty hanging over California's electric experiment, one thing was absolutely clear: for the first time in a century, manufacturers had launched a serious research and commercialization effort on electric vehicles. GM said they had spent $1 billion on the EV1.[1] And GM was just one of many. Ford produced an all-electric Ranger pickup truck, Toyota had its all-electric RAV4 sport utility vehicle—which was later revived in 2012 on a Tesla powertrain. Honda built a car called the EV Plus, and Nissan launched an electric version of its Altra with lithium-ion batteries and a range of 125 miles.[2] In addition to this, Nissan also produced a pint-sized, futuristic two-seater called the Hyper-Mini.[3]

Of course, the automakers did not build these cars willingly. They did so under explicit threat from CARB. GM had shown leadership by developing its all-electric Impact. But those days were long past. Since there wasn't much of a market for electric cars, competition was not a driver. So policy—in other words, CARB—was the sole convective force powering this tornado of innovation. CARB was purposefully making a big ask of the automakers and intent on pushing them to the limit. They wanted to project clear, long-term strategic goals for the industry, while at the same time allowing for certain tactical flexibility—California's regulators had no illusions of omniscience.

But at the same time, CARB did not want to promote policies that were financially ruinous or needlessly punitive.

But the automakers were starting to believe that the ZEV policy was exactly what CARB did not want it to be: punitive and financially ruinous.

At some point every automaker had crossed swords with CARB. And they did so for three overriding reasons. First, there was no discernible market for EVs—interest was high, but customers were scarce. One Toyota North America vice president summed up the problem this way: "there were 'hand-raisers' for both the EV RAV-4 and the Prius hybrid, but while 50 percent of hand-raisers ended up purchasing the Prius, only 1 in 100 ended up buying the RAV-4 EV." Despite the fact that Toyota spent "gobs" of money promoting it, dealers sold only "about 50" RAV4s in the first week. Thereafter, they were only able to sell or lease around five a week.

Second, what EVs automakers sold, they sold at dramatically subsidized rates—which meant car companies lost huge amounts of money on each unit delivered. Many believed that Toyota was already losing money on the nickel metal hydride battery packs they used in their Prius hybrids and that the Prius was little more than a glorified marketing campaign. Pure EVs required batteries that were much more expensive and much bigger.

That points to problem number three: technology was not merely a challenge, it was simply not ready. Modern automotive lithium-ion batteries—with dramatically increased energy density—were half a decade away.

CARB's insistence and the industry's resistance fueled a spectacular fracas between California and the automakers. And halfway across the globe, an Audi engineer named Wan Gang was taking notice.

Revolutionary Road

He had spent a decade in Germany as a student, then as an engineer for Audi, but Wan Gang's thoughts had started to return to his homeland. Wang had led a number of delegations to China for his company and Audi was doing well back home—a black Audi would soon become the calling card of China's elites. But Wan knew that there was something much bigger to come. China was on the brink of transformation, and that metamorphosis would have profound consequences. For the past twenty years, China had been trying to resurrect its decrepit auto industry, and Wan Gang wanted to join the movement. For China, it was deeply humiliating to constantly rely on technology that had been borrowed, bought, or stolen from Japan or the West.

Unlike Japan, China had never built up its own, truly domestic auto industry. Almost all of China's auto technology was of foreign origin. Its early trucks were based on the Soviet ZIS 150—a four-ton military vehicle produced at the Stalin Auto Plant in Moscow.[4] And the ZIS design had actually been copied from Ford years earlier.[5] The plush government limousines that Chairman Mao Zedong and Premier Zhou Enlai commuted in were also knockoffs—based on an old Mercedes.

During the 1960s, while Japan was feverishly consolidating its automotive producers to gain scale and technological competence, China was building miniature clones of Soviet auto factories throughout the country's interior to protect its industry from foreign military attack.

When Deng Xiaoping began his economic reforms in the 1970s, China's government arranged for a manufacturing partnership between a struggling American Motors Company—the maker of Hummer and Jeep—and the Beijing Automotive Industrial Corporation. It set the stage for many more Sino-foreign joint ventures to come. This kind of manufacturing partnership—where foreigners supplied automotive technology and manufacturing expertise in exchange for access to mainland markets—dominated Chinese auto production from the 1980s through the 2010s. Foreign companies worried about handing over their blueprints to Chinese partners, but the market potential was too alluring. So one after the other, foreigners fell in line.

China was a wild new world, completely uncharted, and everyone wanted in on the game. There were Jeeps, VWs, and Citroëns, but also a number of oddballs. One, called Panda Motor Corporation, was funded through a $250 million investment from the Korean reverend Sun Myung Moon's Unification Church.[6]

As Deng Xiaoping's reforms took hold and the country's central government released the reins of economic control, cities and provinces shook off the shackles of central planning and became increasingly entrepreneurial. Many local governments started to build their own automotive concerns—some of them based around the carcasses of Leninist factory relics.[7]

They did not produce quality vehicles. Early diesel trucks had only one cylinder—as opposed to six, eight, or ten in U.S. or European trucks—and they spewed so much black soot that foreigners called them "ink fish."[8] And China's market was still not producing at scale. In 2000, China manufactured fewer passenger cars than Spain—about 600,000.[9] But the next year, car sales began to surge.

China's entry into the World Trade Organization (WTO) was the critical turning point. The WTO—a series of international trade agreements—would prohibit member countries from discriminating against Chinese imports, and the quid pro quo was that China was obligated to reduce its own barriers to foreign imports and institute a number of other economic reforms. This set of promises made the country a significantly more attractive destination for foreign direct investment, and American, Japanese, European, and Korean investors began to inject huge sums of capital into the Chinese economy.

Sharp tariff reductions forced Chinese automakers to reduce their own prices to compete with foreign models. That was the downside for domestic producers. But the upside was that the effect on sales was not linear—a small drop in price often led to a massive surge in sales. When one domestic producer cut its prices by 20 percent, sales leapt 900 percent *the following month*.[10] In 2002, China's economy grew by a healthy 9.1 percent, but auto sales skyrocketed by an astonishing 37 percent.[11]

From 2002, China's auto market multiplied outrageously. Bank lending rules subsidized cheap capital, which allowed Chinese manufacturers—especially large state-owned ones—to finance new factories at bargain-basement rates. As a result, China was quickly catching up to and surpassing the West in manufacturing capacity as it became a new "workshop of the world."

But while China's concrete, steel, and manufacturing capacity—and even the size of its auto market—was overtaking the West, its technology was not. The best cars built and sold in China were all designed by Western companies and manufactured in Sino-foreign joint ventures. Chinese companies needed to develop an eye for aesthetics, the acumen to control quality along deep and complex supply chains, the know-how to test durability and ruggedness over hundreds and thousands of miles, and dozens of other similar capabilities.

There was no single piece of technology that could be bought, built, or stolen to unlock that puzzle. High-quality vehicles were the product of expert design, flawless construction, and orchestration of a vast army of contractors. Thousands of discrete elements had to be integrated, perfectly, every time. That was the genius behind the Japanese auto manufacturing system and key to their global success.[12]

China fell short in all those areas. As a result, China's leadership began to hear a lament that its industry was "big" but not "strong."[13]

Leapfrog: Revolutions, Refugees, and the Education of Wan Gang

Wan Gang's industry acumen, his personal charm, resourcefulness, and innate willingness to "think big" put him in a position to potentially address the vexing riddle of Chinese technological inferiority. Wan Gang was one of thousands of Chinese engineers who had traveled abroad to study engineering and then burrowed into the guts of advanced Western auto companies. This cadre of technical experts provided a potential bridge past Japan, Korea, and the West. Wan was one of many, but he had one somewhat intangible quality that seemed to set him apart from the rest: he had a knack for turning proverbial lemons into something much more palatable. China's leadership made a big bet that Wan could do the same for its expanding automotive industry.

Wan's road to power started as a sixteen-year-old, during the height of China's frenetic, and sometimes brutal, Cultural Revolution. In 1968, as the government whipped China's youth into an almost religious fervor for Mao Zedong, millions of them were also banished to collective farms in the countryside. Wan was expelled from the bustling city of Shanghai to a rural district with no electricity, no hospital, no shops to speak of, and hardly any roads. This would be his home for the next eight years.

There were ritualized beatings of government officials, teachers, parents, and other authorities and also senseless destruction of China's cultural relics by the *hongbing* (紅兵) or Red Guard. Together with these other turmoils, the forced sojourns were designed to upend the order of society—and in that, they succeeded. They were a common fate for the children of urban elites and intelligentsia. But although these forced evictions were traumatic, they sometimes had unexpectedly positive results.

Wan's silver lining was a hands-on practicum in electrical engineering, infrastructure development, and engine technology. He helped build a hospital and also an electrical generator for the community. Wan and his fellow exiles, who numbered about twenty, constructed the community's electrical grid with their own hands.[14]

Personally, Wan developed a fascination with one particular piece of equipment: the village tractor. He spent long hours in a work shed disassembling and reassembling the tractor's internal combustion engine. It was his textbook, tutor, and hobby. In addition to introducing him to engines, his detour into the countryside also taught Wan how to build something out of nothing. It was a useful skill set for an ambitious engineer.

When the "revolution" subsided, Wan returned to Shanghai and matriculated at Tongji University. For graduate school, he traveled to Germany, where he was exposed to some of the world's most sophisticated automotive curriculum at the Clausthal University of Technology. At graduation he had offers from no fewer than six car companies, including Mercedes, BMW, and VW. But he liked Audi—it was the smallest, with the greatest opportunity for growth.

Initially, Wan's home at Audi was in vehicle development. But Audi had an "unwritten rule" regarding promotions: if you wanted to move up, you needed to change departments. So he eventually switched to a workgroup that painted about two thousand cars a day. Although painting sounds basic, it was not. Wan's team used sophisticated robots, was pioneering new environmentally friendly techniques, and attracted the attention of not just company leadership, but high-level German and international politicians.

Wan was eventually promoted to central planning, which gave the Chinese engineer a bird's-eye view of Audi's entire production process. Audi's vehicle lines were inhabited by 1,400 robots that could pump out a car every 62 seconds. The line was a modern marvel of engineering.[15]

Comfortably ensconced as a midcareer executive within the nerve center of one of the world's most dynamic auto companies, Wan felt secure enough to venture back into the academy for a stint as a visiting professor back at Clausthal. But he still maintained his position at Audi.

Away from the galloping drumbeat of Germany's automotive machine and Audi's internal politics, Wan's mind gravitated back toward China's impending automotive boom—he knew it was coming. It seemed obvious that China's rising affluence would accelerate motorization and would lead to a host of knotty social, economic, and environmental problems—just as it had in Japan and the United States. Petroleum imports would bulge, and air quality would take a frightening turn for the worse. Indeed, China's huge population meant that these problems were bound to be more severe than elsewhere. It wouldn't be sustainable.

Wan's big break came when he was asked to host a delegation of Chinese government officials. As a Chinese national, teacher, academic, and engineer Wan was a natural choice to welcome a group of high-ranking Chinese guests. He had performed this ambassadorial role many times. But the consequences of one particular visit were bigger than anyone might have imagined.

China's minister of science and technology, Xu Guanhua, had been searching for potential solutions to just the kind of problems that had been bothering the Audi professor. And as Wan walked him through the halls of Audi, he took the opportunity to explain a plan that could address all China's impending automotive problems—China's technology gap, the oil imports, Beijing's stifling air pollution, and climate change.[16] The crux of this plan was that China should look past the internal combustion engine—it should seek to leapfrog the West, and build the most advanced and cleanest auto sector in the world.

The challenges of oil imports, technology dependence, smog, and climate change were almost too overwhelming to consider in the context of China's industrializing economy. But Wan's novel solution, electric cars, could address all of the above.

To Xu, Wan Gang was a compelling figure. He had spent time abroad—in the belly of Germany's industrial leviathan. He spoke from experience when he told Xu that other countries were already working on replacing petroleum-fueled vehicles with battery-powered cars. At the turn of the century, China consumed only about a barrel of oil per capita per annum, but a developed nation like Japan consumed 15—the United States consumed more than 20.[17] Burning oil at that rate would deplete China's entire recoverable reserves in a single year.[18]

Perhaps the most compelling part of this equation was the opportunity to be at the starting line with global competitors. The race for the electric vehicle had just begun. If China moved swiftly and decisively, it had a chance to jump the competition and avoid another era of technological humiliation.

Xu Guanhua's colleagues on the State Council were mostly engineers and he knew they would understand these environmental challenges and resource constraints as well as anyone.

Shame for Glory

Quietly, Xu arranged for Wan Gang to present his ideas to China's highest ruling body. Walking into that meeting surrounded by the stony-faced rulers of the world's most powerful authoritarian nation must have been intimidating. These were the whales of Chinese politics. And Wan was, by every political and social measure, a minnow. On the surface, Wan was an affable, unassuming automotive expert; he had no political ambitions and wasn't even a member of the Communist Party. But Wan was no political dummy.

Wan was animated by an intense, unquenchable, internal fire. He understood that, if he played his cards right, within the space of a few short minutes Wan Gang—once banished to a tractor shed in the countryside—could change the course of Chinese history.

After that day, the Chinese government hastily engineered Wan Gang's return to China. A well-worn story line claims that he did not even have a job, and simply moved into his mother's house in Shanghai. But in retrospect, it seems much more likely that a decision—in fact, many decisions—had already been made.

The forty-nine-year-old Audi engineer was quickly installed as a professor at Tongji University and put in charge of a secretive government program to develop advanced vehicle technologies. Based on Wan Gang's industrial vision, China's leadership had decided to develop its industry for "new energy vehicles" faster, cheaper, and at a larger scale than the West or Japan. Through generous funding and intense focus, China moved to establish itself as a world leader in electric vehicles.

This much was obvious: the sector was going to have to rely on state support—industrial policy. Since the time of Henry Ford, no automobile industry in the world had ever become internationally competitive without that kind of government intervention. America's innovation policies had been set through federal R&D, safety standards, fuel economy laws, and environmental regulations—as well as a deliberate retreat from public streetcars, enormous investments in roads and other auto-friendly infrastructure, and a sustained engagement in the Middle East to defend the global spigot of cheap oil. Japan had channeled technology, foreign exchange, and loans to their automakers—and they had also kicked out the American competition. The same was true across major European economies and Korea.

But it was easy to make mistakes in this kind of endeavor. In the name of industrial consolidation, Japan's planners had almost stamped out Honda as a car company—which could have cost them dearly in the global race for emissions and fuel economy. On the other side of the world, Brazilian policies promoting localization of automobile production had resulted in cars that were extraordinarily expensive and also low quality. Wan Gang's idea of "leapfrogging" the West—rather than merely catching up—added a new dimension to the challenge.

But China's leaders knew that the government and markets had the potential to effect great transformations—they had witnessed it in the previous two decades. The world was changing, and China had the opportunity to spearhead this transformation.

Poised on the starting line of the next and possibly final heat of the Great Race, they hoped that if China ran hard enough, it might retake the crown from Japan and America. The stakes were more than wealth, power, or global economic leadership. The prize was a victory that could expunge a century of humiliation, and supplant shame for glory. Wan Gang's strategy was a go.

PART II

Leapfrog

9

Sea Turtles, Spaceships, and the Hydrogen Economy

AFTER ALMOST a decade of technology-forcing policies, California's regulators were beginning to have second thoughts. The goal of achieving a zero-emissions vehicle was still there, but the mechanics of making it happen were increasingly unclear. Two decades earlier the Air Resource Board had succeeded in stimulating a global revolution in pollution control by mandating that automakers reach emissions standards that most declared to be impossible. But now it seemed that battery technology was not nearly as amenable to being forced. But although California was poised for a tactical retreat on some of its zero-emissions rules, the state's ZEV program continued to have powerful secondary effects that would reverberate throughout the global economy and propel the industry forward. None of these was more important than the push that the ZEV mandate gave to competitors in Japan and China.

Hearts and Minds

In the early 2000s, California was still the most important and visible force promoting the new industry paradigm—and propelling the Great Race forward. And so one might expect that the California Air Resource Board's 2001 decision to reduce the stringency of the ZEV mandate would have been a great relief to the industry—and especially Detroit. Specifically, CARB had decided to allow automobile manufacturers to offset some of their EV requirements with higher fuel efficiency.

But rather than accept the truce, the automakers parried, and attacked ferociously. This, they thought, was the chance to permanently end the much-hated mandate.[1] GM led the charge and sued CARB. But a judge rejected their lawsuit out of hand. GM could not claim damages because the regulations had not yet taken effect. So GM lay in wait. Once the rules had kicked in, it sued again.[2] And in June 2002, GM's lawsuit won an injunction against implementation of California's guidelines. In the short term, the strategy seemed to be working. But General Motors' attack on California's ZEV regulations was typical of everything that was wrong with the American auto industry. It was tactical, abrasive, and had the effect of alienating not one but many important constituencies.

From the perspective of quarterly returns, or a single product planning cycle, GM's efforts to dismantle California's ZEV program were full of merit. After all, infrastructure was a problem, investments in existing facilities for internal combustion engines were substantial, and batteries were too expensive and bulky to create a truly compelling vehicle. In the innovation industry, EVs would have been referred to as "bleeding edge" technology—a term that is short for "before leading edge." Whereas leading-edge technologies are at the spear point of commercialization, bleeding-edge technologies are not yet ready for the market. Often companies will avoid even the leading edge, preferring to wait until the market has been proven and settling for the role of a "strong second" or "strong follower."

GM's focus on undercutting CARB was infused with the logic that had allowed Toyota and Nissan to whittle away at its market share over the years. It ignored the many practical benefits of the ZEV program. ZEVs were a potential source of technological diversification; they were an investment in R&D and a new transportation design for the twenty-first century. And just as important, they were a ticklish topic with the general public.

Although EVs were still not selling in great numbers, the idea of the EV—a car that didn't pollute and helped America kick the oil habit—was immensely popular. Once the innovative American company that developed the Sunraycer and EV1, GM had morphed into the villain that "killed the electric car." Its high-profile skirmishes with the Air Resource Board helped sharpen that negative image in the minds of many Americans.

While Toyota was investing prodigiously in the hybrid revolution, Detroit was relying on massive, polluting, gas-gulping Hummers, Escalades, Suburbans, and other SUVs for their profits. The lawsuits were a bare-knuckle tactic to protect this business model. American auto companies were perceived to be part of the problem, not the solution. "Instead of sending engineers, we sent lawyers," recalled one rueful GM executive years later.

In 2003, CARB settled yet another lawsuit with manufacturers, again stretching out the time horizon for implementing the ZEV mandate, weakening the program, and allowing a smaller number of fuel cell vehicles to substitute for each battery electric car.[3] Things were going extremely well for GM's lawyers, but not so for America's electric car. Indeed, everything seemed to be going dramatically wrong.

Freedom from Electricity

This wasn't just in California. It was also in Washington—in the Department of Energy and the national labs. Under George W. Bush, Clinton's Partnership for a New Generation of Vehicles was discontinued and transformed into a very different beast: the "Freedom Car"—a program that was cast as part of a larger "Freedom Agenda."

After the terrorist attacks of September 11, 2001, the Bush administration had co-opted the word *freedom* to mean anything that supported its policies. It could be deployed to justify invading Iraq and Afghanistan, cutting taxes, or shifting the focus of an R&D program. It was important for government bureaucracies to show that they were supporting the cause, because Bush had made it clear that if you weren't for freedom, you were against it.

Officials in the Department of Energy had no intention of getting on the wrong end of freedom's lance, so they hurriedly devised a new explanatory scheme to shield their programs from potential budgetary cuts. The justifications for promoting hybrid and electric vehicles had seemed self-evident under the Clinton administration. They ranged from environmental goals, to reducing demand for oil, to promoting the competitiveness of America's auto manufacturers. But now the DOE was forced to defend its vehicle research efforts on the basis of four "freedoms." Two of these were relatively uncontroversial:

- Freedom from pollutant emissions, and
- Freedom from dependence on imported oil

In years past, the first would have been called environmental policy. Now it was a "freedom." The second freedom was just another take on the well-trafficked Washington policy trope of "energy independence." So calling them "freedoms" appropriated the language of the Bush administration, but didn't do very much else.

But the next two "freedoms" that animated Bush's notional "Freedom Car" were much more heavily imbued with the administration's particular perspective on energy and transportation policy. One was the "freedom for Americans to choose the kind of vehicle they want to drive, and to drive where they want, when they want." It was a coded rhetorical rebuttal against California's policy of mandates and electric vehicles. Mandates—and even higher fuel-efficiency regulations—were seen as the government telling citizens what cars they should drive. Electric vehicles had short range, which would supposedly inhibit Americans from driving "where they wanted." And finally, they took time to charge—thus transgressing the third clause of "when they want." By the Bush administration's reckoning, if Americans wanted to drive an 8-mpg Humvee, they should have all the gas stations and cars necessary to do so.

The last freedom was the "freedom to obtain fuel affordably and conveniently." Again, this was a jab at slow-charging electric cars. It was also justification for keeping gas prices low—which would no doubt work against Freedom Car's goal of reducing America's dependence on foreign oil.[4]

The whole program was a rhetorical mouthful and philosophically, many of its components were at odds with one another. Substantively, all this freedom meant that federal research programs moved away from batteries and hybrids, and increasingly focused on incremental improvements to the efficiency of combustion engines and a long-term goal of promoting hydrogen fuel cells.[5]

The shift gave EV enthusiasts heartburn for a number of reasons. The most obvious was that the entire program was based on fossil fuels. (Combustion engines ran on gasoline or diesel, which basically meant oil, and fuel cells on hydrogen, which would likely be refined from natural gas or coal.) This was starkly demonstrated by the changing composition of PNGV's—now Freedom Car's—membership. Formerly focused on auto companies, by 2005 Freedom Car had expanded to include ExxonMobil, BP, Shell Hydrogen, and ConocoPhillips.

It was like catnip for conspiracy theorists—and with good reason. Some argued that including the fuel providers was a boon to the program, but others saw it as a sinister plot.[6] Letting the oil companies into a fuel-efficiency R&D effort, they said, was like letting a fox into the henhouse.

The Bush administration, it seemed, was intent on dismantling much of the previous decade's progress on promoting clean cars.

Wan Gang and His Sea Turtles

Washington's shift toward fuel cells sent a very confusing signal to global manufacturers and research centers. No one wanted to be swimming against the technology tide.

In China, the electric vehicles program was off to a slow and uncertain start. Before Wan Gang's presentation to the State Council, the Ministry of Science and Technology (MOST) had been running an EV pilot program in the southern island of Nanao and gathering data on EV fleets. But it would have been a stretch to call this a Chinese EV research program. The cars were mostly foreign imports designed and built to meet California's standards—though there were a few crude domestic models.[7] In addition to this, a fleet of sixteen-seater buses was deployed on the Beijing campus of Qinghua University— China's equivalent of the Massachusetts Institute of Technology and the cradle of its engineer-laden political leadership. But buses were a lot easier to build than cars. For one, there was much more space aboard for batteries, which meant that power density and design were not great concerns. The buses also followed a set route and at relatively low speeds, so they did not need to be engineered for extreme mileage or driving conditions.[8] This was about as much as China could do at the time.

Wan Gang had far grander ideas.

Wan Gang was part of a rising generation of Chinese business leaders called "sea turtles." In China, social elites fell into distinct classes. For instance, the children of Communist Party leaders were called "princelings." The princelings used their political connections and social rank to accrue wealth and power. But the "sea turtles" were something completely different. The sea turtles generally worked their way up China's social ladder through education. At some point, they would strike out for America, Australia, or Europe for work or study. But just like real sea turtles—which swim the oceans for years and travel thousands of miles—they always returned home to lay eggs on the exact same beach where they themselves were born. Back in China, sea turtles used their cosmopolitan education, skills, and foreign connections to build careers—and businesses.

Over the 2000s, China's stunning economic growth drew legions of sea turtles back to its beaches. These returnees played a critical role in modernizing the automotive sector, and the most influential, by far, was Wan Gang.

In some ways Wan's sea turtle story was quite typical. He left China to study engineering, then after graduation he got a technical job at a foreign multinational and built a solid reputation.

But when Wan returned to China, his story diverged dramatically from the typical sea turtle adventure. Wan's quiet politicking and his presentation to the State Council propelled the "New Energy Vehicles" program into the forefront of Chinese techno-industrial policy. On the strength of Wan's vision, vehicles were folded into China's incubator for critical bleeding-edge technologies: the cryptically named "863 Program." This was the beach where Wan would play for the next half decade. It would serve as Wan's springboard to the top tier of China's ruling echelons.

Keeping Up Appearances

The full name of the 863 Program is the "State High-Tech Research and Development Program." But most Chinese call it 863 because it was born in March 1986—or 86/3. That month, four of China's most prominent scientists—Wang Daheng, Wang Ganchang, Yang Jiachi, and Chen Fangyun—presented a report to the Communist Party titled "on the follow-up study of foreign strategic high-tech development proposals."[9] The study made what should have been an obvious point: China's technology had fallen badly behind that of the West.

The unsurprising assessment was still an embarrassment to the state—and its critique of the Chinese system was a serious risk for its authors. But the China of 1986 was far more open to criticism than it had been under Mao. So, instead of muzzling the scientists and shunning the technology manifesto, Deng Xiaoping and his reformers embraced it. The State Council ordered a vigorous research and commercialization program to be undertaken to target key industrial sectors. These would come to include biotechnology, robotics, deep sea exploration, optical computing, and, eventually, automobiles.[10]

One of the key goals of the 863 Program was not just to develop new technologies, but to develop them domestically without borrowing from abroad. The Chinese spent generously to rope in researchers, universities, and private enterprise—dispensing almost $50 billion in its first two decades.[11]

But although the initial goal was to promote Chinese technology, before long the 863 was as much about Chinese prestige as Chinese progress. In other words, propaganda was a primary objective. Consider China's space program.

863's Wild Ride

In the early hours of October 16, 2003, the crown jewel of China's 863 project, the Shenzhou 5 reentry capsule, glided down from space to earth over the Mongolian grasslands. Shenzhou 5's twenty-one hours in orbit had secured China's place as only the third nation in history to independently launch a human into space. As the capsule door was flung open, a basically robust-looking astronaut named Yang Liwei smiled enthusiastically. The large red communist flag on his snow-white space suit offered the perfect photo op for the proud Chinese nation. "I feel good," he had told his wife and the mission controllers from space. But only a few minutes earlier, Yang had looked gruesomely bad.

When the capsule was first opened, Yang appeared wan, listless, and drenched in blood. The sight shocked and horrified onlookers. Critical mistakes had been made in the design of the capsule, and they had almost cost the space pioneer his life. As the craft took off, g-forces crushed his whole body. "All of my organs seemed to break into pieces," he later wrote. But when Yang landed, the media censors leapt into action. Though it was billed as a live broadcast, the event was actually on a time delay. This gave the censors precious minutes to re-craft the narrative. So Yang was mopped off, strapped back in, and the capsule was resealed for a second "live" take. This time the return was triumphal. For seven years his secret remained intact—a PR success for China's scientific establishment.

Some of this same spirit animated China's EV program. Vehicles were a highly visible and technology-intensive sector. They were an article of prestige for any industrialized nation. China wanted to *appear* to be at the forefront of automotive technology. To do this, China needed to keep a finger on the pulse of the trends in Detroit, Munich, and Tokyo.

Finding "Some Alternative"

In the early 2000s, Wan picked up on Washington's new obsession with fuel cells and became a tireless promoter for the technology at home.[12] "China's oil demands are increasing day by day. According to statistics, each year, about 40 percent of [this] oil is used in transportation," explained Wan to a reporter in 2003. With fuel cells, he added "we can find some alternative . . . we can save that portion of resources, and also protect the environment." The one downside, mentioned Wan, was cost. But he estimated that fuel cells would cost only about 20 percent more than a standard internal combustion engine.[13]

In fact, fuel cells cost a lot more than that and most of their advocates were in for a rocky ride. But not Wan; his career was on a lightning streak. In 2003 Wan Gang was promoted from his post as dean of the New Energy Automobile Engineering Center to vice president of Tongji University. Within a year, he became president of the institution, which was remarkable, not in the least because Wan's new position conferred upon him the rank of vice minister of the People's Republic of China. Rarely had a non–Party member reached such lofty heights.

But while Wan's political intuition was keen, his bead on critical technologies was off. The real action in the auto market was not with fuel cells at all—it was still with batteries. And right next door in Japan, and across the Pacific in the United States, something remarkable was happening.

In the 1990s, the Toyota Prius was an ugly, snub-nosed techno-curiosity with a weak engine and even weaker sales. It had hardly made a dent. But this unfortunate little car had recently been redesigned. The new generation of Prius was bigger, stronger, and boasted a distinctive aerodynamic shape that screamed, "I do not look like you because I am the future!" Its sales were about to take off.

When the second generation of Prius hit the U.S. market, "it caused a great sensation," remembered Frank Liao, the chief technology officer of the Beijing Electric Vehicle Company. With the explosion in hybrid sales, helped along by rising gasoline prices, the future of the auto industry suddenly looked more defined: this was not the decade of the fuel cell; it was not the decade of electrification. Toyota's gamble had paid off. It was the hybrid generation.[14]

10

Crazy Anegawa

WHILE THE Chinese scrambled to get their technical bearings, and American automakers traded blows with CARB, the Japanese focused on maintaining their lead in quality, value, and technology. The Japanese had no interest in fighting city hall—especially in America. So Toyota, Honda, and the rest sat back and watched that drama unfold as mostly passive observers. When Freedom Car got rolling, they were happy to research fuel cells—if only to keep pace with technology trends of the day. But each major Japanese company had its own pet technology—and they didn't need Freedom Car to drive their research agenda.

Although Honda was CARB's golden child, it was also the engine company. Nonetheless, it maintained a deep bench of expertise. Whenever CARB approached Honda with a regulatory challenge, the company's engineers heroically sought to move whatever mountains stood in their way. Unless they believed that the prospects were truly hopeless, they pushed ahead. In California, Honda even beat Toyota to the hybrid market—Honda's Insight launched before the Prius in the United States. But fundamentally, Honda remained intently focused on building the world's best internal combustion engines. No one, not even Toyota, could compete with Honda's combination of quality, technology, and value.

Toyota, on the other hand, was the chosen vessel of the hybrid generation. An unlikely confluence of events had transformed the company from a process-oriented value manufacturer into the world's technology leader in advanced powertrains—and one of the industry's most admired companies. Toyota had been benefiting from a protracted lovefest with the media because of this. And soon Toyota's vaunted synergy drive—the technology that powered the Prius, the Big Green Monster—would make its way into other models as well.

From a technology standpoint, Nissan wasn't particularly differentiated. But to the extent it was, Nissan's calling card was probably performance. Its flagship model was the Skyline GT-R—a legendary Japanese racer not even sold in the United States. The Skyline was fast—wicked fast—but it was certainly not fuel-efficient. Nissan clearly wasn't seen as a champion of environmental vehicles. Yet despite this, Nissan still benefited from the "green halo" hanging over Toyota and Honda—a halo they had earned as a result of their pioneering fuel efficiency, emissions, and hybrid technologies.

Each Japanese company had its own quirks, priorities, and corporate DNA, but many Americans lumped the Japanese automakers together. There were, however, some ways in which the Japanese makers really *were* the same. For one, they didn't have much interest in building EVs. Second, they had even less interest in picking a fight with California regulators. Their environmental credibility was blue-chip and a fight that risked tarnishing this image was simply not worth the prize.

Back in Japan, the likely response to a question on EVs might very well have been another question: "Do we even need EVs when the Prius already gets forty, maybe fifty mpg?" In 2001, Japan's MITI (the Ministry of International Trade and Industry) was supplanted by a new ministry: the Ministry of Economy, Trade and Industry, or METI. And METI was subsidizing hybrids with generous incentives. This really amounted to subsidizing Toyota, for it was Toyota's hybrid that set the standard. In fact, Toyota was so vastly ahead of other automakers in hybrid technology that the rest of the industry's mission became obvious: simply catch up. Without CARB forcing the issue, it certainly appeared that EVs—the kind that plugged into the wall—were not going to happen anytime soon.

But one Japanese engineer didn't get that memo. Perhaps this was because he worked not for an auto company, but for a sprawling nuclear utility. Indeed, the engine that drove Takafumi Anegawa was nuclear power. While much of Japanese society looked on nuclear energy with suspicion—even hostility—Anegawa was different. In nuclear, he saw a solution to his homeland's energy security equation and environmental problems. Nuclear was already integral to Japan's electrical system, but Anegawa thought it could do more—especially in transportation. But even the Tokyo Electric Power Company (TEPCO)—Japan's largest provider of electricity and nuclear energy—could not simply move forward on this vision alone. It needed to secure the support of various stakeholders within Japanese society. These ranged from the national bureaucracy, to industrial conglomerates, to local government officials. The general public was also an important constituency, but one that was bound to be difficult to win over. But Takafumi Anegawa had a vision for how all this might be accomplished. The crux of this vision was a "nuclear car."

This nuclear car, he reasoned, could convince Japan's wary citizens that relying on domestic nuclear energy was, in fact, preferable to depending on energy supplies from the notoriously unstable Middle East or Russia—a country with which Japan had an ongoing territorial dispute and with which it never signed a peace treaty after World War II. To Anegawa, one thing was beyond doubt: hybrids couldn't make his dream a reality. So, in the midst of the hybrid revolution, and against all the odds, he decided to push ahead on EVs. They called him Crazy Anegawa.

The Long Shadow of Fukushima

A lifelong nuclear engineer, Anegawa was passionately devoted to the cause of atomic energy. However, from the time he was a young man, Anegawa also realized that Japan's utilities needed to find creative ways to communicate the benefits of nuclear power to the Japanese people. They were fighting an uphill battle. Japan's most devastating war had ended with a cataclysmic nuclear holocaust, and the Japanese were said to have a "nuclear allergy." This meant that they did not like nuclear bombs, they did not like nuclear aircraft carriers or submarines, and they did not like nuclear electricity. In fact, they didn't like nuclear anything.

But Anegawa was different. The energy shocks of the 1970s cemented his belief that only nuclear power could deliver Japan from the thrall of Middle East petrocracies. His studies, career, and even his family life were absorbed into this passion.

Anegawa's first assignment with the Tokyo Electric Power Company was a three-year stint working on core and fuel safety in a reactor complex called Fukushima Daiichi, in northeastern Japan. The reactor at Fukushima Daiichi was an old model, without some of the safety mechanisms of newer plants, but this didn't bother Anegawa. In fact, he liked working at Fukushima. The town was small and rural, surrounded by farms and rice paddies—what the Japanese called *inaka*. It reminded him of the town where he had grown up. Anegawa settled into the rhythm of *inaka* life, got married, and raised his children in the shadow of the Fukushima nuclear plant.[1]

But eventually Anegawa got called back to Tokyo. Again his job focused on core safety. In other words, Anegawa was responsible for managing the complex reaction that caused nuclear fuel to break down and produce heat—heat that was ultimately used to spin massive turbines to generate electricity for the lights of Tokyo's Ginza district, office buildings across the city, and the factory workshops of Toyota, Honda, and Nissan. These nuclear reactions played out on a subatomic scale, but with consequences so powerful that they had the potential to destroy civilizations. They were beautifully complex, nonlinear, and could run wildly out of control.

Core safety was a hot topic through the 1980s. This is because in 1979, a close call at the Three Mile Island nuclear complex near Harrisburg, Pennsylvania, had reminded the world that producing electricity from uranium entailed the sustained containment of hazardous nuclear forces. Although no one had actually been injured in the accident, during the crisis the reactor complex had teetered on a knife's edge between malfunction and catastrophe. In 1986 the nuclear disaster at Chernobyl, Ukraine—deadly and vast in comparison to the scare at Three Mile Island—confirmed nuclear energy's capacity to destroy lives and property and to render entire regions poisoned for generations.

And in Japan, three additional external threats needed to be considered in the context of nuclear safety. Earthquakes and typhoons were part of the cadence of Japanese life. Just like Japan's homes, the country's fleet of nuclear reactors had to be hardened against these. But there was another associated threat—though one that was much more rare. It had to do with an earthquake at sea and the resulting tsunami. Seawalls were built to protect TEPCO's nuclear plants against these fabled disasters. But they were not a front-of-the-mind issue—after all, truly devastating tsunamis were very rare and rarity bred complacency.

Despite the fact that Japan was seated in a tricky corner of the globe, it had maintained a relatively high degree of nuclear safety. Japan had not suffered a Chernobyl or a Three Mile Island. There had been an accident at a uranium processing facility in 1999 that killed two workers and exposed about four hundred to low-dose radiation.[2] It was a serious event, no doubt, but one that failed to shatter the so-called "myth of absolute safety" that permeated Japan's nuclear culture.

Still, many Japanese remained profoundly ambivalent to their country's growing reliance on nuclear energy. In 2008, only about 40 percent of Japanese supported nuclear power, while almost 80 percent believed that lax security at these power plants made them a target for terrorists.[3] But despite the average citizen's reservations, Japan's nuclear dependence was set to increase—from about 25 percent in 2010 to 50 percent by 2030.[4]

To Anegawa, this baked-in growth was a good thing—an excellent thing. And nuclear's position was made sure by the fact that, like Anegawa, much of Japan's technocracy was firmly in its corner. At TEPCO the atomic genie was venerated, almost worshipped. Despite the country's demonstrated interest in cutting edge environmental technologies, Japan's utilities would much rather work on reactors than play around with renewables. "They like nuclear, they hate renewables," confirmed one high-level METI official regarding Japan's options for low-carbon diet.[5]

TEPCO's EV program was part of a larger effort to ensure a more central position for nuclear power in Japan's energy mix. It was largely the result of Anegawa's hunch that, with the right technologies, the public might eventually learn to think like TEPCO—to stop worrying and learn to love the atom.

Cars, Trucks, and Boats

In 2001, the forty-four-year-old Anegawa was stuck in a very technical and academic funk. He was preparing a conference paper called "Internal Gap Lattice for ABWR-II Reactor" for a nuclear conference in Hollywood, Florida. But Anegawa kept getting distracted by a much more entrepreneurial thought. If TEPCO were going to expand nuclear power generation, he reasoned, it would help to show the Japanese people that nuclear power was a solution to the country's broader energy issues—including energy security and climate change. There had to be value added beyond the traditional electricity-dependent sectors. Japan's cars, trucks, boats, and planes still relied on world oil markets, and Anegawa wanted to change this.

Transportation was, in some senses, the final frontier for Japanese energy security. So Anegawa wrote up a bold, transformative proposal for his superiors at TEPCO. The crux of this strategy was for the company to lead Japan in the electrification of automotive transportation. "I am not a battery scientist," he later recalled. "But I could tell that battery chemistry was progressing." Lithium-ion batteries had been developed and commercialized in the United States and Japan over the previous thirty years. But in 2002 they were just reaching the point of viability for automotive applications. As a rule of thumb, lead-acid batteries—which had been used in electric cars from the days of Edison up to the EV1—produced about 40 watt-hours of power per kilogram. The next generation of batteries was nickel cadmium, and they didn't do much better. Nickel metal hydride made a huge leap, to perhaps 80 watt-hours per kilogram. But a lithium-ion battery could achieve around 160 watt-hours per kilogram—four times better than lead acid, and about twice as much as nickel metal hydride.[6]

In addition to the emerging technical potential in batteries, Anegawa also knew that TEPCO's ability to bring together a wide variety of stakeholders from across Japan's industrial world might be substantial enough to organize an ecosystem of automotive, battery, and electric companies into a transportation environment where EVs could thrive.[7]

"In other companies—especially overseas companies—such a crazy bottom-up proposal would never be accepted," Anegawa remembered.[8] But at TEPCO, it *was* accepted. When no one stepped forward to lead the new program, Anegawa offered to do it himself.

Other nuclear engineers thought he had made a huge mistake—which is why they called him "Crazy Anegawa." But Anegawa had come to the conclusion that lithium-ion batteries were a game changer. A friend at Mitsubishi, Hiroaki Yoshida, had sold him on the concept and Anegawa's confidence was reinforced by the proliferation of lithium-ion cells in consumer electronics. Cars, he figured, were the next logical step.[9]

For TEPCO, EVs held out the prospect of a vast new market for nuclear energy. If Japan's industrial planners from METI could be convinced that EVs were a viable prospect, they would also have a wide range of reasons to support the technology. Secure, clean, nuclear energy could displace hundreds of billions of dollars of imported oil. EVs also held out the possibility of helping Japan's automakers assert industrial leadership in the twenty-first century.

On the Ropes: Japan's EV Industry After California

For a year or two Anegawa's program didn't look like much. He worked alone. Much of his time was spent studying batteries or knocking on the doors of potential industry partners. Some of his projects were fanciful—for instance, he built his own prototype electric vehicle, the ugly little "An1," which he entered into an electric car race. It finished last. But Anegawa's enthusiasm was unquenchable—even as he was spurned by what seemed to be the entire industry.[10]

Part of the problem with launching the EV program was that both carmakers and regulators thought Anegawa's timing was all wrong. Most major automotive companies had established EV programs in direct response to the California mandate in the 1990s. However, many of these research-and-development programs were disbanded as CARB loosened its EV mandates and adopted a "portfolio approach"—focusing on super-low-emission vehicles, hybrids, and a much smaller number of fuel cells and EVs.[11] Because the strictest elements of the mandate only applied to companies designated as "large-volume" manufacturers, smaller companies—like Mitsubishi and Kia—had little incentive to research plug-in electric vehicles. Larger companies were thrilled to be rid of California's burdensome regulations.

From TEPCO's perspective, gasoline and fuel cells pointed to a much less clean and secure source of energy than nuclear power. But when they made this argument outside the company's walls, they were swimming against the industry tide—Washington, Sacramento, Toyota, Honda, GM, BMW, and even METI were all focused on hybrids and fuel cells. A flood of government funding was deluging hydrogen-focused research, and the "smart money" was not on EVs.

The "Two Bests": Toppling Toyota and Honda

Anegawa needed to overcome not only huge technology hurdles, but also the opposition and interests of the incumbent technology leaders. In Japan this could be reduced to two companies, Toyota and Honda (aka, the hybrid company and the engine company). Japan's two largest auto producers were not only the locus of future-oriented fuel cell research, development, and deployment activities, but they were also the guardians of the most successful commercial power trains. One TEPCO employee called these the "two bests." Toyota had its Big

Green Monster, the Prius, which was the best hybrid system in the world. And Honda had the best engine technology in the world. Both companies intended to keep their lead.[12] If Toyota and Honda were not on board—worse, if both of them decided to oppose EVs—then METI was unlikely to support TEPCO.

Within the industry, Toyota was renowned for a somewhat insular mind-set. Toyota's global headquarters was a ninety-minute train ride from Nagoya, in a sleepy *inaka* province called Mikawa. This area was the home to the founder of the Tokugawa Shogunate, Tokugawa Ieyasu, and for one Toyota executive the importance of this legacy could be summed up in two words: conservatism and stability.

Hybrids had been an uncharacteristically gutsy gamble for Toyota. METI had propped up the technology through market incentives for a decade in order to level the playing field with regular cars. But despite METI's market crutch, Toyota had to invest billions of dollars in hybrid platforms and it lost money for years before its "HEVs" (aka hybrids) finally became profitable.[13]

All of this presented a problem: Toyota had taken a risk, it had invested, it had won that bet, and now it wanted to reap the rewards. And METI was also invested in Toyota's success, for it had supported these efforts along the way with rich and sustained subsidies. So as the prospect of EVs materialized, Toyota officials adopted a strategy that would have looked relatively familiar to their competitors in Detroit: from Tokyo to Washington, D.C., they pulled out the stops to oppose plug-in technology. They urged Washington and Tokyo to focus on "the sustainable present" —in other words, hybrids.

In some senses Toyota was right. EVs were a long-term prospect—like hybrids in the 1990s. Hybrids were an immediate and even economical solution. To convince METI of the EV's viability, Anegawa would need partners with the resources, initiative, and technology to challenge these two "bests"—and METI's preconceptions. If EVs were going to be successful, they would need to reach critical mass, and it would be impossible to achieve this on any foreseeable time horizon without at least one major auto company—ideally more than one auto company—supporting his plan.

Mulling his options, Anegawa knew Toyota was the ideal partner. The company had a deep historical interest in electric vehicles.
As early as the 1920s and 1930s Toyota Loom Works was investing
significant sums to develop EVs. Even then, it was already clear that
Japan was critically short of petroleum, and Sakichi Toyoda surmised
electrics might be a good long-term bet. In fact, he had set up a large
cash prize for the individual or company that discovered a better battery. He himself used to commute to work in one of the company's
electric prototypes—there were six.[14] During the early years of the Allied forces occupation, production of passenger cars was banned, but
electric vehicles were considered acceptable—they were a loophole.
So Toyota and other auto companies built passenger vehicles based on
lead-acid batteries. Toyota spun off its electrical components division
into the company DENSO, which built and sold about fifty EVs with
a respectable 121-mile range. In 1949, the number of EVs produced
in Japan exceeded that of gasoline-powered cars. But that year, the
Korean War caused a spike in lead prices (lead was necessary for bullets, mortars, and batteries), thereby dramatically increasing the cost
of Toyota's EVs. The Allied forces' General Headquarters also removed
the ban on passenger car production, so Japanese automakers reverted
to the internal combustion engine, and DENSO eventually dropped
EVs.[15] Two decades later, the oil crisis again stimulated research in the
area, but interest in EVs retreated with the global oil price.

But Toyota's real comparative advantage came from the company's
stunning success with hybrid electric vehicles. Toyota understood
how to design, fabricate, and integrate batteries, inverters, and electric motors into automobiles. In particular, its control system that
synergized the battery and electric motor was extraordinarily sophisticated.

Unfortunately, Toyota was not interested. Indeed, their interests
were just the opposite. The ministry was essentially supporting a
Toyota (and Honda)–endorsed vision of the near and medium-term
future. It was hybrids, more hybrids, and efficient ICEs for the next
decade or so. Fuel cells were the solution for the long run. This was a
future in which nuclear power and TEPCO had no part.

But EVs were a different story. Not only would they allow a dramatic expansion in nuclear power; they would increase plant utilization during off-peak hours. EVs could charge at night, while lights and other appliances were turned off. This could allow TEPCO to potentially sell a lot more electricity without building any expensive new generation plants. But it wasn't just self-interest. Anegawa simply didn't buy the whole "hydrogen economy" story that Toyota and Honda—and America—had been selling. Anegawa thought that fuel cells had major obstacles in terms of cost, infrastructure, hydrogen storage, and the carbon-free production of hydrogen fuel. In fact, there was a running joke in the automotive community that hydrogen was the fuel of the future, always had been the fuel of the future, and always would be the fuel of the future.

Engineers chuckled over this punch line, even as they sought to disprove it. Nonetheless, METI had invested heavily with the Japan Automobile Research Institute and Japanese car companies to build out a hydrogen-refueling infrastructure and bring pilot hydrogen commuting to the streets and highways of Japan.[16] By 2004, there were ten experimental hydrogen-refueling stations across the nation. But fuel cell vehicles still cost millions of dollars to make. With such an unfavorable cost profile, all the infrastructure in the world wasn't going to tip Japan's markets.

Searching for Hercules in Japan

Any automaker challenging Toyota and Honda—and METI—would be sticking its neck out, and building a viable EV system would be a herculean feat. Seeing as a company was likely to 1) lose money and 2) incur the wrath of the two most powerful automakers, there didn't seem to be much to gain.

But Anegawa was lucky: Japan was perhaps the only place in the world where numerous companies existed with the potential to confront such a powerful status quo. There was Nissan—the number-three automaker in Japan and number six in the world—and Suzuki, as well as Mitsubishi, a comparative bit player in autos but a giant in industry, chemicals, robotics, and technology. Then there were smaller companies—Subaru, Isuzu, Mazda, Kawasaki, Yamaha, and UD Trucks—that were less prominent, but still world class in their automotive manufacturing capabilities.

Most people today believe that Nissan was the electric pioneer. But actually it was Subaru and Mitsubishi that broke the logjam.[17] And they didn't do it for purely regulatory reasons. Because of their size, California ZEV regulators didn't require Mitsubishi and Subaru to build EVs. They only forced GM, Ford, Chrysler, Honda, Nissan, and, of course, Toyota.[18] Nonetheless, Subaru and Mitsubishi were the companies where TEPCO's Anegawa found potent pockets of support.

These two companies were driven by a complicated series of institutional factors, including technological ambition, recent corporate failures, competitive impulse, and a desire to build a distinctive public identity as an electric pioneer. They were also driven by powerful personalities who became emotionally vested in the EV concept.

At Mitsubishi, Hiroaki Yoshida was something of an EV fanatic. He had been investigating the potential of EVs since 1994.[19] Yoshida created an EV based on the company's Libero platform in the 1990s and called it, rather uncreatively, the "Libero EV." But the vehicle was a mess. Yoshida felt "embarrassed" by its short range, long charge times, and technical problems. Nonetheless, he bounced back. His team soon prototyped the world's first "plug-in hybrid" electric vehicle, naming it the Chariot EV. It had lithium-ion batteries and an all-electric range of 60 kilometers, as well as an onboard internal combustion engine to recharge the battery. This vehicle was specifically aimed at the California ZEV mandate. But since the state relaxed its regulations, Mitsubishi never put the costly vehicle into production.[20]

Yet even after California eased its standards, Yoshida didn't give up. His passion for electrics took on a life of its own. With company backing, he set a world record for the most miles traveled by an EV in twenty-four hours at the Mitsubishi Motors Car Research & Development Center Proving Ground. He wanted to prove to the world that the obstacles of charging and distance could be overcome. So through a marathon of 70-kilometer dashes and twenty-minute quick charges, he completed 2,142.3 kilometers in a day.[21]

Still, by the early 2000s, Yoshida knew that proposing a new EV program was a bust. In fact, it was a proven means of incurring the wrath of senior executives. No EV had ever made money, none was likely to in the near future, and Mitsubishi's management was not in the mood to spend more yen on Yoshida's expensive hobbies.[22] So Yoshida cut his own path. He still had a sizable research budget under his control and when Anegawa told him TEPCO wanted to push EVs into the mainstream, Yoshida secretly dug into his accounts to develop a new EV for Anegawa. The EV program was a taboo—a subversive corporate secret. It was also an uphill battle.

When Yoshida's team approached battery and motor companies for components, they encountered the same skepticism Yoshida experienced internally at Mitsubishi. As Kenichiro Wada, who later led commercialization of Mitsubishi's EV, recalled, "we visited so many candidate suppliers, but almost all the suppliers said 'sorry, we cannot do that.' Many people said, 'it's the hybrid generation, not electric.' "[23]

In the face of rejection, the team pushed ahead. They continued until the bill of parts for Yoshida's prototype began to take shape. "Fortunately, GS Yuasa and Meidensha said, 'Okay, if you ask so many times, we will make you some sample parts.' Not production parts, just sample parts!" remembered a still exasperated Wada.[24]

Even with sample parts, the results were encouraging. New technology was enabling a vastly improved EV system; foremost were the lithium-ion batteries that would extend the range of Yoshida's prototype. But other elements, like the more powerful, more efficient, more compact permanent magnet electric motors made from so-called rare earth elements, would also empower the design. These motors could be fit in the wheels of the car, leaving more space for passengers inside. Yoshida and Wada believed the new system was a game changer.

After putting the final touches on their "Colt EV," Yoshida's team decided it was time to take the next critical step. It entailed some substantial risk for the rogue lab. They trumped up some excuse to invite Yoshida's boss, Tetsuro Aikawa, the corporate general manager for product development, to the R&D center where the vehicle had been furtively fashioned. On the way out Yoshida casually suggested Aikawa test-drive their new Colt EV. Aikawa was surprised by the project. But he held his judgment in check. In fact, it piqued his interest.

"There are two kinds of people in car companies," recalled TEPCO's Anegawa. "There are mechanical engineers, and people who like to drive." Aikawa liked to drive. When he stepped in, Aikawa pressed the accelerator and the car responded with a smooth, "torquey" pull.[25]

By the time Aikawa stepped out of the car, the question of whether Mitsubishi would have another EV program was settled. The car could perform. It was slick, and it had the potential to provide a path past Toyota's dominance in hybrids and Honda's in engines. Just as important, it could provide something Mitsubishi was sorely in need of, a positive story line for the global media to latch on to.[26]

A "Halo Car"

Mitsubishi had not been doing well. In 2003, it had lost $1.3 billion and its partner DaimlerChrysler refused to inject any more cash into the flagging enterprise. From an image perspective, this was the least of Mitsubishi's problems. "Mitsubishi has been rocked by scandals for nearly a decade," wrote a *New York Times* auto columnist in 2004. "In Japan, there were payoffs to gangsters and cover-ups of defects; in the United States, there were falsified sales reports and a *huge* sexual-harassment settlement involving the Illinois plant. Lax lending practices, which helped to lift sales for a while, have come back to haunt the company; analysts say $1 billion in loans may have to be written off."[27]

There was also one other problem: Mitsubishi cars were not very fuel-efficient. Unlike Toyota, which had a suite of models with fuel economies ranging from 25 to 46 mpg, the vast majority of Mitsubishi's fleet clustered around 20 mpg—only one car sold in the United States broke the 25-mpg barrier.[28]

The company's stock had dropped almost 90 percent from 1999 to 2004. In the course of just one year, Mitsubishi Motors Corporation was twice bailed out by its sister companies—Mitsubishi Heavy Industries, Mitsubishi Corporation, and Mitsubishi Tokyo Financial Group—each time to the tune of about $5 billion.[29] The time was ripe for change.

Further, the company's CEO, Hideyasu Tagaya, who had been an ardent worshipper of the internal combustion engine, exited, creating an opening for what would eventually be called the "iMiev"—or Mitsubishi in-wheel motor electric vehicle.

In addition to shaking off its overall corporate malaise, the company wanted to demonstrate a new commitment to reducing carbon emissions. Increased efficiency could be one part of that solution; EVs could provide another.[30] And so, Mitsubishi got on board. But Mitsubishi, TEPCO, and Subaru (which also joined TEPCO's EV development project) would, without question, need the support of METI if they were to succeed. If Toyota could not deploy a hybrid without ten years of subsidies from METI, this motley industrial crew would most definitely need financial and policy support. They would need to fund *huge* capital investments for battery plants, enormous R&D efforts, and a broad swath of new infrastructure.[31]

EVs Within Reach

In order to secure METI's support, a credible argument had to be made that an EV system was indeed within reach. This was a complex process. TEPCO, Mitsubishi, and Subaru knew they would have to court academics, industry, and other specialists in order to make their case—for these were the kinds of people METI would enlist in studying their decision. The lobbying effort would need to include tactile evidence to rebut naysayers from Toyota and Honda as well as the general trend of industry thinking. Before they initiated their tactical approach to METI, the consortium wanted to be relatively comfortable with respect to their supply chains, scaling, and actual cars.

Once all these issues were more or less settled, TEPCO, Mitsubishi, and Subaru showcased their EVs to every backer they could find.[32] Mitsubishi was showing off a prototype called the Colt EV. Subaru's car was called the R1e.[33] Both cars looked great, and handled well. Government officials, bureaucrats, even delegates from the U.S. Society of Automotive Engineers were invited to the company's proving grounds to test them. To jump-start the industry, TEPCO commissioned Subaru to deliver a fleet of one hundred electric cars. The first deliveries were slated for 2006.[34]

The cars won many converts. Among these was the governor of Kanagawa Prefecture—which later instigated some of the most aggressive EV subsidies in the country.

The Dream Machines

The consortium's challenge was to utterly dispel a broadly held perception that EVs were technologically and economically impractical. By 2006, Kanagawa's governor, Shigefumi Matsuzawa, was convinced. The future of the automotive industry was at hand and he had driven it.

Kanagawa's capital, Yokohama, is a major industrial port city a short train ride from Tokyo. The prefecture's governor was a staunch environmentalist, techno-enthusiast, and an early passenger of the Subaru R1e. "When I was a child," blogged Matsuzawa, "electric cars were the stuff of dreams and futuristic societies in science fiction novels. But through the wonders of technology, these dreams are becoming a reality." In the fight against global warming, he offered, "[these cars] have the potential to become an environmental trump card."[35]

In fact, Matsuzawa had driven two EVs that year—both powered by the new generation of lithium-ion batteries. One was an electric supercar—the Eliica—developed at Keio University in Tokyo. The name stood for Electric Lithium Ion Car. It was the brainchild of Keio professor Hiroshi Shimizu—a brilliant, dynamic, and somewhat eccentric researcher with a passion for EVs. Eliica was Shimizu's second attempt at an electric supercar; the first, completed in 1998, was called KAZ. The Eliica was sportier than KAZ, but they shared a lot of mechanical DNA—DNA Shimizu would jealously call "much better than Tesla's." The Eliica drove on lithium-ion batteries, had eight wheels, 640 horsepower, and could go from zero to 60 in about 4 seconds. While *Car and Driver* called it a "dream machine," many others thought it was bewilderingly ugly.[36] But it was certainly fast. "Many people changed their mind [about EVs] after driving Eliica," remembered Shimizu. "They changed their mind in three seconds of acceleration."[37]

But Eliica's radical design, high cost, and almost comically outsize specifications made it little more than a curiosity—practically outrageous, but not outrageously practical.

Then, in September of that same year, Matsuzawa drove Subaru's R1e. It looked somewhat similar to a 2012 Fiat 500, but had only two seats. While the range of the R1e was relatively short—only fifty miles—to Matsuzawa the car seemed eminently reasonable. The same month, he announced that Kanagawa would work with METI to create a set of subsidies that could jump-start the EV industry nationally and make his prefecture a leader in developing and deploying EVs. "[I] want Kanagawa to create policy that will allow it to lead in promoting the deployment of these environmentally friendly vehicles," Matsuzawa wrote.[38] Matsuzawa, his office, his city, and its industrial base would become intimately identified with Japan's EV project. Not just as technology enthusiasts and policy pioneers, but as the home of Nissan.

Convening the Mandarins

The conversion of Governor Matsuzawa was a great victory for TEPCO. Like Matsuzawa, many METI officials also participated in that same series of trial runs. For them, too, EVs were no longer science fiction.[39]

In spite of Toyota's protests, METI decided to convene a series of seminars to reexamine the economics, science and consumer logic of EVs. It assembled a committee of mandarins from industry, academia, and various ministries of the bureaucracy to scrutinize the relevant issues.[40] In 2007, the committee recommended that METI support full electrification of passenger cars and published its "New Vehicle Strategy 2010"—a detailed road map to support the EV sector.

METI set targets for electric vehicle deployment and worked with industry to model the subsidies that would be required to reach these goals. Based on this plan, the Ministry of Finance approved a budget for the program and submitted it to the Diet as part of a larger budgetary package. There was no partisan debate on the matter. The program was based on sound, sober policy analysis. In Japan, that was the bureaucrat's job, and it was generally not seen as the politician's role to meddle.[41] If anything, the politicians would push METI to do more to support Japan's advanced manufacturing sector.

Into the Mainstream

METI's incentives for EVs were *very* generous. The subsidy was designed to cover up to 50 percent of the incremental cost of purchasing an EV as compared to a gasoline vehicle (up to 1 million yen—more than $10,000 in 2010).[42] Combined with Japan's high gas prices—and comparatively cheap electricity—that put the economics of EVs within reach. When the iMiev (pronounced "I my EV") eventually launched, METI's million-yen subsidy brought the price of the car down from about $48,000 to just above $35,000. It paved the way for steady growth of Japan's EV sector.

TEPCO's original consortium moved toward the daunting challenge of commercialization. At Mitsubishi, development was handed over to Kenichiro Wada, an executive with a background in automotive interior design and electronics integration. The iMiev was Wada's first time being responsible for a complete vehicle and he was not altogether comfortable with the prospect. "Why me?" he asked Yoshida. "What if I mess it up? I've never done this before!" Wada protested. "That's okay," returned Yoshida. "It's never been done before. If you make a mistake, no one will know."

By 2007, Mitsubishi's Colt EV prototype was well on its way to being transformed into a production vehicle that *Motor Trend* magazine admiringly deemed "quite cute."[43] And it was. In 2011, essentially the same car would be released in the United States, marketed simply as the "i." At the same time, Subaru was just a year out from completing development of its Stella EV.[44]

But this insulated and collaborative greenhouse for electrification created by TEPCO, Subaru, and Mitsubishi was about to transform into a much more Darwinian landscape. METI's subsidies attracted a new field of competitors. Striding confidently into the arena was Japan's third-largest auto producer, Nissan.

Not Quite First: Nissan Joins the Fray

Installing a Lebanese, Brazilian-born executive as the head of one of the country's largest auto manufacturers caused quite a stir in Japan's business circles. When Carlos Ghosn took the helm of Nissan in 1999, he did so as part of a new alliance between that company and his employer, the French automaker Renault. At first the Japanese didn't know quite how to treat him. When the newly appointed CEO entered the stage at the Tokyo Motor Show, the electric organ welcomed him by vamping a few bars of "The Girl from Ipanema." It was a joke, but Ghosn's mission in Japan was deadly serious.

Nissan was a bloated, inefficient, and mismanaged company. Everyone knew radical change was necessary. The company was $17 billion in debt and some speculated that Ghosn was solicited to do what had to be done, but could not be done by a Nissan company man—slash budgets, eviscerate programs, and transform a lethargic Japanese institution into a leaner international beast.[45] He planned to cut 21,000 jobs and reduce Nissan's capacity by at least 30 percent. "There is no alternative," Ghosn told his Japanese audience. "Failure is not an option." [46]

Ghosn was certainly no environmental warrior. Hybrids, EVs, and other programs all came under his unsentimental knife—and he lambasted Toyota incessantly for investing in money-losing hybrids. Despite this, when Ghosn tore down Nissan's EV program, he retained its lithium-ion research group.[47] "I was really struck by those engineers when I met with them," he said. "They thought that an electric car could be feasible and affordable. I had no clue, but I was very impressed by their passion."[48]

Nissan was not as technologically proficient or as profitable as Toyota—especially when it came to hybrid vehicles—but this was part of the reason why it was willing to take the risk on producing a consumer EV. Toyota had won the hybrid technology race, and in order to produce a competitive hybrid electric vehicle Nissan was forced to license Toyota's technology. "We had hybrid technology that was competitive with Toyota's, but perhaps it was not as economical," admitted a Nissan manager in 2011.[49] But by 2007, thanks to Ghosn, Nissan was once again in the black. Now it needed a brand, and a route past Toyota's Big Green Monster.

In comparison to Mitsubishi or Subaru, the scale of Nissan's resources was inescapably vast. In 2007 Nissan formed the Automotive Energy Supply Corporation together with NEC to develop and motorize the technology that would eventually power what the company called its "Leading Environmentally-friendly Affordable Family Car," known to Americans as the Nissan LEAF.[50]

The LEAF claimed to be "the world's first mass-produced mainstream electric vehicle."[51] However, this was not really accurate—Subaru and Mitsubishi were years ahead of Nissan. What is true is that the scale of development, publicity, and deployment that Nissan set out to achieve was beyond the capabilities of smaller players like the Mitsubishi Motor Corporation.

At $36 billion, Nissan's market capitalization was easily five times that of Mitsubishi. In August 2009, Nissan opened its new headquarters adjoining Yokohama Station—the capital of EV-obsessed Governor Shigefumi Matsuzawa's prefecture. Silhouetted by Yokohama Harbor with a giant wind turbine on the horizon, the glistening waterfront skyscraper was the command center for Nissan's 240,000 global employees.

Nissan's headquarters boasted a cavernous showroom that vied with the Tokyo Motor Show for sleek modernity and elegance. Its legendary $90,000 GTR Coupe racer dominated an elevated section of the floor space flanked by two of the company's most recent concept cars. Dozens of other glistening showcases were arrayed against a four-story cascade of windows overlooking the waterfront. A phalanx of beautiful young Japanese women in slim-cut white dresses—who also served as Nissan's models at major auto shows around the world—hovered close by to answer questions and introduce the car's features for visitors. On any given day, there was a good chance that the Tokyo Broadcasting Station or Nihon Television would drop by for a shoot. Soon the LEAF would occupy the heart of this industrial temple.

But while this public face was impressive, the company's inner workings were, if anything, more spectacular. Plans were made for the LEAF to be built just down the road in Nissan's massive Oppama plant—a facility that epitomized Japan's remarkable "just in time" manufacturing system. So complex was this mechanical organism that the company had two distinct sets of engineers: one for cars, and the other entirely dedicated to designing, evolving, and sustaining its mighty manufacturing machine.

In Oppama individual orders for cars and SUVs poured in from around the world. Over the course of less than twenty-four hours each of these would be custom-built by 1,700 men and women on and off the factory floor. Henry Ford's conveyor belt was still the centerpiece of the operation, but much of the rest had evolved beyond recognition.

Chassis, doors, fenders, and electronics flew through the air on Oppama's double-decker line—hanging high above the primary assembly rigs. At one end of the plant, cars started as hollow metal frames sitting on large accordion boxes that rose and fell to accommodate workers of different height and build. They then snaked their way through dozens of workstations where they were customized for Nissan's global customer base with various sound systems, performance packages, colors, and other features.

Inside the chassis, the car's guts are all wires, computer boards, airbags, engines, and differentials. They were bolted, riveted, and locked together like the world's most complex jigsaw puzzle before being papered over with the soft marshmallow seats and smooth interior panels we see every day as the consumer face of these machines. In total, 30,000 pieces were mated together in the course of eight hours—about one piece every five seconds.

Unlike simple mass production, there was essentially zero inventory. The progress of each piece was synchronized with a designated car or truck. It was almost as if the factory went to market each morning to pack a "lunch bag" for every chassis. Each of these "lunch bags" was ferried around the plant by a robot carrying bins filled with pieces for a specific car. Once its bins were empty, the robot wheeled back to the staging ground to be mated with another vehicle. It was a scene that made it easy to imagine an autonomous transportation network in the not too distant future.

What made this even more amazing was that if something went wrong—at any moment—the line stopped. Each worker had the power to still this pulsating industrial calliope. The exquisitely coordinated organism—the machine that changed the world—screeched to a halt until the problem was resolved.

At the end, cars were bumped onto a set of steel rollers and accelerated to 80 mph to test the alignment, braking, and emissions. A Juke crossover or Cube roared with power until a big green "OK" popped up onscreen to certify that its systems were fit for market. After that final way station, it was ushered forth into the daylight. Chassis entered the building as hollow metal boxes and exited just hours later as shiny new cars.

Three times a week, a large oceangoing boat pulled up to Nissan's private loading docks to accept as many at five thousand cars and SUVs for shipment to America and the world.

Soon, Nissan's juggernaut would be ready for the LEAF. Just north of Nissan headquarters sat Nissan Stadium, with a capacity of 72,000 . . . just another inescapable sign that Nissan played in the big leagues or it didn't play at all.

Over the next four years the Nissan-Renault Alliance would plow

$4 billion into designing and promoting its flagship EV—almost as much as Mitsubishi Motors' entire market cap.[52] Although the company was a latecomer to the EV game, its budget and goals were aggressive—many of them more aggressive than those of METI, Mitsubishi, or Subaru. For instance, Nissan wanted Japan to have 5,000 quick chargers for EVs deployed in Japan by 2015, while METI did not expect to hit that number until 2020.[53] Nissan did its part to make this happen by installing 800 DC fast chargers in Nissan dealerships around Japan—a number that was many multiples of what the U.S. federal government funded between 2008 and 2012 or even existed in the United States.

It was the beginning of a high-stakes courtship between Nissan and the electric car. "You want to make sure your passion is not a weakness," said CEO Carlos Ghosn. "You need to make sure that your passion is a strength."[54] Whatever the future, Nissan had invested billions and there was no turning back.

NEC: Subaru's Heartbreaker

To the industry as a whole, it was a godsend that such a sizable player could pour this scale of resource into EVs—not hybrids, but pure EVs. And Mitsubishi took pains to promote the idea that the LEAF was not a head-to-head competitor. The iMiev was in a different class than the LEAF, appealing to the "kei-car" market, smaller vehicles that plied the streets of crowded cities like Tokyo. The LEAF was almost a full-size sedan. Together, said Mitsubishi, the companies could make a much more effective case for continued government support than Mitsubishi and Subaru could on their own.

But for Subaru, Nissan's entry into the EV market had very tangible, and negative, consequences; mostly these centered on Nissan's decision to poach Subaru's battery supplier, NEC.

Over the 1990s and early 2000s, Nissan's capabilities in lithium-ion batteries were improving dramatically, and the company's battery research group was among the best in the world. However, when Nissan finally made the decision to develop the LEAF and push an EV toward commercialization, it realized that the complexity of implementing and producing economical, high-quality lithium-ion batteries was beyond its reasonable capacity. Nissan began to shop around for a partner and found one with the experience it required—NEC. There was only one problem: NEC was Subaru's EV development partner.

But for NEC the bigger, richer, more experienced auto company proved irresistible. In the words of one friend of Subaru, "NEC broke Subaru's heart and married Nissan." Nonetheless, by some estimates it was a marriage made in heaven. On the one side, NEC ensured that battery cells and battery packs were of high and consistent quality. Nissan ensured that their motorization proceeded smoothly and on a grand scale. That scale would drive down prices and defray investment costs. Joining up with a sophisticated battery producer also had the effect of tying the success of the battery manufacturer to the long-term durability and success of the product. For its part, Nissan was content with a 51 percent stake in the companies' joint venture, the Automotive Energy Supply Corporation (AESC). The results were basically good—although the LEAF battery did not travel quite as far as initially advertised and lost some capacity in extremely cold or hot weather. In 2013, after 90,000 units in global LEAF sales, there had not been a single fire in an AESC battery pack. "That's huge," exclaimed Kiho Ohga, manager of Nissan's ZEV program.

Nissan's entry into the EV space was a clear signal to regulators, competitors, market analysts, journalists, and the public that electric cars were, again, on a roll. A company like Nissan could withstand a few years of lackluster sales to gain the technical and market acumen to succeed. Furthermore, its investment in EV technology would translate into increased competitive pressure for players like Toyota and Honda, as well as Korean, American, and European companies. One other thing Nissan's involvement would do is up the ante for METI. This was an enormous company. Many people felt that in the eyes of METI, Nissan really was too big to fail.

11

I'll Be Back

California Returns

ONCE AGAIN Japan was winning both the race for technology and for public opinion. Over the early 2000s, oil prices shot through the roof, and more and more Americans started worrying about climate change—their angst fueled by hot weather and later Al Gore's global warming documentary, *An Inconvenient Truth*. At the same time, batteries were getting cheaper, safer, more potent, and more powerful. Nissan, Mitsubishi, and Subaru were surging ahead, but California's establishment was having a difficult time getting back in the game. At every step, they were blocked by Detroit and Washington. The state government in Sacramento, which had previously been the maker of technology markets for the automotive sector, suddenly found itself stymied.

Clean Cars (aka Pavley)

California's failure was not for lack of ambition. In 2002, a Democratic assemblywoman named Fran Pavley had introduced AB 1493—a bill to limit greenhouse gas emissions in California autos. Specifically, it called for the state to enforce "the maximum feasible reduction of greenhouse gases emitted by passenger vehicles and light-duty trucks." State officials called the rules the Clean Car Standards, but automakers nicknamed the bill "Pavley." It was a step change in CARB's regulatory reach.[1] Under the aegis of Pavley, CARB would require them to reduce CO_2 emissions by 30 percent by 2016. For practical purposes, it put California in the business of regulating fuel economy *qua* CO_2 emissions. Pavley was skating right up to the line of California's legal rights under the Clean Air Act. Combined with another state assembly bill, AB 32, California was launching a systemic effort to dramatically curb greenhouse gas emissions within the state's economy. And California wasn't alone. Seventeen other states were following its lead.

In years past, GM might have filed a knee-jerk lawsuit. But rather than rush to the courts, they waited for the law to take effect in 2004, gathered their strength, and then tried to make an end run around California's judiciary.[2]

Automakers were becoming more sophisticated in their battles with California. GM knew that if they sued the Golden State, they would have to face CARB—a technically formidable body that was bristling with battle-hardened lawyers and ready to clash. On the other hand, if they roughed up a less formidable foe—if they sued a state that had adopted California's rules and won—that would throw the entire venture into doubt. They settled on Vermont. And the automakers also sued two other weaklings: New Mexico and Rhode Island—both of which had adopted California's standards.

The industry contended that only the federal government had the authority to regulate fuel economy.[3] This was arguably true. And automakers hoped to keep it this way, because neither Congress nor the National Highway Traffic Safety Administration (NHTSA) had raised fuel economy standards for cars since the time of the first oil crisis in 1975.[4] For trucks, the increases in fuel economy had been minuscule.

But things did not go as planned. In a 240-page decision, the federal judge appointed to the case rebuked every single one of the automakers' claims.[5] Some months earlier, the 2007 Supreme Court ruling on *Massachusetts v. EPA* had allowed that CO_2 was a pollutant—which by extension meant that it could be regulated by the state of California under Section 177 of the Clean Air Act. Functionally, the regulation would be indistinguishable from fuel economy. But legally, California was now clear to begin implementation of AB1493 as well as another greenhouse gas regulation it had passed called AB32. All California needed was a "federal waiver" for its policies—which it had never before been denied.[6] It soon became clear, however, that under the Bush administration, there was a first time for everything.

Iron Man 1

But even in the face of federal opposition, the political and technological momentum behind the EV industry was again rising. In California this tide was personified by two iron men: Arnold Schwarzenegger and Elon Musk. Both of them seemed unlikely champions.

A decade earlier, Schwarzenegger had driven the transformation of the HMMWV—the Hummer—from a military workhorse to a status symbol of 1990s consumerism. He was the "Hummer guy." But in 2003, with the recall of California's governor Gray Davis—during which much political blood was spilled—the Golden State's megalithic action hero threw his hat into the gubernatorial race. Schwarzenegger won—crushing the dreams of Congressman Darrel Issa, who had spent close to $2 million of his own money on recalling Davis. Arnold liked to speak in bold, declarative sentences that were charged with braggadocio and left little room for compromise. But on the issue of clean cars, one could sense a creeping evolution. It started with another one of his retrofitted Hummers.

Schwarzenegger liked to think of himself as a "have your cake and eat it, too" environmentalist, so he focused on technology solutions to pollution and global warming. He did not intend to transform his own lifestyle to live a meeker existence. Things like eating less meat, or living in a smaller house, or, perhaps, driving a smaller car, were simply not part of Arnold's vocabulary. But at the same time, it was clear that America's love affair with oil was imposing costs—political, environmental, and health—upon the United States. In his own bizarre way, Arnold wanted to be part of the solution. And so he did what any reasonable Austrian, Mr. Universe, movie star turned politician would do: He built himself the world's first hydrogen-powered Humvee. Just like his street-legal Hummer, Arnold's hydrogen Hummer was another first, but it was clearly not a practical solution for the everyday Californian. Arnold had to do better.

Although Schwarzenegger's evolution on the issue of clean cars may have had a political element to it, before long there was every evidence that his dedication to the causes of clean air and global warming was sincere. Arnold still liked big cars, but he also understood the importance of clean cars. After he won the election he became, at least indirectly, the guy responsible for deciding how many Californian kids had to die of smog-related asthma and lung conditions. He also had to decide what California's role would be in the creeping crisis of global warming. And so he had to decide how far to pursue the matter of California's "special authority" with America's ultimate regulators in Washington. His answer? Pretty damn far.

It was the role of a lifetime. In the movies, Schwarzenegger had played an action hero who saved lives. But now he had the opportunity to play a real-life action hero on a national and even global stage. "Fighting the feds on the clean air standards . . . fighting for California . . . He loved that role," remembered CARB chairman Mary Nichols. California's fight for clean air was good politics, and the clash with Washington and international automakers was exhilarating to boot. "This is fun stuff, and they all get bitten by it," Nichols said.

But the waiver that would allow California regulators to set new emissions standards was taking a long time to materialize. By the end of 2007, it had been two years since the governor had initially requested permission from the Bush administration. Washington was slow-walking the process, and Arnold's blood was beginning to boil.

On November 8, 2007, standing in front of the state capitol, Sacramento's iron man marshaled a phalanx of scientists, CARB board members, and politicians to launch a shot across Washington's bow. Shoulder to shoulder with CARB chairman Nichols and Attorney General Jerry Brown—formerly and subsequently governor—California's entire political establishment launched a fusillade. Schwarzenegger made it clear that he would make the EPA's life miserable if it did not approve California's waiver. "We will sue!" he threatened. And what if they lost? "We sue again, and sue again, and sue again, until we get it. We're going to win!" he swore.[7]

Iron Man 2

Just south of San Francisco, another iron man was quietly making his own declaration of intent. Elon Musk was not a bodybuilder, nor a movie star, nor a politician. He was a nerd. But in his own way, he was just as intense, just as driven, and just as much of a celebrity as California's iron man governor. Musk was Edison meets Generation X. He had "big ideas," he was brilliant, and he had swagger.

This was the nerd made good. So much so that he served as the real-life inspiration for a bit of Hollywood iconography. Tony Stark, the fictional genius cum inventor cum action hero from the film versions of *Iron Man*, was based on Musk. Just like Stark, Musk was a bold, pugnacious visionary—a serial entrepreneur with a unique genius for realizing impossible technology dreams and a penchant for dating models and movie stars. "Everything he touches turns to gold," remarked one of his admirers. To the innovation community, Musk would become the consummate rock star.

Musk had three impossible dreams that he believed would change the world. "When I was in college," said Musk, "I decided I wanted to be involved in things that would have a significant impact on the future of humanity. And the three things I could come up with were the internet, sustainable energy (both production and consumption), and space exploration, particularly the extension of life beyond Earth to multiple planets."[8] He'd already cofounded PayPal—a critical node of the global e-commerce system—and this had netted him a few hundred million. But rather than retiring to some remote island in the Caribbean or a Manhattan loft, Musk decided to risk it all on dream number two: the electric car.

The beginnings of the all-American electric car company are steeped in controversy. But what seems clear is that the idea had a number of fathers, and its early execution was a synthetic process. The key company players were Musk and a small-time entrepreneur named Martin Eberhard. The team named the venture Tesla Motors—after the tragic genius Nikola Tesla, who invented the alternating current electricity that powers our world today. Eventually Musk would come to dominate the undertaking and building Tesla would severely test the boundaries of his own genius and entrepreneurial strength.

Never slaves to convention, Tesla's founders developed a business plan that was brash, gutsy, and, in the end, dazzling. They would build the company in three phases. During phase one, the company would make an electric car so hot that they could sell it to wealthy Americans for as much as a small home. During phase two, the company would produce a luxury sedan so spectacular that it would outperform the finest internal combustion vehicles of the day, and sell that car slightly downmarket for only a tad less. But during phase three, Tesla would transform the world with an affordable people's EV for the masses. That would signal the beginning of the end for oil sheiks and petrocracies.

From a technical standpoint, Tesla Motors' origins could draw a straight line back to AeroVironment and the GM-sponsored Sunraycer. Tesla's original IP came from a company called AC Propulsion, the brainchild of AeroVironment's contractor Al Cocconi—the ingenious inventor who had worked on GM's solar racer. In the early 2000s, when Musk met the team at AC Propulsion, they showed him the electric supercar Cocconi's team had built. It was something of a sideshow—a bit akin to Hiroshi Shimizu's Eliica. But Musk was enormously intrigued. In AC Propulsion's speed demon he saw the beginnings of a product. Eberhard had independently arrived at the same conclusion.

And so, Musk and Eberhard went into business together. The next few years would not be easy. Tesla's founders were not "car guys" and had taken on a formidable task. No one had ever done what they were trying to do. As for Musk, his fortune and reputation were both invested. As costs began to spiral out of control, the entire venture teetered on the brink. Musk is the first to admit that it almost cost him his sanity. More than once, internal tensions boiled, and eventually led to a power struggle between Musk and then-CEO Eberhard.

When their internal spat went public, litigation ensued and Musk took to his blog to denounce his cofounder. Eberhard, said Musk, had brought little but pain to the automotive startup. "The facts are that when I requested through AC Propulsion to meet Eberhard, he had no technology of his own, he did not have a prototype car and he owned no intellectual property relating to electric cars. All he had was a business plan to commercialize the AC Propulsion Tzero electric sports car concept," said Musk, adding that "three years later, when Eberhard was asked to leave Tesla, most of the work that he had been paid to do had to be redone." Whatever the truth, Musk succeeded in ousting Eberhard and took for himself the role of CEO.

As CEO, Musk's goals were radical, but some of his engineering decisions were relatively conservative. For instance, Tesla's first model—the Roadster—was built on the chassis of a Lotus Elise. That framework was fitted with an electric motor and a pack consisting of 6,831 Panasonic lithium-ion battery cells.[9] In some senses, it was more of a kit car than an electric innovation. Still, the Roadster boasted screaming acceleration (zero to 60 in under 4 seconds) and a sinuously sexy exterior. Thousands plunked down deposits of up to $50,000 to reserve a spot in line, and the vast majority of those depositors held tight as the projected price for Tesla's new electric car climbed.

The base price for Tesla's Roadster was $109,000—about three times as much as the Elise. Yes, it looked good. And it was already starting to develop Silicon Valley cachet. But one Honda executive remarked disparagingly that, as far as he was concerned, the Roadster was "not even a real concept car, but more of a science project."

Even with all of Tesla's borrowed technology, there were embarrassing problems. For a $100,000 vehicle, the car's componentry was somewhat shoddy. Its door locks, radio dials, and window triggers felt cheap and plasticky. The tiny back trunk sometimes came unhitched, prompting one well-practiced—and optimistic—salesman to note that it was secured by "not one, but two latches," as he leaned heavily on a half-secured trunk. Then there was the battery. For one, it was enormously expensive. But it was also high-maintenance. The company's stock plunged after a popular automotive news site published an article called "Tesla Motors' Devastating Design Problem: It's a Brick." What was this design flaw? If allowed to fully discharge, Tesla's batteries would be permanently dead—they would "brick." To combat this deficiency, Tesla set up a system to monitor its vehicles in real time. They even dispatched employees with extension cords to garages in order to charge them up if need be.

The perceived business risk was substantial enough to win Tesla the dubious distinction of being "the third most shorted stock on American stock exchanges." People were betting big against Tesla. Yet as Tesla's silent Roadsters started slipping onto California freeways, they made an indelible mark on the global automotive landscape. The car was real, and the Tesla brand had a growing fan base.

In America, electric cars were surging back from the brink of obscurity. And Tesla was not alone.

As a young man, Henry Ford quit his job as chief engineer of the Detroit Edison Electric Company to contest the first heat in The Great Race: automotive mass production. Ford's internal combustion engines and sturdy buggies won the day and steamrolled Thomas Edison's electric vehicles. By 1921, Ford was producing over a million vehicles a year.

2

On September 1, 1923, a violent earthquake struck Tokyo. Lit stoves ignited houses made of wood and paper, and petroleum tanks spilled a black and burning torrent into the harbor of Yokosuka. Reconstruction created a new demand for imported vehicles from the United States and marked the beginning of a mass market for automobiles in Japan.

3

The Toyoda men harbored a well-known obsession with automobiles. Though the Toyodas had been to the United States and meticulously studied the art of mass-production—walking the assembly lines of Ford's River Rouge plant—the issue of scale was insuperable. Without government support, it was madness to challenge America's industrial titans.

4

Toyota exports its first truck to China. The decision to develop Japan's own domestic auto sector was, ultimately, strategic and political. As Japan's military clawed its way deeper into the Asian continent and Pacific islands, Japan's economic planners ejected GM and Ford, effectively transferring their market share to the likes of Toyota, Nissan, and Isuzu. This laid the industrial foundation for Japan's military conquest.

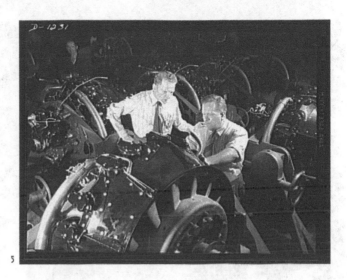

5

The automotive industry became the beating heart of America's "arsenal of democracy." It was so important to the war effort that federal agents occupied company headquarters, leading the aging and, by this point, slightly deranged Henry Ford to believe they were trying to kill him.

Chrysler was the largest tank producer of the war, and together Ford and Willys-Overland produced 2.5 million military trucks and 660,000 "jeeps." In total, the auto industry built some 4,131,000 engines for tanks, planes, and other military vehicles.

6

The Allied Forces' industrial hegemony was absolute. Combined, Japan, Germany, and Italy produced about 437,000 vehicles in 1938, while the UK produced 445,000. The United States produced 3.5 million automobiles. In this sense, the decision by Japan and Germany to declare war on the United States is almost unfathomable.

7

"The enemy has begun to employ a new and most cruel bomb," said Japan's Emperor Hirohito in his first ever radio address. Resistance, he declared, would "lead to the total extinction of human civilization."

8

The imposing, bombastic, but basically benevolent General Douglas MacArthur (left, with Emperor Hirohito) received the title Supreme Commander of the Allied Powers (SCAP) in Japan. He exercised absolute control over the country's military, civil, and economic future from the Allies' General Headquarters.

9

The seeds of Japan's dominance in quality and cost were planted by two individuals: Taichi Ohno and W. Edwards Deming. Japan's embrace of quality-control guru Deming (right) stood in sharp contrast to Detroit's ambivalence to his methods.

10

In the 1950s, a major labor dispute with leftists almost brought Toyota to its knees. Rather than risk hiring communists, Taichi Ohno streamlined Toyota's production with ruthless intensity.

The 1950s and 1960s were an era of economic growth, glamour, and industrial dominance for the United States. Broad-based prosperity and rising incomes provided a platform for a booming automotive industry.

The 1950s also marked the beginning of a long period of industrial decline—during which American quality began to slide—and the beginning of America's smog epidemic. The Los Angeles Optimists Club even donned gas masks in protest of the horrible pollution that veiled the city.

To the scientist Arie Haagen-Smit, the source of LA's pollution couldn't have been more obvious: cars. But a group of oil and gas companies declared that the science was still uncertain. They funded the Stanford Research Institute to refute his research and undermine his credibility.

Soichiro Honda was a fierce competitor, and he reveled in his plans to destroy the industry's comfy equilibrium. "The fighting spirit . . . is my nature" he once proclaimed.

Japan's entry into the Great Race was confirmed at the 1961 Isle of Man TT—the Super Bowl of motorcycle racing. Flabbergasted Brits looked on as one sleek 250cc Honda finished, then another, then another. Honda swept the podium in both the 125cc and 250cc divisions.

In 1975, when Eiji Toyoda was called to testify in front of the Diet as head of the Japan Automobile Manufacturers Association, he said that the regulators should slow down on pollution controls. The celebrated industrialist was pilloried by the media, politicians, and environmental groups. It was a public relations fiasco.

By 1980, Japan had surged past Germany to become America's largest source for automotive imports. It now accounted for 80 percent of foreign autos sold in America. Twice, Japan's economic planners had saved its automakers from American competition. Now it was Detroit that needed protection.

The 1970s were a period of traumatic evolution for the energy industry. Two oil crises, the environmental movement, economic stagnation in the United States, and a tumultuous geopolitical landscape all played a role. Nuclear power was part of Japan's response to the crippling series of oil shocks.

18

19

Born in Ohio to immigrant Jewish parents in 1922, Stanford Ovshinsky was a consummate outsider. But Ovshinsky understood the environmental and geopolitical dangers of relying too much on oil. He invented a new family of semiconductors, hydrogen fuel cells, thin-film solar cells, and batteries. The *Economist* magazine called him the "Edison of our age."

20

As Deng Xiaoping (pictured with President Gerald Ford at left) began his economic reforms in the 1970s, new auto technology was at the top of Beijing's wish list. After failing to partner with Toyota, China arranged for a manufacturing partnership ("joint venture" or "JV") between the American Motor Company (maker of Jeep) and the Beijing Automotive Industrial Corporation. It set the stage for many more JVs to come.

21

22

In 1974 newly elected Governor Jerry Brown (*left*) and his team were high on victory and intent to change the world. Twenty-eight-year-old lawyer Mary Nichols (*right*) and other members of the California Air Resource Board were an important part of the plan. They purposefully pitted American makers against their Japanese rivals, all in pursuit of cleaner air.

23

The twenty-seven-year-old engineering prodigy Yoshitoshi Sakurai (right) helped Honda dominate the global race for emissions controls as well as the F1 racing circuit. Later, he likened his advanced telemetric control systems to the brain of Brazilian racing legend Ayrton Senna (left). "[Senna's brain] could simulate . . . RPM of [the] engine, gear position, braking point [and] steering," he said. So too could Sakurai's computers.

Paul MacCready (*left*) was hailed as the "Engineer of the Century." He was not only a visionary, he could implement. Built for GM, MacCready's Sunraycer (*below*) was crushingly dominant in its race across the Australian Outback. His next invention, the all-electric Impact, would set in motion a series of events that would transform the global auto industry.

24

25

Clinton's Partnership for a New Generation of Vehicles (PNGV) had intended to build an American "supercar" with 80 mpg. Under George W. Bush (right), PNGV was transformed into a very different beast: the "Freedom Car." The program's "four freedoms" were a coded rebuttal against California's technology-forcing mandates. That hostility toward California's goals eventually put Bush at loggerheads with the state's Republican governor, Arnold Schwarzenegger (left).

26

27

The Prius was part moonshot, part defensive bulwark against PNGV. By the early 2000s Toyota's "big green monster" had become an industry standard against which America could not compete.

28

29

Behind Wan Gang's enigmatic smile was an iron determination to break a century of Chinese dependence on foreign oil and Western technology. The ultimate goal was to leapfrog Japan and the United States so that the world's biggest markets for automobiles would import cars from factories in China rather than the other way around.

Just as China was joining the Great Race, America beat a sudden retreat. When California loosened its EV mandate in the early 2000s, thousands of EVs were unceremoniously crushed. The incident sparked innumerable conspiracy theories and even a hit documentary, *Who Killed the Electric Car*.

30

31

For a year or two, Tokyo Electric Power Company's (TEPCO) EV program didn't look like much. Auto companies were thrilled to be rid of California's burdensome regulations, and TEPCO's Takafumi Anegawa, the nuclear engineer turned EV Don Quixote, was spurned by what seemed to be the entire industry.

By the early 2000s, Mitsubishi's Hiroaki Yoshida knew that proposing a new EV program was a surefire means of incurring the wrath of senior executives. But when Anegawa told him TEPCO wanted to push EVs, Yoshida secretly dug into his budgets and built one anyway.

32

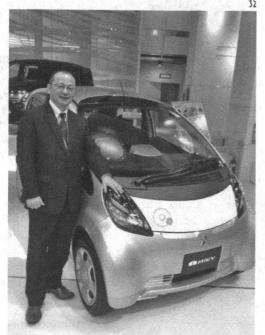

Mitsubishi's Colt EV was eventually transformed into a production vehicle called the iMiev—a car that *Motor Trend* magazine admiringly deemed "quite cute." (*Below*) Here the iMiev undergoes deep-water testing.

33

34

Elon Musk served as the real-life inspiration for Hollywood's Tony Stark, the fictional genius-cum-inventor-cum-action hero from the movie *Iron Man*. Like Stark, Musk was a bold, pugnacious visionary—a serial entrepreneur with a genius for realizing the impossible and a penchant for dating models and movie stars.

35

Bob Lutz (left) was not your typical American auto executive. Born in Zurich, Switzerland, in 1932, his father was VP of Credit-Suisse Bank, and his cosmopolitan upbringing showed. The Volt was a direct outgrowth of Lutz's consuming insecurities, fixation on the media, fondness for muscle-car styling, and unwillingness to compromise.

36

Before the LEAF, Nissan's technology calling card was probably the Skyline GT-R—a legendary Japanese racer. CEO Carlos Ghosn carved away Nissan's corporate bloat, but he retained its lithium-ion research group. "I was really struck by those engineers. . . . They thought that an electric car could be feasible and affordable. I had no clue."

The Big Three provided one of the lasting images of political ineptitude during the financial crisis. Alan Mulally of Ford, Robert Nardelli of Chrysler, and Rick Wagoner of GM each flew to Washington, D.C., in his own private jet to ask the Democratic Congress for life-sustaining funds.

The powerful trio was greeted with disdain and disbelief. Representative Gary Ackerman, a Democrat from New York, saw "a delicious irony in seeing private luxury jets flying into Washington D.C., and people coming off of them with tin cups in their hand. . . . It's almost like seeing a guy show up at the soup kitchen in high hat and tuxedo. It kind of makes you a little bit suspicious."

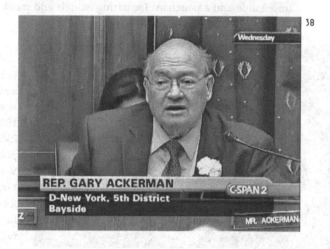

China's leaders confidently stated their intentions to leapfrog the West into the age of electric cars. Some in America weren't so sure.

GM would be saved, but Chrysler, had to "prove its right to exist," remembered Fiat CEO Sergio Marchionne. "I wasn't given a dollar of equity . . . and everything we were given was secured. . . . [M]y private parts were attached to that security." In other words, Fiat was taking a huge gamble.

40

41

The Great Recession was a crisis, but it was also an opportunity to restructure failing automakers and invest in new technology. One DOE official remembered that "a lot of stuff people wanted to do for ages, there was finally funding to do."

42

Obama embraced a very different philosophy on science and energy than Bush. Nobel Prize winner Steven Chu was made secretary of energy, and there was a quick rethinking of the federal government's relationship with manufacturers. Suddenly the administration had massive, cohesive, and direct leverage over the U.S. auto sector. But they had little time to act.

Just as Japan seemed set to establish its unquestioned dominance in the new electric age, disaster struck. The Great Tohoku Earthquake, its accompanying tsunami, and the Fukushima nuclear crisis rattled the very foundations of Japan's industrial edifice.

43

44

The Fukushima nuclear disaster turned TEPCO into a hated villain, and it was attacked from all sides. But nuclear energy provided the baseload of TEPCO's power supply, and abandoning it was unthinkable.

45

Nissan had just launched its $4 billion people's EV—the LEAF. It was supposed to be a rolling media sensation. Enormous publicity was built into the car's development plan. But in the context of Fukushima, such a rollout would be both impossible and highly inappropriate. "Promotions of EVs were cut," remembered a Nissan exec.

By the mid-2000s, China's air pollution was becoming a national crisis. In major cities, stifling clouds of smog obscured not only urban skylines, but often the other side of the street.

46

47

With the Olympics close at hand, MOST's pacesetters were in desperate straits. No Chinese company had a firm grasp on the critical technologies for building an EV: advanced batteries, motors, and inverters. Along with iconic pieces of architecture like the Bird's Nest stadium, the Chinese wanted to show that they were winning the Great Race to build the car of the future.

48

49

Before the *Mizuki* incident, China had been Japan's largest supplier of critical industrial building blocks called rare earth elements. Afterward, this flood slowed to a trickle. China's government also actively promoted boycotts of Japanese goods. Newscasters read off lists of Japanese brands that should be targeted by patriotic Chinese citizens. Protesters destroyed Japanese cars on the streets, and in the ensuing months Japanese auto sales dropped an estimated 40 to 50 percent.

50

In May 2012, Elon Musk's SpaceX capsule successfully docked with the International Space Station. Tesla's stock was also skyrocketing. When Tesla beat analysts' expectations for sales, it triggered a "short squeeze." Stock prices soared higher and higher. From $37 at the beginning of April, past $40, then $50. By mid-May, Tesla shares were flirting with $90. By summer 2014, it shares were trading above $250.

51

In September 2014, America's most successful EV manufacturer announced plans to build a massive battery factory in the United States that would import significant swaths of technology from the Japanese company Panasonic. Tesla and others are now in pursuit

of not only electric but also autonomous vehicles. These car robots will provide an economic edge to the societies that embrace them that may even outstrip the importance of the jobs linked to the automotive manufacturing industry. As the Great Race surges ahead, America, China, and Japan are all very much in the running.

12

Challenging the Big Green
Monster

FOR BOB Lutz, Tesla was a symbol of everything wrong with America.
It's not that there was anything fundamentally wrong with Tesla's
business model. Nor were there any fundamental flaws with the technology—at least not that he could ascertain. The problem, as far as Lutz
was concerned, was that the electric supercar was being pursued by a
Silicon Valley startup and not Detroit—more specifically, not General
Motors. In the Great Race for technology, GM was losing.

In so many ways, Lutz was not your typical American auto executive. The distinctions started early. Born in Zurich, Switzerland, in
1932, Lutz came to the United States when he was only seven years
old. He was no Ellis Island immigrant. Lutz's father was vice president
of Credit Suisse and his cosmopolitan upbringing showed. Lutz spoke
five languages and as a young man he returned to school in Lausanne
for his secondary education. But Lutz also had an aggressive streak
of American patriotism and Yankee style that defined who he was—
much more so than his European roots. He had no accent and flew
fighter jets for the Marines during the 1960s.

Lutz also earned both his undergraduate degree and an MBA at the
University of California, Berkeley. But to interpret his alma mater as
an indication of Lutz's politics would be a mistake. Lutz was almost
obtusely conservative, belligerent, and impervious to facts he did not

like. In Lutz's 2011 book, *Car Guys vs. Bean Counters*, his antiscience screed on global warming caught many by surprise.

> Nowhere has my faith in media integrity been destroyed more thoroughly than in the so-called "global warming" discussion. Resolutely parroting the now-discredited prophecies of Al Gore and his absurd movie, *An Inconvenient Truth*, hardly any of the so-called mainstream media ever gave fair coverage to the large and growing army of CO2-caused AGW (anthropogenic, or human-caused, global warming) skeptics. Every network (Fox excepted) and every major newspaper gives endless coverage to disappearing glaciers (they've been melting for almost four hundred years), polar bears on ice floes (hello—they can swim! And far from being "endangered," the population is up sharply), rapidly rising ocean levels (they aren't), and higher ocean temperatures (they're actually lower).

Almost every fact in that paragraph was either a funhouse mirror of reality or patently false. Even by the standards of Detroit, Lutz had a chip on his shoulder.

Bob Lutz was an unreasonable man. But his outsize personality sometimes got him his way. The Chevy Volt was a direct outgrowth of his consuming insecurities, fixation on the media, penchant for muscle car styling, and unwillingness to compromise.

Unlike some Detroit types, Lutz moved around between companies. He started at GM, but in 1971 became executive vice president for global sales at BMW. He then held senior leadership positions at Ford, and eventually Chrysler, where he pioneered such models as the Ford Explorer and Dodge Viper.[1] Lutz's creative DNA was very much a part of the American industry. In fact, he took great pride in American cars, and American manufacturing. And there was absolutely nothing Lutz detested more than getting soaked by the Japanese—particularly Toyota.

Of all the Japanese competitors, Toyota was the most injurious and insulting. Through the early 2000s, Toyota's rise seemed inexorable. Long dominant in small, fuel-efficient cars, and comfortably ensconced in the luxury car segment with Lexus, Toyota was also moving aggressively into the truck and SUV market—where GM took its biggest profits. But at the same time as Toyota was clawing away at GM's market share in heavy, gas-guzzling trucks and SUVs, the company simultaneously benefited from an ironclad public perception that it was the most environmentally progressive car company in the world.[2]

The Toyota Prius was casting a halo over the company's entire line. In 2001, Toyota received a pleasant shock when Leonardo DiCaprio took his Prius to the Academy Awards. "We were very much surprised," remembered one of the car's designers. "We checked, and he had already bought four Priuses. He bought his own first, then a car for his wife, then for his father-in-law and mother-in-law." And so did Cameron Diaz, Bonnie Raitt, and Larry David.[3] By 2003, the car's iconic position as the ultimate badge of environmental awareness was practically emblazoned on the Walk of Stars. A PR agency had even contacted Toyota to procure five Priuses (or Prii, as Toyota calls them) for the Oscars—allowing environmentally conscious celebrities to eschew their ostentatious limousines for Toyota's fuel-sipping green machine.[4]

Many did not appreciate this environmental showboating. *Car and Driver* mocked the display of "pop royalty . . . Meryl Streep, Ted Danson (who made his fortune leading a gang of pathetic boozers in the alcohol-soaked sitcom *Cheers*), the serially deranged Richard Dreyfuss, and Jeff Goldblum" cavorting around in their Prii.[5]

But what *Car and Driver* missed was that this was the beginning of something very big—a long, upward hockey stick in Prius sales. The car sold 24,000 units that year, but the next year sales doubled. And they doubled again the year after that.[6]

By 2003, Bob Lutz knew that Toyota had done his company enormous damage. "For every savior (Prius)," he wrote, "there must be an Antichrist, and the mainstream media found it in the Hummer H2, GM's smaller, 'civilianized' version of the legendary military vehicle." According to Lutz, the anti-Hummer narrative was entirely unjust. But that was beside the point. *The point* was that the most obvious way to reverse that harm would be to tangibly refute the thesis of Japanese environmental and technology dominance. Just as the EV1 was winding down, and the automakers were gaining a reprieve from the hated ZEV mandate, Lutz began to think that GM should build another electric car.

But even for Lutz—operating as a high-level executive from the inside—contending with the inertia of General Motors and its panoply of entrenched interests was intimidating. And so, for a time, the gunner held his fire.

There were seemingly infinite reasons not to build another electric car. And as in any large organization, it was always easier to say no than yes. Saying yes would mean risking GM's cash, its reputation, and careers. If things went wrong, GM might be dragged through the mud again—as an electric car serial killer. If they went right, GM might be forced by regulators to build thousands of uneconomical EVs—just as it had with the Impact and EV1.

But for Lutz, the rise of Tesla was too much to bear. "Suddenly there was the Tesla announcement: 200 mile range, 0–60 in four point something seconds, 140mph top speed, 6,831 laptop batteries," recalled the irritated industrialist. "I basically said, now wait a minute. I've accepted everybody's arguments of why we can't do this. But here's this small startup company in California and they think that they can get all of these figures."[7]

Reviving the electric drivetrain wasn't about environmentalism—though the green image of EVs certainly didn't hurt. It was about beating Toyota and recasting GM's image in the American psyche. Of course, GM wouldn't actually be leading the new wave of EV development. By 2004 the Japanese—Mitsubishi, TEPCO, and Subaru—were well into designing their next generation of EVs. But Lutz felt little need to acknowledge that inconvenient truth—that would be giving the Japanese too much credit.

Bush-Whacked

On the other hand, the regulators at the California Air Resource Board knew that Japan's EV program was surging back. When CARB saw that the technical case for EVs was rapidly building strength, it decided to double down on its earlier ambitions—once again ratcheting up the pressure on manufacturers. But for CARB to succeed, Washington would have to get out of the way. Schwarzenegger was pounding on the EPA, but the Bush administration was still blocking his path forward.

But 2008 was an election year, and by the following spring levers of the executive branch were in very different hands—Barack Obama's. Just as important, the automotive industry had gone from truculent to supplicant. Gas prices were skyrocketing, the economy was tanking, and so were sales of gas-swilling trucks. As the crisis accelerated, worry became panic, and soon desperation. Detroit needed Obama's help. But in order to get that, they were going to have make peace with the regulators in California.

PART III

Three Crises

13

"Scared Shitless"

America's Industrial Implosion

N 2008, signs of weakness in the U.S. economy started with the New Year. In January, layoffs began to outpace new job growth and a few months later the failure of the ninety-year-old investment company Bear Stearns presaged the collapse of the financial sector. Over the summer, the crisis continued to build strength and eventually it came to a head in September, when the investment bank Lehman Brothers disintegrated under the weight of a bankrupt portfolio—composed of assets that had been hidden from the public through malfeasant accounting.[1]

John McCain, Barack Obama's Republican opponent, gave a stump speech two days after what came to be known as the "Lehman Shock." There he made the inopportune comment that "the fundamentals of our economy are strong." The Republican candidate was dogged by the statement for the remainder of the season.[2] For, in short order, it became clear that the fundamentals of the economy were perilously weak. When the crisis reached a crescendo around Christmas, monthly job losses spiked to over 700,000. Together with the international financial system, the world economy was in tailspin.[3]

Georges Doriot, the father of America's modern venture capital ecosystem, once said that every startup experiences a crisis—a 3 A.M. phone call that makes you sweat cold bullets and stare into the remorseless, reptilian eyes of failure. Such moments force an entrepreneur to examine the fundamental strengths and assumptions of his enterprise. Sometimes things end in a bang, sometimes a whimper but—sometimes—you pull through. Between 2008 and 2012, America, Japan, and China each confronted a potential "game-over" scenario for its national EV project. For America, it was not just EVs at risk. It was the auto industry itself and, indeed, the global economy.

The Lehman Shock

The intensity of the crisis demanded quick action, but this was a role that the Bush White House and Congress only grudgingly fulfilled. One exception to this was Treasury secretary Hank Paulson, who pled for government intervention with great fervor, telling Congress that Lehman's collapse ten days earlier would "look like nirvana" if it failed to act on the crisis.[4]

At the urging of the Treasury, both the legislative and executive branches moved quickly to bail out the banks. Critics saw the Wall Street bailout as "the most barefaced money-grab since Goldfinger, the James Bond villain, tried to rob Fort Knox."[5] Some accused Secretary Paulson of looking out for his buddies at Goldman Sachs. But most mainstream economists agreed that—however unjust—the bailout was necessary to protect the integrity of the global financial system. By early October, the federal government had passed the Troubled Assets Relief Program (TARP) to purchase bad assets from banks in an attempt to shore up their balance sheets.

But the chaos was not relegated to New York. The effects of the Lehman Shock were felt far beyond Wall Street. For one, people abruptly stopped buying cars. Buyers were, in the words of one GM executive, "scared shitless," and so was management. What was worse for the Big Three was that sales of trucks, which were more profitable than cars, fell precipitously. By 2009, trucks accounted for less than half of an already desiccated pool of U.S. auto sales—a far lower proportion than in recent years.

Detroit had been nursing a flesh wound for the past decade. But now it was suddenly confronted with a vivid, public, and entirely predictable reckoning.[6] Within months, GM and Chrysler would both be unable to finance their daily operations. There was a credit freeze. In other words, no one would lend to anyone else, because they had no confidence they would be paid back.[7] This meant that, after bleeding cash, the two besieged automakers (GM and Chrysler) would simply close their doors, cease to operate, and drag down the supply chain—bringing Ford with them.[8]

This could be predicted with such certainty because of the way U.S. auto manufacturers financed their operations. They could not just stop producing cars if demand dried up—for at any given moment they owed billions. Take the representative example of GM. When the company produced a car, it was sold to a dealer the same day. That transaction was often financed through GM Financial, the manufacturer's financing arm. The vehicle was loaded on a truck or train and shipped to a showroom. About a month later, GM would pay its suppliers. That "float"—the outstanding cash owed to GM's suppliers—was $20–30 billion at any given moment. Theoretically, a shortfall in revenues could be financed, but amid the crisis, there was no one willing to lend. Without access to functional capital markets, GM knew exactly how much outstanding debt it had, and how long it had to pay it.[9]

When car sales evaporated, cars began piling up in parking lots rather than rolling onto trucks and trains bound for dealerships. Management knew it had about thirty to forty-five days to figure out what to do before eating into its cash reserves and, eventually, defaulting on financial obligations. If GM could not pay its suppliers, then it would have to file for bankruptcy, an option initially perceived as so destructive to the brand that it was not seriously contemplated.[10]

Washington's Cool Response

In the face of these snowballing challenges and with the backdrop of a massive government infusion to the financial sector, the automakers decided to seek help from Washington. From an economic and political perspective, there was a powerful logic to supporting the auto companies. But when they went to Washington, GM, Ford, and Chrysler so irked members of Congress that the legislators almost allowed the industry to fail.

It was one of the lasting images of political ineptitude of the financial crisis. Alan Mulally of Ford, Robert Nardelli of Chrysler, and Rick Wagoner of GM each confidently flew to Washington, D.C., in his own private jet to ask the Democratic Congress for life-sustaining funds. Their reasoned explanations of the importance of the U.S. automotive industry, in terms of employment and the industrial structure of the Midwest, were eclipsed by their lavish mode of transportation.

The powerful trio was greeted with disdain and disbelief. Sialoquent congressmen vented their rage one by one. Representative Gary Ackerman, a Democrat from New York, mordantly stated that there was "a delicious irony in seeing private luxury jets flying into Washington D.C., and people coming off of them with tin cups in their hand, saying that they're going to be trimming down and streamlining their businesses. . . . It's almost like seeing a guy show up at the soup kitchen in high hat and tuxedo. It kind of makes you a little bit suspicious . . . couldn't you all have downgraded to first class or jet-pooled or something to get here? It would have at least sent a message that you do *get it*."[11] Popular consensus seemed to be that these executives did not "get it."

Detroit's collapse had been decades in the making. Thirty years earlier, in 1979, Chrysler almost went under. But it was buoyed by $1.2 billion from the federal government. Since then, American automakers—both unions and management—had repeatedly side-stepped the tough reforms that would have set them on a more sustainable course. But in 2008, the scale of the problem was much bigger. The Big Three were collectively asking for $25 billion.

Congress rejected their pleas. One reason was that the U.S. auto industry had succeeded in alienating almost every major interest group in one way or another. There was a general consumer perception that their goods were substandard, Republicans thought their unions were feckless, and the industry's decades of lobbying against fuel economy increases and emissions regulations had enraged many environmental groups. The Midwest, where most American autos were produced, was politically important geography filled with swing states that could decide a presidential election, but it did not have a congressional majority in the House or Senate. So Congress tossed the political hot potato to the White House.

Congress had just passed the TARP, or Troubled Assets Relief Program, which appropriated $250 billion to purchase nonperforming assets from banks. The TARP's goal was to provide liquidity to the banking system so that banks would not fail and credit markets would continue to function. Capitol Hill told the automakers to go ask the administration for some of that money instead.[12]

But when automakers approached Treasury secretary Paulson for TARP funds, they were met once again with stiff resistance. Paulson's background was in the financial sector and that was where he laid his priorities. "That money is for the banks," he told GM.[13]

There was, however, a pool of funds that Secretary Paulson and his team thought might be available. A year earlier Congress had appropriated $25 billion in loan guarantees for what was called the Advanced Technology Vehicles Manufacturing (ATVM) loan program. The program had been authorized under the 2007 Energy Independence and Security Act as a sweetener to help auto manufacturers reach their fuel economy goals. Since George W. Bush did not particularly value the program, his people told the industry that the administration would work with them to make that money available for their immediate needs.[14] For this to happen, company execs would have to go back to Congress, which was not on particularly good terms with Detroit, and ask for the authorizing legislation to be amended.

Electroshock Therapy

Detroit was certainly in ill repute on Capitol Hill. But it did have one thing going for it—the Chevy Volt. Though still in development, Bob

Lutz's Volt had already started to acquire a Prius-like sheen. It symbolized the "good GM"—and the "good Detroit."

The Volt was GM's technology flagship, it was its environmental flagship, and it was its promise of corporate renewal. But despite the enormous symbolism the Volt had acquired, it was somewhat ironic that the car was not really the product of a fundamental strategy decision by GM. It was more the product of one man's pique—Bob Lutz who was sick and tired of getting hosed by Toyota—and a media-brokered shotgun wedding.

Lutz hated the Prius—he hated it with a seething passion. He hated its pathetic acceleration and he hated its sterling green image. He hated the idea that humans should have to "conserve" energy. He hated its stupid name and its stupid face. Deep into the 2000s, he hated the fact that the media was still heaping praise on Toyota for the Prius. "The mood in the auto press was all Toyota, Toyota, Toyota," recalled Lutz. "Toyota saves the planet! Only Toyota does intelligent things! Old Rust Belt America is too dumb to think of anything!"

He needed to get out from under the shadow of Nagoya's Big Green Monster. Somehow, Lutz needed to "send a strong technological statement" that GM was every bit the powerhouse that Toyota was.[15] What Lutz did not want was some wimpy little Japanese mongrel of a car. Instead, Lutz pushed like mad to get GM to build an electric concept car that was tough, muscular, and would take advantage of all that torque available through an electric powertrain. He wanted an electro-American muscle car.

After seeing that Tesla was on track to deploy its electric supercar, GM finally allowed Lutz his druthers—at least in the form of a concept car. And so, at the 2007 Detroit Auto Show, GM unveiled the Chevy Volt. It was a mock-up, a hollow shell, but it was a vessel of Lutz's competitive ambition. There was no economizing or apology for the road concealed within its contours. The Volt sported a massive Porsche-like nose, with an aggressively slanted windshield. It made the Ford Mustang look like a wimp. But unlike the gas guzzling Porsche or Mustang, the Volt promised to run on electricity. And, at least in theory, that would make it enormously efficient.

In the run-up to the 2008 oil crisis, with gas prices headed toward historic highs, the Volt's allure was electromagnetic. It was the talk of the town. It looked as if GM, which had been convicted in the court of public opinion as executioner of the electric car, was back in the technology game—and in a big way.

Except that it wasn't. This was a concept car. Every year, hundreds of concept cars get built. Precious few ever see the glint of an assembly line's robotic arm. This was especially true for the most radical concepts—of which the Volt was certainly one.

But that year in Detroit you might say that GM lost a certain amount of creative control over the company's development decisions—it was overtaken by events. The public reaction was too strong and by teasing the EV concept, GM had condemned itself to actually building the vehicle. It risked another round of media flogging should the concept fail—or simply fail to materialize. And so Lutz got his electric car. If Japan could build a historic hybrid and Tesla could design an electric supercar, Detroit could build the Chevy Volt.

"Is This for Real?"

In 2007, GM started scouring the world for an engineering dream team to make the Volt a reality. Sitting across the Atlantic Ocean in GM's German headquarters was an exec who would be critical to the task.

Michael Farrah had worked on the EV1 in the 1990s, and he had the experience in electronics and integration that would be necessary to build a new generation of American EVs.[16] Farrah was also deeply passionate about the potential of the electric car. All in all, he seemed like the perfect fit. But when Detroit rang him to ask if he wanted to join the Volt development team, Farrah's answer was a surprisingly emphatic "Hell no!"

It wasn't that he didn't believe in the concept; he just didn't believe in GM's sincerity. "I've been on programs like this before," he told them. "They're not real."[17]

After seeing the company crush a thousand EV1s, Farrah had good reason to be skeptical. Only in this case, the project *was* "real." Management let Farrah conduct his own due diligence on the Volt and everyone he asked told him that this was not a test.

Farrah knew that if GM was truly committed, it could bring extraordinary resources to bear. But the timeline was daunting. GM intended to have the Chevy Volt in showrooms by 2010.[18] It was an absurd ambition.

Yet at the same time, there was something reassuring about the laundry list of development goals. The whole thing was risky, the whole thing was a gamble, the whole thing was very un-Detroit—very un-GM. In order to make it possible, the Volt's team was going to have to junk the methodical product planning cycle that had come to characterize the industry and move toward a much faster, more innovative posture. Like an EV, Farrah's team was going to have to offer maximum torque from the starting line.

"You guys are not going to be held to the normal GM bureaucracy," Lutz told them. "[S]pend money when you need to spend it. You have a problem, call us on the phone." The pace was exhilarating. "Next week" was a common scheduling tactic in the industry. But with this project there was "no next week," remembered one giddy engineer. Everything had to happen in parallel, and money was not an object.[19]

By 2008, the Chevy Volt technical team had swelled to a staggering five hundred people—including an army of battery, electronics, and code specialists that far outstripped anything you might normally expect to see.

GM was also bringing in new partners. It was not equipped to build its own batteries—given the complexity of the tasks already at hand, that would have been suicide. But they still had to test the battery systems built by other manufacturers and to integrate them into Volt's drivetrain.

To get around the vexing issues of range, the company had decided to opt for a design it dubbed a "range extended" EV. This included two electric motors, an elaborate planetary gear transmission, and a 1.4-liter, four-cylinder internal combustion engine. On electric power alone, the Volt would run about forty miles, after that, the internal combustion engine would power its electric motors. Run in reverse, one of these motors would produce that magical booster of electrical efficiency—regenerative braking. GM's engineers figured that the Volt's battery range would be sufficient for about 80 percent of daily trips in America.[20] But the beauty of the Volt was that its engine would also cover the off day when a customer wanted to travel beyond the forty-mile electric range.

The downside was that yoking these two systems together into a performance package would not be cheap or easy. Over the past decades, cars had become increasingly computerized. But the Volt was going to take this trend to an entirely new level. Its control system required approximately 10 million lines of code. As a point of comparison, the F35 joint strike fighter—perhaps the world's most advanced fighter aircraft—required only about 7 million.

As the project wore on, the development team's elation slowly turned to trepidation. Deadlines were slipping, battery packs were leaking, and sparks were flying when and where they should not. And through the entire undertaking GM was granting unprecedented media access. Journalists were taken on tours of battery labs where test packs were strung with wires, and roped with tubes spurting orange liquids.

"Can GM pull this off?" one reporter repeatedly asked. Without exception, he received the same response, "Failure is not an option."[21]

Lost in the technical maelstrom—but not on GM's leadership—was the fact that the optics of the Volt project were just as critical to GM's survival as the mechanics. For while the drama of the Volt's development was taking place in GM's technical centers around the world, a much larger narrative was playing out in world energy markets, the global economy, and on Capitol Hill.

14

Dark Green

Money, Power, and the Stimulus Melee

N EARLY December 2008, after his thrashing by the congressional panel, a chastened Rick Wagoner rolled up to Capitol Hill in a prototype Volt. It was GM's love letter to a Democratic Congress. "The auto industry is an important one for the economy, and obviously it's under tremendous pressure—in part because of the global financial crisis," he stammered to reporters across from the Capitol Building. "We're going to be changing technologies . . . and it would be a shame to see the U.S. fall out of that race."

But despite GM's effort to put on its best face, its proposal to divert funds from the Advanced Technology Vehicles Manufacturing (ATVM) program for an automotive bailout went over like a lead balloon. The Democrats didn't like the automaker/administration plan one bit. It was still Hank Paulson's design.

For the Bush administration, ATVM was not a priority, but for the Democratic congressional leadership it most certainly was. The Democrats' message to automakers was crystal clear: "Keep your hands off ATVM." That money was appropriated for a specific purpose.[1] With that, the House adjourned for the winter recess, thereby calling the White House's bluff. The House as good as dared the administration not to sustain the automakers using TARP-appropriated funds.[2] The tactics could not have been much tougher. Democrats wanted to modernize Detroit, but they were gambling with the future of American auto manufacturing itself.

Faced with the potential loss of 2 million jobs, the Bush White House first balked, then blinked, and then funded $17.4 billion in loans to the automakers as part of an initial $35 billion automotive rescue package.[3] This was the beginning of TARP's Automotive Industry Financing Program (AIFP).

The Bush administration's decision to rescue automotive companies was heavily contested. Vice President Dick Cheney and many Republicans in Congress opposed it, but Bush went ahead anyway—unwilling to go down in history as the president who destroyed America's automotive economy. He compromised on his free market "principles" on both autos and banks. In addition to the immediate threat of job losses, Detroit's failure threatened to overwhelm the Pension Benefit Guaranty Corporation—which insured the pensions of major U.S. employers. This would create an even bigger financial disaster.[4]

But whereas the banks received a $700 billion rescue package, the Bush administration did the bare minimum necessary to keep Detroit afloat. In the words of one Republican strategist, Bush "punted" the issue to the next administration.[5] The Obama team would have to catch the ball and run with it.

Team Obama Returns the "Punt"

Most economists soon believed that Washington would have to go beyond damage control to avoid a depression. It needed to enact a large Keynesian fiscal stimulus program. In January 2009, this consensus, combined with the intensity of the crisis, provided the incoming Obama administration with unprecedented power over the economy and a unique opportunity to advance its industrial vision for America. In the parlance of a subsequent State of the Union speech, it provided an opportunity to invest in new technology and to "win the future." But even as the administration was confronting the daunting task of planning and dispensing a $745 billion package responsibly and within a very compressed window of time, it needed to deal with the intensifying exigencies of Detroit.

For the Obama White House, the need to save Detroit was never in question.[6] Instead, the debate centered on tactics. The new administration brought in a team of investment bankers and charged them with overseeing Chrysler's and GM's reorganizations. The goal was not only to save the automakers, but set them on a road toward long-term profitability. It would require a whole-scale revamping of their capital structure. Led by the private equity mogul Steve Rattner, the team suggested GM and Chrysler each declare bankruptcy. It was a bitter pill—a few months earlier the automakers had not even wanted to consider that possibility.

But their options boiled down to: bankruptcy with the federal government's help, or bankruptcy without the federal government's help. So they forged ahead. One reason a bankruptcy supported by Washington was so much more attractive was that the kind of bankruptcy each carmaker filed for would be critically important. A Chapter 11 bankruptcy would allow each company to keep its assets, adjust debts, and devise a repayment plan for its creditors. It would also allow the company to remain in operation.[7] But for that to happen, there would have to be financing to carry them through bankruptcy proceedings. And Washington was the only place that such financing could be had. If adequate funding could not be drummed up, it would force a Chapter 7 filing and stop all operations. Such a move would have a massive domino effect, forcing hundreds of suppliers into bankruptcy or out of business. Under that scenario, GM estimated that the job losses would have been one to three million—and concentrated in a region that was already one of the most economically depressed in the country.[8]

The Obama administration supplied both General Motors and Chrysler with an additional package of loans, worth $45 billion—for a running total of $62 billion. They also helped them develop a plan for filing a Chapter 11 bankruptcy that could prepare the automakers to return to profitability.[9]

But although both companies were bailed out, only one was really *rescued* by Washington. Chrysler was forced to merge with the Italian automaker Fiat. "Treasury and the U.S. government made a pretty clear decision back in the Spring of 2009 as to who was going to survive as a child, and who was going to go onto a life support system to find out if they could make it to Christmas of that year," remembered Fiat's CEO, Sergio Marchionne, on the fifth anniversary of the bailout. "I wasn't given a dollar of equity . . . and everything we *were* given was secured. I think parts of my private parts were attached to that security." In short, Fiat was taking a huge gamble, and Chrysler had to "prove its right to exist."[10]

On the other hand, GM couldn't fail. It was too big, too valuable, and too intertwined with the overall industrial fabric of the nation. One executive remembered the bankruptcy planning as a kind of "Socratic method." The automakers would approach Rattner's team with proposals, ask if they sufficed, and then he would tell them to go back and try again.[11]

The eventual cost of the automotive bailout was more than $81 billion. For this the government acquired a 9.85 percent stake in Chrysler and a 60.8 percent stake in GM.

Dispensing the Stimulus

One deputy assistant secretary at the DOE recalled the period as "exciting" and "frantic."[12] The first influx of cash, the Automotive Industry Financial Program (AIFP), was administered under the Treasury's $750 billion TARP mechanism. But billions more were going to be channeled through the DOE as part of the $840 billion American Recovery and Reinvestment Act (ARRA, or the "stimulus"). There was also that pot of cash that the Democrats in Congress had protected, the ATVM loan program. The DOE's Phyllis Genther Yoshida, who had been deeply involved in both PNGV and Freedom Car, remembered that "a lot of stuff people wanted to do for ages, there was finally funding to do." Partially as a result of this, there was a quick rethinking of the federal government's relationship with manufacturers. Suddenly the administration had massive, cohesive, and direct leverage over the U.S. auto sector. They also had very little time to act.

The "New Industrial Policy" of the Obama Administration

Up until the stimulus there were significant institutional and philosophical barriers preventing the federal government from engaging in more aggressive automotive research and development. Many Americans worried that antitrust regulation—which barred U.S. companies from collaborating on certain R&D efforts—was putting American manufacturers at a structural disadvantage against international competitors. By the 1980s Japan was seen as the biggest threat. In response, various pieces of legislation, notably the Stevenson-Wydler Act of 1980, had smoothed the legal path to public-private and inter-industry collaboration.[13] But anything that went beyond testing and validation, into commercialization, "wouldn't pass muster with OMB. . . . Republicans call it industrial policy, you couldn't do industrial policy."[14] Clinton had tried to push government research further downstream with the Partnership for a New Generation of Vehicles by justifying the effort as just this kind of "test and validation program."

But in 2008, the Obama administration decided that, contrary to Republican belief, it *could* do industrial policy—even if they didn't call it that. Some new ideas came in with the transition team, and early on, team Obama made clear that they were predisposed to support electric vehicles. Obama's energy plan, released in August of the election year, made a goal to put "1 million Plug-in Hybrid cars—cars that can get up to 150 miles per gallon—on the road by 2015." The fervent hope was that those cars would be "built here in America."[15]

Lifesaver, Pork Barrel, Treasure Chest

The stimulus was part lifesaver, part pork barrel, part treasure chest, and part grab bag. With business drying up, everyone wanted a piece. The fracas included the massive auto companies that were now partially owned by the government, foreign conglomerates trying to purchase a piece of the action, labs, small companies, and entrepreneurs scrambling for a transformative capital infusion.

In some ways, this was one of the strengths of the U.S. approach. It enticed an incredible diversity of actors into the race. But the feds sometimes had a hard time telling the difference between promoters and innovators—and to be fair, so did Wall Street and Silicon Valley. Many poor decisions were made and many of the prominent battery and automotive startups funded by the stimulus did not fare well. That said, there were also some pathbreaking successes.

The stimulus was animated by diverse and sometimes conflictual goals. Channeling government largesse toward economically strategic regions was one. Seeding new industries was another. Then, of course, there were the twin goals of increasing U.S. energy security and reducing carbon emissions.

Early on, savvy operators understood that a strong letter from a powerful congressman or senator might mean the difference of millions of dollars in government grants or loans. So too could the decision to site a project in a specific state or congressional district.

The Big Three

One priority for Washington, of course, was the traditional auto sector. Two of the Big Three—General Motors and Chrysler—were now partially owned by the administration and Obama was politically vested in their success—and transformation. Ford, of course, did not get a bailout. Through a bit of luck and strategic foresight, it had already begun an enormous restructuring prior to the crisis. Ford called it "The Way Forward." By 2008, it was already raising debt, closing plants and selling off assets such as its Hertz rental car business. Ford amassed significant amounts of cash to aid in that process. But while Ford passed on the federal bailout, it got something else: an ATVM loan for $5.9 billion. It also benefited from the rescue of its supply chain.

Even for the auto industry, where cash flows were calculated in billions, federal infusions of cash were jaw-dropping. TARP's loans to GM and Chrysler finally plateaued above $80 billion. Through ARRA the Big Three also received hundreds of millions in grants for electric vehicle research.[16] Of course, this money was not without strings. The government used it to influence and incentivize the behavior of America's automakers and to promote higher mileage standards and environmental technologies.

By May 2009, the Obama administration had "persuaded" automakers to desist with their legal challenges to California's emissions and fuel economy regulations, and agree to an acceleration of the hard-won fuel economy hikes from the 2007 Energy Independence and Security Act—a bill championed by a small Washington, D.C., group called Securing America's Future Energy, or SAFE. By 2016 fuel economy would surpass 35 mpg, and the 2025 standards would eventually be ratcheted up to 54.5 mpg.

It was a big deal. In a White House Press release, EPA administrator Lisa P. Jackson congratulated the president on solving a "supposedly 'unsolvable' problem." Congressman Ed Markey said the president had conquered "the energy and economic policy equivalent of a Rubik's Cube." Perhaps. But he had done so by taking a toy that had already been smashed to bits, and reassembling it—not through any particular mathematical genius or cunning. The energy team of the Obama administration had all the leverage in the world and they would have been fools not to use it. They had the chance, so they put the screws to Detroit.

Venture Capital Groups and Portfolio Companies

America's automakers took the most stimulus money from government coffers—other than the banks, of course. But there were also others who benefited richly. Among these was a set of brand-new entrants into the automotive world: the venture capital (VC) companies.

VC groups invest in the commercialization of technologies that are usually somewhat novel and have market potential. Some of the most prominent firms include Kleiner, Perkins, Caufield & Byers (KPCB); Sequoia; Draper, Fisher, Jurvetson (DFJ); and New Enterprise Associates (NEA). In the world of electric vehicles, KPCB, DFJ, NRG, and Technology Partners were the big dogs.

The business model of VCs is to raise large tranches of private capital—what they call "funds"—and then invest that capital in a number of companies with the potential for a rich three-to-five-year payback. These funds range from a few tens of millions to perhaps a billion dollars for the biggest VC players. Most VCs trace their origins to the veterans of the tech companies of Silicon Valley (for example, Fairchild Semiconductor and Hewlett-Packard) where expecting a three-to-five-year return is entirely reasonable. But in the mid-2000s, some of these investors forged into the sectors like energy and autos—where investments often take significantly longer to mature.

In 2009, this is exactly what was happening. Some of Silicon Valley's most storied investment groups had bet heavily on green technology remaking the energy world. In 2007, two partners at KPCB penned an editorial for *Fortune* calling the transformation of the energy sector the "single largest economic opportunity of the 21st century." The Internet, they said "represents a similar disruptive burst of energy and creativity, where we helped visionary entrepreneurs create companies like America Online, Netscape, Amazon and Google."[17] It was an interesting, and slightly blurry, premise. For "energy" encompassed a wide variety of industries ranging from coal mining, to electrical generation, to end-use efficiency (for example, home insulation), to transportation and automobiles.

The energy world was, in so many ways, more complex than that of information technology (IT). In IT, most of the money was in making and marketing new virtual platforms out of computer code. And new platforms generally replaced old platforms that were obviously inferior. In energy, that was not necessarily the case. Many of the benefits of "clean tech" accrue to society, not the individual—such as reduced pollution or decreased national energy imports. Yet huge sums of money had gone into "clean tech" in the 2006–2007 time frame on the strength of this Silicon Valley thesis. After three years VCs were ready to get out. The problem was, between the financial crisis and the extended timelines inherent in manufacturing innovations, VCs were trapped and strapped. They were running out of time and money.

Sympathetic designers of the stimulus directed billions of dollars toward VC-backed ventures, in part because they wanted to promote innovative companies. But some also accused the government of channeling funds toward investors who were close to the Obama campaign. The critics were not all partisans. "The processes were not followed consistently for all applicants and that inconsistency opened up the program to criticism of bias," said Frank Rusco, the program director for energy at the Government Accountability Office (GAO).[18]

According to Rusco, the DOE approved loans, on a provisional basis, without carrying out marketing studies or legal studies, or examining the technical merits or commercial merits of many projects. "These are things you would just *do* before you went out and said 'we're committed to loaning this money.' "[19]

Early on, VCs with close connections to Washington and the Obama campaign set about establishing relationships that would help their companies through the review process for government grants and loans. Portfolio companies associated with well-established VCs fared better than average during the grant and loan review process. In 2009, the *Wall Street Journal* reported that "venture-capital firms are hiring law firms and attending seminars to help their start-ups snare a slice of the stimulus pie." The industry had decided to "embrace . . . bureaucratic Washington."[20]

Some of these companies turned into lightning rods for political controversy—and fodder for those who were critical of government's new role in the economy. Solyndra became the archetype for a VC-backed company of dubious worth that worked through Washington to secure massive amounts of government funding. When it went bust, its $535 million government-backed loan went underwater. A firestorm of controversy and allegations of political impropriety ensued.

Another typical case is that of the VC firm Kleiner, Perkins, Caufield & Byers (KPCB). The firm was a heavy hitter in Washington. Some of its partners were substantial donors to the Democrats and one served on President Obama's Economic Recovery Advisory Board (now called the Council on Jobs and Competitiveness). KPCB had a $500 million green energy investment portfolio—and much of that portfolio was in trouble.[21] Washington came to the rescue. Almost half of the eligible companies listed in KPCB's green energy portfolio achieved some level of stimulus funding—an extremely high number compared to the standard success rate for startups. Together, grants, tax credits, and government-secured loans awarded to KPCB—dispensed mostly through the DOE—totaled at least $680 million, including some very dubious EV prospects.[22]

Geographically, KPCB's portfolio companies were exceptional: most of them were located in California as opposed to the Midwest. But one of the largest DOE awards to a KPCB company went even farther afield, to an EV startup based in Finland called Fisker Automotive.

Fisker was the product of a failed design pitch to a young Tesla. Elon Musk and his team didn't like Fisker's plug-in hybrid. They wanted to optimize a purely electric car. And so Henrik Fisker took his luxury plug-in car concept and decided to try to build it on his own.

In 2008, the company had no product and no track record and wanted to make its early vehicles in Europe. Nonetheless, Fisker's funders succeeded in securing a $529 million U.S. government loan. The company promised to establish a future factory in Vice President Joe Biden's home state of Delaware, and there were rumors that the vice president had pushed aggressively for the Fisker project. "The workers here have always been the best in the world," commented Biden at an event celebrating the planned opening of a Fisker plant at an abandoned GM factory in Delaware. The former Delaware senator promised the company's founder that his state's people would once again prove themselves.[23]

The company's sports car, the Karma, cost about $95,000, and achieved only 35 miles on its battery before transitioning to a gasoline-fed engine that could run at about 20 mpg. It was not affordable, not made in America, not exactly environmentally friendly, and ripe for criticism in many other respects.[24]

But critics of the DOE loan programs often made the mistake of lumping Fisker together with another DOE awardee: Tesla. True, Tesla was also building a two-seater all-electric sports coupe, costing $110,000 and had its eye on the luxury vehicles market, but by the time the stimulus rolled around, Tesla had already sold thousands of Roadsters. Indeed, Tesla was a much better bet, but it was also incredibly desperate for the DOE's cash.

Tesla applied for a $465 million loan to carry out the next stage of its business plan—its all-electric, luxury, Model S sedan. And they played the typical Washington game of cultivating relationships with the DOE labs and bureaucracy. "But all companies do that, it's not just them," remembered one DOE official. Still, Tesla played the game particularly well. Many people questioned whether it was appropriate to fund such luxury items with large taxpayer subsidies. But in the case of Tesla, unlike Fisker, there was a business and technology road map to bring EVs to the masses.[25]

As Easy as A123

The president's men and women loved to trumpet the fact that when they entered office, "the U.S. produced less than two percent of the world's advanced vehicle batteries." In response to this, ARRA underwrote thirty new American facilities for manufacturing advanced automotive batteries and their components. These plants received almost $2.4 billion from the U.S. government. "By 2012," they said, America would boast the "capacity to produce an estimated 20 percent of the world's advanced vehicle batteries."[26] But there was a serious problem embedded within this boast: industry analysts were concerned that America's battery manufacturing capacity would grow so large, it would overwhelm automotive demand.[27] And indeed it did.

Front and center in Obama's electrification plan was the battery company A123. It had strong VC backing, deep connections to the DOE, good access to Capitol Hill, and high-paid Washington lobbyists—everything one needed to succeed in the stimulus.

A123 had originated out of the Massachusetts Institute of Technology and was initially funded through a DOE program, unrelated to the stimulus, called the Small Business Innovation Research (SBIR) program. A123's first SBIR award launched it onto a track of progressively escalating DOE investment. During the stimulus it secured funding worth $254 million. The first $249 million was to build a manufacturing facility for automotive-grade lithium-ion batteries in the economically depressed community of Livonia, Michigan.[28]

But things started to get strange when A123 invested $20 million in Fisker Automotive, on the condition that it use A123's batteries in its flagship EV, the Karma. Generally, a new technology company like Fisker would want to minimize its technology risk by purchasing components from a proven manufacturer. By cross-investing, Fisker and A123 were multiplying their technology risk—if one risky startup failed, both could fail. The Fisker investment was a harbinger of things to come.

On August 5, 2009, A123 was awarded its grant from the DOE. The next month the stock made its initial public offering, raising almost $400 million, and by October the company's market capitalization had climbed to $2.3 billion—trading at $25 per share.[29] For a time, A123 looked like the ultimate clean-tech success story.

But by the end of 2010, A123 stock had plunged more than 90 percent to about two dollars.[30] And things were about to get worse. In early 2012 it announced the recall of $55 million worth of faulty battery packs sold in Fiskers and other vehicles.[31] And by the summer of 2012, A123 was headed for bankruptcy.

The company announced that it had executed an agreement under which a Chinese auto parts company called the Wanxiang Group would buy 80 percent of A123 for $450 million—a small fraction of its earlier valuation.[32] In the end, the Wanxiang Group got an even better deal than that. They scraped up the assets of the "all-American" battery company at bargain-basement prices after it had already gone bankrupt. And then they changed the name. In the spring of 2013 a group of DOE officials heard that the company was to be renamed B456 and thought it was a macabre April Fool's joke.

To critics, the stimulus looked like classic big government clientelism. It looked like powerful VC groups from liberal California using their connections and resources to aggressively pursue government handouts.[33] They were willing to go to great lengths and they were succeeding in getting money, but the results of these investments were clearly uneven.

No "Perpetual Motion Machines"

Of course, these investments were no easy task. And it is vital to remember that the purpose was not to fine-tune an asset portfolio for a new American sovereign wealth fund, but to salvage and stimulate the U.S. economy. In the wake of the financial meltdown the entire point of the stimulus was to move massive volumes of money out the door as quickly as possible. The fact that this ended up being a "green" stimulus was an added bonus. Responsibility for administering the "green" portion of these funds was delegated, overwhelmingly, to the Department of Energy. It was a process that was bound to be flawed and problematic. In many cases, DOE programs were responsible for handing out more than ten times the amount of their usual operating budgets. Still, DOE made a number of decisions that made it worse.

Foremost among these was requiring applicants to submit their development proposals according to a rigid paper-based format and on a very tight timeline. Policy makers knew they were under a microscope. As a result, the administration was petrified of funding a "perpetual motion machine." However, once a funding opportunity was announced, reviewers at the DOE were banned from communicating with companies. This was standard policy for DOE funding opportunity announcements (FOAs) and the practice was instituted to reduce chances for corruption or impropriety.[34] However, the stimulus was executed on an extraordinary timeline and under extraordinary circumstances. In many senses, hewing to this set of regulations had the effect of boosting players with entrenched connections and who already understood the system. Some suggested that the DOE mostly funded safe research to which they had previous exposure.[35]

Reviewers often came from the department's National Laboratories or other parts of the DOE's technical establishment and were best acquainted with a specific universe of companies and technologies that had maintained close interaction and communication with the DOE. Under normal circumstances, the DOE would have held a series of "pre-solicitation meetings" to become better acquainted with groups that were interested in funding. But in this case, there was no time. It ended up that "a lot of these things were programs that we'd already done, but we just expanded the size of them."[36] People or companies with preexisting relationships had an advantage. "People go with known people . . . but not necessarily the known technology," commented one government official after the fact.[37]

200,000 Cars

In addition to all this, the United States also offered tax subsidies for EVs. An up to $7,500 per vehicle subsidy (dependent on battery size) was offered for the first 200,000 electric vehicles per manufacturer. This policy applied to EVs with a minimum battery capacity of 4 kilowatt-hours. A car with 16 kilowatt-hours or more, like the Chevy Volt or Nissan LEAF, received the full $7,500 tax credit. One senate staffer involved in devising the credit described the process as old-fashioned sausage making. "We didn't think $5,000 was enough, and we didn't think we could get $10,000, so we decided to go for $7,500," remembered Amit Ronen.[38] Altogether this arrangement worked out to a hefty maximum subsidy of $1.5 billion per automaker, foreign or domestic.

In addition to the EV credit, the federal government offered significant incentives for installing EV chargers—subsidizing 50 percent of home charger costs up to $2000 in 2010 and 30 percent of the cost of a home charger up to $1,000 in 2011. But all of these were offered as tax rebates—which, ironically, meant that they only benefited wealthier people with larger tax liabilities.[39]

There was also a $230 million program called "The EV Project." It partnered with California, Oregon, Arizona, Texas, Tennessee, Washington State, and Washington D.C. to deploy 14,000 free in-home and public chargers. The project was anchored by $99 million in DOE money through a grant to a company called ECOtality. There was also an additional $130 million of matching investment from private partners. But this was not for research and development as it is generally conceived of. It was half market study, half infrastructure deployment. The underlying justification was that data gained from these subsidies could be used to promote further EV deployment.

Like many stimulus-era programs, its management left something to be desired. The Idaho National Laboratory, responsible for administering the program, created stringent non-disclosure agreements with every single recipient of "EV Project" funding. These agreements said that DOE was not allowed to distribute this precious taxpayer-funded data beyond its own research confines.[40] And this meant that the costly data was not much use to the industry as a whole, and left the taxpayer holding an unfulfilling $99 million tab. In another questionable incident, the bulk of fast chargers planned through the program were contracted through a partnership with the oil and gas company BP. After four years, almost none had been installed. ECOtality filed for chapter 11 bankruptcy in September 2013, and BP was still sitting on the money, and its hands.

The rollout of charging infrastructure was disappointingly slow. In fact, as of spring 2012 two-thirds of the EV Project's DC fast chargers were located at a single Cracker Barrel restaurant in Lebanon, Tennessee.[41] In comparison, by early 2013 Japan had already deployed around 1,700 fast chargers nationally—in an area approximately the size of California.[42] Fast chargers were particularly important because they allowed consumers to gain the confidence to drive their EVs much longer distances without fear that the vehicle would run out of batteries. What might take six to eight hours with a normal level-1 charger could be accomplished in twenty to thirty minutes with a DC fast charger—thus assuaging concerns that an EV driver would be stranded without power.

"Halftime in America"

The stimulus was an enormous opportunity. The Obama administration used its unique moment of leverage with the industry to push through a program of aggressive automotive industrial policy. But these policies were, of necessity, hastily planned. They were open to accusations of clientelism and heavy influence from Washington lobbyists. Yet, for all its flaws, the Obama program represented the possible beginnings of a new industrial strategy for the United States. Whether or not these programs would be allowed to continue depended largely on the outcome of a national dialogue that would culminate in the presidential election of 2012.

Both sides of this debate were unwittingly presaged by an intense, gravelly voice, stepping out from a dark, forbidding alley, on a cold winter night in February 2012. "It's halftime," the voice said. "Both teams are in their locker room discussing what they can do to win this game." As the camera angle panned left, a long shadow drifted forward. "It's halftime in America, too," Clint Eastwood told a rapt audience of 100 million Americans watching the 2012 Super Bowl.

Chrysler, which had just survived America's economic catastrophe through Uncle Sam's firm hand-holding, wanted to send a message: it was strong again, it was ready to roar back. Amidst the rat-tat-tat roller-coaster ride of thirty-second slapsticks, Chrysler's "Halftime in America" stretched on for what seemed like an eternity—two minutes. It culminated in an impassioned, unmetered, patriotic rap and battle cry for American resurgence. "This country can't be knocked out in one punch. We get right back up, and when we do, the world's gonna hear the roar of our engines," Eastwood assured an audience still reeling from the effects of the Great Recession.

It was potent stuff.

But the spot was roundly criticized by Republicans and Fox News as a not-so-subtle endorsement of the Obama administration—by both Chrysler and Eastwood himself. It was a controversy that probably would have died in a few weeks, except for Eastwood's next foray into U.S. politics seven months later—this time very much intentionally at the Republican National Convention.

Hailed as a secret weapon by Republican strategists, Eastwood emerged onto the convention stage into a sea of red, white, and blue. The audience was smaller than at the Super Bowl, but it was broadcast to a politically pivotal demographic of 30 million Americans obsessed with politics and U.S. elections.

Eastwood shuffled out with a bit of a smirk, carrying an unexplained empty chair. Rather than staying on script, he decided to improvise a profane, slapstick chastening of President Barack Obama—using that empty chair as a stand-in.

> "What? What do you want me to tell Romney?"
> "I can't tell him to do that . . . he can't do that to himself. You're absolutely crazy."

Slack-jawed political analysts watched, aghast at the spectacle taking place just minutes before Mitt Romney himself was scheduled onstage. It was, without doubt, the single indelible moment of a largely forgettable Republican convention.

Beyond the Kafkaesque quality of his monologue, Eastwood's appearance underscored a serious point: if Obama was reelected, it really was halftime for both Detroit and a potentially transformative raft of Obama administration energy policies. If, however, Obama lost, then it was game over—at least for the next four years. Obama's green transportation and energy agenda would be treated like a bad joke by the Republican Party. There were two clear roads ahead.

Despite the battle scars from Solyndra, Fisker, A123, and others, Obama still placed a great emphasis on the importance of the clean energy sector, and certainly EVs. "[T]here are few breakthroughs as promising for increasing fuel efficiency and reducing our dependence on oil as electric vehicles," he told a crowd of college students during the run-up to the 2012 election. "Soon after I took office, I set a goal of having one million electric vehicles on our roads by 2015. We've created incentives for American companies to develop these vehicles, and for Americans who want them to buy them."[43] Joe Biden's famous summary of the administration's first-term achievements was that "GM is alive, and Osama bin Laden is dead." The Obama administration was lumping GM's survival together with bin Laden's demise within its pantheon of achievements. So it clearly meant to sustain its focus on America's auto sector.

On the other hand, if Romney won the presidency, there was little doubt that he would seek to withdraw government support for EV innovation and deployment. Romney embraced the Republican narrative of a bankrupt clean-tech sector. He even called Tesla a "loser"—lumping it together with the failed solar company Solyndra and a struggling, soon to be defunct, Fisker. The businessman candidate was rooting, very publicly, against one of America's most innovative and promising companies.

So for EV enthusiasts all over the world, Mitt Romney's wistful late-night admission on November 6 that his wife, Ann, "would have been a wonderful first lady" came as an intense relief. In a poetic turn just a week later, Tesla's Model S became the first vehicle to be unanimously voted *Motor Trend* Car of the Year. This prompted a characteristically vindictive Elon Musk to muse that Romney was correct about "the object, but not the subject" of his slander. Translation: "who's the loser now?"

Electric car sales were starting from a low base, but they were on a steep upward climb. The United States had gotten a shaky start, but any serious observer of the EV sector knew that while America was not exactly winning, it was most definitely in the race.

15

Cataclysm

The Demons of Fukushima

O N A chilly November night in 2011, a steady rain watered Tokyo's upscale Chiyoda district as puffs of fog wafted through a chest-high metal fence. Half a dozen police officers stood guard over a dark, sprawling complex. Not ten yards away, a heavily armored police trans-port sat parked, with another behind it.

"Move along," one policeman told a passerby, while another apolo-getically explained the security measures. The building was the main office of the Tokyo Electric Power Company (TEPCO), which owned and managed the Fukushima nuclear complex. Six months earlier, a disaster at Fukushima had threatened to destroy the country's east-ern megalopolis—Tokyo—and transform northeast Japan into a new Chernobyl. Only, unlike the former Soviet Union, Japan was not a ram-bling continental empire with living room to spare. It was 130 million people packed into a mountainous archipelago the size of California.

At 8 P.M. a steady stream of gray suits began to trickle, then pour out of the building and hurriedly atomize into the anonymity of Shin-bashi Station. Yet almost as many were returning to work—tired faces, almost all men. On a good night, the occasional passerby would hurl an expletive toward a fleeing executive. On a bad night, the entire complex would be besieged by throngs of militant antinuclear activ-ists.

At 8:15, Fumihiko Anegawa emerged for a meeting to discuss Japan's EV program. In Japan, those who knew EVs knew Anegawa. He was widely hailed as the visionary behind the country's modern electric vehicle movement. But for the moment, the prominence of TEPCO's innovative EV effort was massively eclipsed by the festering nuclear accident at Fukushima.

Over dinner at a nearby Chinese restaurant Anegawa explained in slow, steady, deliberate tones the difficulties that had befallen Japan's EV initiative and his beloved nuclear industry over the past ten months. He spoke with the shell-shocked tone of someone who had seen war. Anegawa was so intensely focused that he failed to notice a small earthquake as it rattled through the building.

Like the United States, Japan was also hit by the Great Recession. But Japan's automakers were in a fundamentally stronger position than those in America. There were problems, to be sure. For instance, Toyota had been dogged by a controversy regarding "unintended acceleration" in its cars (caused by floor mats jamming the gas pedal). And both sales and stock prices took a serious hit during those lean years. For Toyota sales plunged 20 percent from 2008 to 2009, and its stock valuation fell by almost 40 percent. But the company still had $25 billion of cash on hand at the peak of the crisis and retained the confidence of the investor community. As a result, Toyota—unlike GM—could easily finance any eventual shortfall. Other Japanese carmakers also suffered setbacks. Nissan's sales fell by more than 30 percent and Honda sales also fell. But among Japan's major automakers there were no bankruptcies. In short, the situation was dire, as opposed to cataclysmic. Strong automakers and steady government policy allowed Japan's EV programs to continue to gain strength.

But just as Japan looked set to establish its unquestioned dominance in EVs, disaster struck. The Great Tohoku Earthquake, its accompanying tsunami, and the Fukushima nuclear crisis they instigated were enough to shake the foundations of any industrial edifice. Anegawa had fought to make EVs the perfect complement to cheap, safe, carbon-free nuclear power. Along the way, he had secured the support of Japan's powerful economic planners and some of its manufacturing giants. But with the Fukushima nuclear meltdown, his vision was slipping away. Indeed, Anegawa's atomic dream had transformed into Japan's nuclear nightmare and his beloved reactors were in dire straits. The fate of Anegawa's EVs also hung in the balance.

It had all started eight months earlier, miles beneath the ocean floor.

Acts of God and Man

On March 11, 2011, at 2:46 P.M., the Pacific Continental Plate lurched violently under Japan's main island of Honshu, setting off a chain reaction of disastrous consequence. Shock waves exploded from the quake's epicenter forty-two miles off Japan's northeast coast, radiating across the Pacific Ocean but also toward the Japanese mainland.

Three miles off the port of Matsushima, the captain of a Japanese coast guard clipper noticed the horizon start to bend upward before him. The image was surreal, but demanded speedy and concrete action. The captain pulled his vessel toward the rising colossus, gunned the engines, and held his breath as the ship climbed directly into the mountainous swell. His massive vessel seemed small as it rocked perilously skyward before cresting the huge wave and speeding down the far side of its watery peak.[1] Up above, a Japanese Self-Defense Force pilot watched the tsunami break as it approached land and sent out a tense, terse, terrified warning: "Tsunami! A huge tsunami is coming!"[2]

During those perilous minutes, two fateful swaths of mass drew inexorably closer: a giant rolling scythe from the sea and the quiet coastal towns of northeastern Japan. In Japan's maritime communities, fortifications were in place, and seawalls protected ports, shipyards, and neighborhoods. But in many places the scale of the disaster overwhelmed these defenses. Despite historical records of massive tsunamis, almost no one anticipated the magnitude of the deluge. The quake lowered coastal elevations by as much as two feet and in some places there were indications of waves over one hundred feet tall. Cluttered black rivers rushed inland and wiped out cities; cars were swept away by coursing rapids of brine and earth; houses and community centers were ripped off their moorings; thousands of lives were subsumed in the turgid, muddy torrent.

Sprinkled across Japan's eastern shoreline, dozens of nuclear reactors hummed with furious intensity. Eleven of them were directly in the path of the giant waves. At Onagawa, just north of the quake's epicenter, the waves crested above fifty feet and wiped out 1,500 of the city's 10,000 residents. Yet the city's nuclear plant had been built on high ground and shored up by thirty-foot seawalls. Survivors flocked to it, and hundreds sheltered there in the days and weeks to come. But 110 miles south, at the TEPCO Fukushima nuclear generation complex, the situation was much less sanguine.

Masao Yoshida was the director of the Fukushima Daiichi power station—where he was responsible for the smooth operation of the nuclear power plant and also the health and safety of the six-thousand-plus TEPCO employees who manned the facility. He was also responsible for ensuring that this gigantic nuclear machine bore no ill effects for the surrounding community.

As the ground started to shake beneath him at 2:46 P.M., Yoshida tensed up. He hoped the shaking would soon stop. But the rumblings intensified. Yoshida wanted to dive for cover, but the tremors soon grew so intense that he couldn't move. The ceiling of his well-apportioned office ripped in two.

Just a week earlier there had been a training drill for workers on how to respond in case of a major earthquake and Yoshida silently prayed that everything would go according to plan. The operators controlling the plant's six reactors would have to shut each one down. All of these actions had been drilled extensively, but nothing was certain. As the plant headquarters continued to shudder around him, Yoshida tried to focus on the actions he would take in the minutes and hours ahead. More than anything, he needed to get to the Emergency Operations Room to command a response—and quick.

Inside the main control room for reactor units 1 and 2, engineers dropped to the floor or lunged for something to grab hold of. Within moments Ikuo Izawa, the manager on duty, knew this was no normal quake. He screamed to his subordinates, "Scram! Scram!" signaling them to manually shut down the galloping reactors. "Unit One, scram!" he bellowed, but the clatter of steel and concrete drowned him out. Still, his workers knew what to do.

"Unit One, half scram!"

"Unit Two, half scram!"

They verbally confirmed.

"Unit One in scram!"

"Unit Two in scram!"

They screamed into the deafening melee. They triggered backup cooling systems run by diesel generators in the plant's basement. Everything seemed to be going according to plan. But in fact it was too little, too late.[3]

Fifty-foot waves crashed over eighteen-foot seawalls, destroying power lines and flooding the basement where emergency backup generators were stored. Within an hour the waters destroyed all of Fukushima's major safeguards. Temperatures and radiation levels spiked, and the carefully calibrated nuclear reaction used to produce electricity ran violently out of control. With cooling systems off line, nuclear fuel rods liquefied into molten radioactive puddles and began smoldering their way through containment structures.

Sitting at a conference in Geneva, Switzerland, Takafumi Anegawa received a phone call from his chief deputy, Hiroyuki Aoki. The Fukushima reactor had failed, Aoki told him. And its backup systems were in shambles. "I couldn't believe it," remembered Anegawa, and he took false comfort in the thought that "Aoki-san doesn't know the details of nuclear power plants."

But Aoki had no use for Anegawa's cool analytical skepticism. Conducting a meeting in the middle of a TEPCO conference room, Aoki had watched his wheeled whiteboard whip back and forth fifteen feet. "I think we all assumed we might die," he remembered. Four of the crippled reactors were burning, and eastern Japan was hurtling toward an existential nuclear crisis. Fukushima was now an atomic time bomb—a terrifying man-made accouterment to Japan's worst natural disaster since the Great Kanto Earthquake of 1923.

It was time for Anegawa to come home.

Japan's Backyard

Both plant operators and Japan's political leaders in Tokyo struggled to digest the calamity. The following day, as Prime Minister Naoto Kan testified in front of the opposition Liberal Democratic Party on his administration's reaction to the quake, tsunami, and nuclear incident, Fukushima's seismic isolation room was suddenly concussed by a massive jolt. Aftershocks had been roiling the Japanese archipelago for twenty-four hours, but this was more powerful and violent than anything they had yet experienced. The room crashed into disarray. Workers were knocked off their seats, ceilings collapsed, and the facility's air filtration system was destroyed—flooding the building with highly contaminated dust and gases. As poisonous clouds billowed into the command center, workers lunged for air filtration masks and a sinister gray ash sifted steadily downward.

Much of the explosion was captured on live TV and soon Naoto Kan received a barrage of questions about the explosions at Fukushima. The clueless prime minister had no idea what was happening. He had no inkling that TEPCO's Fukushima reactors were, one by one, self-immolating. From a political perspective, the optics were bad: Naoto Kan looked like a man out of his depth—and he was.

But no one knew what had happened. On site some thought one of the reactor containment vessels had exploded—which would mean certain death by radiation for all of them. From the Emergency Operation Room, TEPCO employees could clearly see that the fifth floor of the Unit 1 reactor building had been blown to bits.

What had actually transpired was the lesser of two evils—the reactor containment vessel had not burst. When internal pressures had exceeded certain limits, the reactor vessel had begun to vent hydrogen into its containment structure. The blazing hot containment vessel didn't mix with the large volumes of captive hydrogen. And suddenly: *crack!* The huge reactor building popped like a concrete balloon—with terrifying force—expelling radioactive gas and water into the surrounding atmosphere and ocean.

"When that first [hydrogen] explosion occurred, I really felt we might die," plant manager Yoshida later recalled. But when Yoshida realized none of his colleagues had been killed, it steeled his resolve to fight on. "I felt awful for those injured, but I felt like Buddha was watching over us," he said. But despite Yoshida's courage, the situation was spiraling out of control.

"What the Hell Is Going On?"

That afternoon in Tokyo the prime minister was heard screaming at TEPCO's CEO, *"What the hell is going on?"* Throughout this series of events, TEPCO's president Masataka Shimizu, and the plant manager, Masao Yoshida, had been placing dueling calls to the Kantei—the prime minister's office. TEPCO's president reportedly wanted to abandon the doomed Fukushima plant entirely, which would have protected his employees, but also would have led to a full-scale meltdown, and likely a chain reaction throughout reactors along Japan's east coast as they too were abandoned. Tokyo would have to be evacuated and incalculable damage would be done to Japan's environment, society, and economy. On the other line, plant manager Yoshida pled for time. He claimed he could control the demons of Fukushima—if only he was allowed to keep a team on site.

Yoshida's proposal involved flooding the reactors with seawater and jury-rigging new systems for cooling the containment vessels. But the Kantei was worried—too much had already gone wrong. They wanted to know what the possible effects might be of flooding a red-hot nuclear reactor—could it cause them to explode? For Yoshida, exigency trumped prudence. He knew the situation was dire and there was no margin for error *or* delay. But Yoshida also knew that the Kantei would order him to halt the injections of sea-water until he had presented convincing analysis that it was the safer course of action.[4]

Always his own man, Yoshida was not overawed by Naoto Kan's executive power. On March 12, a stormy Kan had paid an early morning visit to the site, and Yoshida was phlegmatic and frank regarding the situation. When the prime minister badgered Yoshida to vent the reactors and release the pressure in the containment vessels, the engineer calmly explained that he was not yet ready. But TEPCO, explained Yoshida, had assembled a "kamikaze crew" for the task. That word caught Kan's attention, and the prime minister backed off.

Before his conference call with the prime minister's office Yoshida gathered his staff for an internal strategy session. "Look," he told his team. "The head office might tell us to suspend seawater injections. If that happens, I will put on a show and tell you to do just that . . . but I want to you keep injecting. Do you understand?"

And so, in front of TEPCO's top leadership and Japan's civilian government, Yoshida gave the order to postpone flooding the reactors until the possible effects had been thoroughly examined. Then he flipped off the cameras and forged ahead. If mutiny was the price of success, then so be it. He was no longer taking orders from Tokyo. He was the only force holding back Fukushima's nuclear inferno. Even in the face of death, he would not retreat.[5]

Eventually the prime minister overruled TEPCO's president and assented to Yoshida's strategy of containment. As Kan gave the go-ahead, Yoshida's plan was already well under way. Nonessential workers were evacuated and workers in their twenties and thirties were ordered to leave—they had their whole lives ahead of them.

With grim determination Yoshida led a small army of senior TEPCO employees into combat. The English-language press called them the Fukushima 50. In fact, the number was greater. The "50" battled on as radioactive fires blazed out of control and fuel storage pools boiled around them. As they toiled, TEPCO's senior managers and engineers were slowly poisoned by radiation. Hydrogen explosions continued to rip through the work site.

Surrounding the plant, mass confusion reigned as radiation levels spiked and contradictory information, or the complete lack thereof, panicked tens of millions across Northeast Asia. Government warnings conflicted with those from TEPCO, which conflicted with those from the U.S. Embassy in Tokyo. An exodus of foreigners clogged airports and Japanese nationals fled to regions far away from the terror. For months the rolling Fukushima disaster continued.

Takafumi Anegawa raced back to Japan to confront the burning challenges of Fukushima. His expertise could not be spared. Back in Japan, Anegawa set to work trying to stabilize the maelstrom of nuclear particles cascading off Fukushima's reactor cores. "Nuclear energy is a kind of 'not in my backyard' business," remembered Anegawa. "But in this case, 'my backyard' became all of Japan."

The Twisted Myth of Absolute Safety

The nuclear disaster turned TEPCO—which had been a respected keystone of Japan's economy—into a hated villain. Nuclear power provided the baseload of TEPCO's power supply, and for TEPCO, abandoning nuclear energy was unthinkable. But by the time the disaster at Fukushima was over, many believed that TEPCO had effectively forfeited its right to atomic energy. "Both TEPCO and NISA [of METI] were aware of the risks, [but] no attempts were made to amend existing regulations," said one parliamentary investigation.[6] Fukushima, said another critic, was the result of a "twisted myth of absolute safety"—a myth that precluded efforts to enhance the safeguards for Japan's nuclear plants.[7] Indeed, consensus developed that the tsunami was an act of God, but that serious missteps by both TEPCO and METI had intensified its destructive force. "In my judgment, [Fukushima] was a natural disaster, but also a human disaster caused by METI and TEPCO," explained Masahisa Naitoh, a former head of energy policy at METI and now chairman of the Institute of Energy Economics of Japan.[8]

Soon TEPCO was not only putting out radioactive fires, but battling for its own corporate survival. Cleanup and evacuation efforts sapped

its resources. Nuclear energy was the backbone of TEPCO's generation fleet, as well as its strategic plan for Japan's low-carbon future. By
June, TEPCO's stock price had tumbled 90 percent and bankruptcy
ensued—wiping out $39 billion of shareholder value. Just compensa-
tion for victims of the disaster was incalculable and the psychological
pressure often unbearable. While testifying before parliament, ME-
TI's chief, Minister of Trade Banri Kaieda, broke into sobs as he was
berated by the Liberal Democratic Party opposition for his handling
of the affair.

Amid all this, TEPCO had little bandwidth for electric cars. And
abandoning Anegawa's nuclear-powered EVs seemed like the smallest
of tragedies. They had been a nice idea—a bold idea. But at the end of
the day, they were marginal.

The Torch Is Passed

TEPCO slashed research personnel and funding wherever it could—
including its flagship "CHAdeMO" electric fast-charging network.
Some of these projects were taken over by private sector partners from
around the world, while others were put on ice. Japan's industrial
giant had been brought to its knees, but as TEPCO fell it passed the
torch—and chairmanship of the CHAdeMO consortium—to Nissan.
"After Fukushima it was our turn to carry the baton," remembered
Kiho Ohga, the general manager for Nissan's Zero Emissions Planning
Division. "They couldn't."[9]

Kiho Ohga was on the top floor of Nissan's headquarters—its executive floor—the day of the quake. This was where CEO Carlos Ghosn
and the other top brass resided. Fortunately, Nissan's state-of-the-art
building was engineered to withstand the most intense earthquakes.
The entire skyscraper was built on giant rollers that allowed it to sway
and absorb the seismic battering. But for those inside, that skyscraper
overlooking Yokohama Station felt anything but secure. All hell
broke loose. Desks, bookshelves, and filing cabinets were flung about
and secretaries were histrionic—screaming with terror throughout.

"Everyone was in a panic, running around. But there was nowhere to go," Ohga recalled.

Just three months earlier, Nissan had launched its $4 billion EV—the LEAF. It was supposed to be a rolling media sensation. Enormous publicity was built into the car's development plan. But in the context of Fukushima, such a rollout would be both impossible and highly inappropriate. "Promotions of EVs were cut," remembered Ohga. Launching the LEAF in Japan was going to be a much more fraught endeavor than any of them had expected.

Since many blamed lax regulation by METI's energy division for the nuclear disaster, one might say METI was responsible for destroying Anegawa and Nissan's years of painstaking work. In that sense, the leadership team at Nissan and the EV team at TEPCO had every right to be furious with the nuclear bureaucracy. But the irony was that in the wake of the tsunami, TEPCO, METI, and the automakers were now more interdependent than ever. On top of widespread damage to factories, chemical, and other industrial facilities, automotive sales had plunged. Now more than ever, they needed METI's help.

In April auto sales were 51 percent below what they had been a year earlier. Dramatic floods in Thailand, where many Japanese automakers had established factories, stymied overseas production, and the climbing yen made it hard to export profitably from domestic factories. Amid the confusion, METI's task was clear: help automakers recover as quickly and completely as possible, and marshal their resources to aid Japan's recovery.

But how to think about promoting EVs in the midst of an electricity shortage? Because of the nuclear power shutdown, Tokyo—perhaps the most energy-efficient city in the world—was being asked to reduce its electricity consumption by approximately 15 percent over the following months. That meant a long, hot summer. TEPCO would also need to ration its technical expertise, human capital, and financial resources. As a first step, the Diet passed a METI-designed measure to backstop TEPCO and begin to compensate the 160,000 evacuees from the Fukushima area. When the electric giant's survival appeared increasingly untenable, TEPCO was effectively nationalized.

After shutting down Japan's entire nuclear sector for inspection, the bureaucracy devised a plan to reduce peak electricity demand—so as not to overload Japan's limping electrical system. It forced some factories to operate at night, and others on weekends. Strict energy-saving measures were instituted in office buildings around the country and Japan's government adopted a dress code called "cool biz"—or in some cases "supercool biz"—where suits and ties were jettisoned for short-sleeve shirts worn open. This allowed office buildings to turn down their air-conditioning. Lights went off throughout the city when they were not absolutely necessary and Tokyo shaved about 18 percent off its electricity demand.

Together with METI, Nissan sought out a means of using Japan's fleet of EVs to aid in recovery. Roads had been destroyed and gasoline could not be shipped to some of the hardest-hit regions. However, in many of those areas, electricity was restored much sooner. So Nissan dispatched a convoy of LEAFs to be used by doctors and rescue workers to aid in the recovery.

Within weeks, Nissan and METI had started collaborating to accelerate plans to deploy a vehicle-to-home (V2H) system that would allow an EV to power a Japanese home for up to two days in case of a blackout. Electric vehicles, they reasoned, could be used as a strategic energy storage asset—making them even more attractive to Tokyo-area residents weary of postquake blackouts. Within two years, about 10 percent of new LEAF owners were purchasing the V2H units.[10]

In December, METI also reinstated an "eco car" subsidy it had marshaled during the recession in order to boost the domestic auto industry. It was now expected to combat the aftereffects of the natural disaster, a stubbornly high yen, and the flooded Japanese auto factories in Thailand. It worked. Domestic auto sales surged by 40 percent year over year for the month of January.[11]

The "China Threat"

Japan's situation would have been harrowing with any two or three of these challenges. But in addition to all this, China started making trouble.

Many had assumed the threat from China would come in the form of high-quality, low-cost manufacturing. Japan's economic and business leaders had consequently urged the country's powerful bureaucrats to do what they could to help domestic carmakers maintain their technology lead. A desperate editorial from the *Nihon Keizai Shimbun*, Japan's premier business paper, was emblematic of how elites viewed the China threat—it was existential. It read:

At the end of 2009, Beijing announced a target of increasing the share of electric cars in overall domestic production to 10% in 2015. The government has also created a subsidy program to boost sales of electric vehicles by providing up to 60,000 yuan (770,000 yen) [US$8,800] per unit. . . . Beijing has apparently decided to catapult the nation's auto industry into the electric age by skipping the transitional era of hybrids. . . . China is bent on taking the leadership in carmaking by taking advantage of the revolution now taking shape in the industry. Japanese carmakers need to respond to China's moves by developing electric vehicles that can compete favorably with rival Chinese offerings in this crucial market.[12]

In response, Japan's next round of subsidies matched the generous Chinese incentives. But Japan and China's industrial conflict was about to become hotter as China increasingly sought to undermine its geopolitical and economic rival.

Until 2009, the market for electric vehicle batteries was highly consolidated among two players: Toyota and Panasonic had a joint venture called the Prime Earth Vehicle Energy Company and the other player was the Sanyo Electric Company, Ltd. Together these two constituted about 95 percent of supply. Prime Earth manufactured all of Toyota's EV batteries, in addition to batteries for Hino, Daihatsu, Honda, and Ford.

When Panasonic moved to take over Sanyo in 2008, U.S. antitrust regulators went on alert. But the Federal Trade Commission was satisfied by Sanyo divesting a few nickel metal hydride battery manufacturing plants. China's Ministry of Commerce, which oversees antitrust issues, took a broader view. It homed in on assets related to batteries for electric and hybrid electric vehicles. Panasonic spent months trying to placate the Chinese. This was something completely new; China was now seeking to regulate EV battery makers in Japan. It foreshadowed a much more intrusive approach by China into the Great Race—and Japan's economy.

In the fall of 2010, China again upped the ante—this time with geopolitical consequences. Both Japan and China laid claim to a small string of islands south of Okinawa and just north of Taiwan. In Japan, they were called the Senkaku (sharp tower) islands, and in China the Diaoyutai (fishing shelf) islands. In English they are sometimes referred to as the Pinnacle Islands. Ownership was important for four reasons: first, the owner could claim their strategic territorial waters; second, the island chain was surrounded by rich fishing grounds; third, there were potentially significant hydrocarbon deposits in nearby seabeds; and finally, there was the ever-present burden of history and national prestige.

When a Japanese coast guard patrol boat, the *Mizuki,* discovered a large Chinese fishing vessel sailing in a disputed littoral surrounding the islands, it approached and called for the Chinese ship to vacate Japan's territorial waters. The Chinese vessel refused. As the two crews drew closer, the Chinese fishing captain showed no signs of deference. The two boats paralleled each other at perilously high speed, and suddenly the Chinese captain pulled a hard starboard maneuver, smashing into the Japanese coast guard vessel. The hit sent black smoke billowing from the Japanese ship and a high-speed chase ensued. It ended only when coast guard officers boarded the Chinese ship, arrested its captain, and confiscated the boat.

Japan's leadership was indignant at the brazenness of the assault—after all, the island chain had been in Japanese or U.S. hands for more than one hundred years. But China's highest officials reacted with a fury that was exponentially greater. China's president, Wen Jiabao, called for Japan to release the captain and ominously warned that Japan would suffer severe "consequences" if it did not.[13] Before long, those consequences materialized.

Soon Chinese state media was avidly promoting boycotts of Japanese goods. Newscasters read off lists of Japanese brands that should be targeted by patriotic Chinese citizens.[14] From 1995 through 2011, China accounted for 45 percent of Japan's growth in exports, so these boycotts were absolutely material, and Japanese auto producers were particularly hard hit. Protesters destroyed Japanese cars on the streets, and in the months after the Mizuki incident Japanese auto sales dropped an estimated 40–50 percent. As a defense against these jingoistic outbursts, Chinese owners of Japanese cars emblazoned their rides with People's Republic of China flags and patriotic slogans, many declaring that the disputed island chain belonged to China. To help bolster sagging sales, Nissan went so far as to offer a vandalism guarantee on vehicles sold in China.[15]

Other consequences were more insidious, but no less damaging. The motors that propelled Japan's new generation of EVs were smaller, stronger, and lighter than such systems had previously been. But the secret to their strength lay in a palette of Chinese minerals called "rare earths." Rare earths are a critical building block for everything from hard disk drives to weapons guidance systems, and by 2010 China had secured an effective monopoly over the sector, producing around 97 percent of the world's supply. For EVs, the most critical rare earth was a soft, silvery metallic substance called neodymium, which dramatically enhanced the efficiency of permanent magnet motors. America's last operation for extracting rare earth elements was the Mountain Pass Mine, overlooking the highway between Los Angeles and Las Vegas. But it had been shut down years earlier over environmental concerns.

In China, environmental concerns had a distinctly marginal effect on business decisions. From the red soils of the country's southeast, large, environmentally destructive rare earth mining and processing operations disgorged almost the entire world's supply of neodymium. For Japan's high-tech, manufacturing-intensive economy, that supply was critical.

In the first half of 2010, Japan was the world's largest importer of rare earth elements. But after the boating incident, the stream of China's rare earth exports abruptly dried up. It was like cutting off oxygen to Japan's high-tech manufacturers—without rare earths, they could only survive so long. In the second half of 2010, Japan's imports of rare earths plunged by a spectacular 70 percent compared to the same period a year earlier.[16] Some companies resorted to importing the elements through illegal smuggling operations that funneled this industrial contraband through Vietnam and China's southeastern neighbors. But this was hardly a solution.

Japan protested, while Chinese officials coyly denied there was any export ban. Perhaps, they suggested, nationalistic Chinese companies might be holding back these industrial building blocks of their own accord—in retaliation for Japan's arrest of the Chinese fishing captain. For a host of reasons, this was not believable; for one, a number of the firms trying to export rare earth elements to Japan were foreign-owned. One American analyst called China's actions "gunboat diplomacy."[17]

China's manipulation of this market was also noted with some consternation abroad. "You used to be able to buy rare earths from China," said the U.S. Department of Energy's Pat Davis. "Now you can buy magnets. Next year, who knows?"[18] In response, the United States committed $120 million to a new research hub aimed at innovating past this dependence on Chinese supply. It also approved the reopening of Molycorp's rare earths mine at Mountain Pass.

In Japan, the reaction to this economic assault was also immediate. Japan's state-controlled Japan Oil, Gas and Metals National Corporation (JOGMEC) had been aware of the country's growing vulnerability for years, and starting in 2007 JOGMEC had sought out alternatives to Chinese supplies in Vietnam, Peru, and Kazakhstan. They had also started stockpiling some of the most critical rare earth elements. Now these efforts accelerated spectacularly.

Diplomatic and trade representatives from METI and JOGMEC fanned out across the globe searching for alternative rare earth suppliers and procuring long-term supply agreements for whatever was available. METI also worked with high-tech manufacturers on a crash research project to encourage rare earths recycling and technology solutions for Japan's acute dependence on China. Finally, Japan scoured the seabeds surrounding its home archipelago for alternate sources of supply. In March 2013 those efforts paid off. Japanese researchers announced that they had discovered "astronomically high [levels] of rare earth minerals" on the ocean floor—so high that lead researcher Yasuhiro Kato thought his team "must have made a mistake."

Still Waters Run Deep

Amid this percussive series of crises, it was hard not to admire the resourcefulness and resilience of the Japanese. Despite the earthquake, the tsunami, the viciously high yen, a global economic disaster, and all of China's meddling, Japan was still dominating.

Nissan LEAFs, Mitsubishi "i's" and Prius plug-ins were populating showrooms across Europe and North America. Even with higher electricity rates than before the nuclear shutdown, electric cars were selling well at home. METI also collaborated with Mitsubishi and Nissan to deploy a massive number of "fast charging" stations across the country, allowing a Nissan LEAF or iMiev to add 40 or 50 miles of range in perhaps fifteen minutes. In France, Peugeot purchased and rebranded Mitsubishi i's for sale in the European market, while Renault—Nissan's European partner—leveraged Nissan's EV technology in an attempt to lead Europe.

In the summer of 2010, the McKinsey Global Institute published a ranking for "EV readiness" across the world. Japan, it reckoned, was not really in the running—somewhere behind France, Germany, the United States, and even China. How wrong it was. By the summer of

2012, McKinsey's narrative had been smashed to bits. Japan was number one. That year, Japan's automakers sold more than 60,000 plug-in electric vehicles and controlled about 90 percent of the global market for hybrid and EV batteries.

To some, especially those in California, this didn't come as much of a surprise. It certainly wasn't for Roland Risser, who ran Pacific Gas and Electric's EV program in the 1990s and is now head of buildings technology for the U.S. Department of Energy. "The Japanese have always been ahead," he mused with some jealous admiration from his Washington, D.C., office overlooking the glassy waters of the Potomac River. "They just don't talk about it much."[19]

16

Lucky Eights

China's Olympic Scramble and Economic Noncrisis

W AN GANG, China's prophet of automotive innovation, was rarely at a loss for words. He had an envious ability to "strike a good balance between technology and politics." And Wan Gang's political talents paid enormous dividends after his return to China. Starting in 2007 he occupied a throne within the inner sanctum of Chinese power as the minister of science and technology.[1] As he ascended the ranks of the Chinese state, he maintained his passion for electric vehicles. In the words of one Chinese auto executive, "this was Wan Gang's pet project." As the ultimate insider, Wan Gang now had the power, authority, and budget to promote his dream.

Although Wan was not a Communist Party member, he was very attuned to the Party's needs. He had to be. China was hosting the Olympics in 2008 and the country's leadership had promised to make theirs a "green Olympics." Beijing's entire industrial system was going to be curtailed for weeks to brighten the city's typically noxious summer skies. Citizens wouldn't be allowed to drive, either. But none of this was particularly impressive to an international audience. All it did was show that China could coerce its people into bending their lives out of shape so that Beijing could fleetingly obtain clean air for its international guests. But Western countries had already come to take clean air for granted and their clean air came through advanced technology and regulation. So for China, there were no bragging rights to be had by telling its citizens not to drive.

This was yet another reason why the Chinese put so much focus on their electric vehicles program. For almost a decade, the Olympic deadline dictated the form and pace of electric vehicle research in China.

China produced more than 9 million cars and light trucks in 2008 and the next year it would become the largest automotive economy in the world. The government needed to show its people—and wanted to show the international comunity—that it was leading the technology race against air pollution. The Olympics forced Chinese automakers to move further, faster than they otherwise would have.

The Olympic Scramble

By 2006, Wan Gang's Ministry of Science and Technology (MOST) had selected a group of industry partners for China's national EV program. These included First Automotive Works in Beijing, Dongfeng, Chery, and SAIC. In return for being brought into the 863 Program, these companies were expected to deliver EVs in time for the games. But by 2007—the Olympics close at hand—MOST's pacesetters were in trouble. No Chinese company had a firm grasp on the critical technologies for building an EV: advanced batteries, motors, and inverters (which helped motors and batteries "talk" to each other). China also lacked the supply chain for many of the more sophisticated hybrid elements. To meet the August 2008 deadline, a huge amount of progress would have to be made.[2] With a polished degree of understatement, Ouyang Mingao, who coordinated the Olympic effort for Qinghua University and served as one of China's top advisors on new energy vehicles, remembered the lead-up to China's games. "Of course we had some pressure," he recalled. "That was a very important event."

It was so important that some of the initial plans to showcase strictly domestic technology were stretched. For instance, Chery Automotive called in an England-based engineering and consulting shop named Ricardo for help. Ricardo was one of the three "A teams" of global automobile engineering (the others were German-based FEV and their Austrian rival, AVL). Ricardo's consultants were where automakers turned when a project was too complex, or resources were too short, for a company's internal engineering staff. For instance, Ricardo was the company responsible for customizing the spunky, compact powertrain inside BMW's Mini Cooper. But even for Ricardo, the Olympics deadline was tight. "This wasn't a moveable feast," remembered the Ricardo project manager. The Olympics were right around the corner.[3]

To fulfill the requirement of deploying a Chinese hybrid vehicle, Chery and Ricardo decided to develop a "bolt-on" system, where a hybrid drive would be attached to the driveshaft of an existing model. It would not be pretty. A more sophisticated approach would have been to integrate the hybrid elements directly into the car's driveshaft. But that was simply out of the question. There was no time. From the perspective of Toyota or Nissan or Ford the device was risible. Ricardo itself was not wild about it. But, from Chery's perspective, the hybrid system was a thing of beauty—a huge technology leap. And it was also the ticket to beating the deadline.

In the last months of development, Chery told Ricardo that it would need a fleet of fifty of these bolt-on hybrids for the games. Again, time was absurdly short. But there was no point arguing—and good money was to be made. So Ricardo got to work. Technical issues bedeviled the cars until the last moment. Ricardo and Chery engineers burned the midnight oil installing the hybrid drives, debugging their algorithms, and road-testing them. In the end, the cars were delivered on schedule. But Ricardo was so concerned about their reliability that Chery hired and trained special drivers to pilot the cars—just in case something went wrong.

After the games, Chery's sentiment was that the entire program had been a smashing success. But Ricardo did not seem nearly as enthused. In fact, they were slightly embarrassed by the final results. A Ricardo executive later conceded that the vehicle was really "halfway through development."

In addition to China's hybrid and electric taxis, the Olympics also had a fleet of China's hallmark electric buses. Because the Beijing bus manufacturer Foton could make only 46 in time for the big show, the United Nations Development Programme donated four lithium-ion powered buses to the games—bringing the total count to 50 and helping China's electric vehicle fleet creep past the 500 mark.[4]

"10 Cities, 1,000 Vehicles"

China's image-obsessed government pulled out all the stops for the Olympic debut. Fourteen thousand performers participated in the opening ceremony alone. Two thousand and eight drummers pounded through a spectacular synchronized countdown to the Olympic torch lighting; at the finale dozens of dancers seemed to defy gravity as they played effortlessly across a magically illuminated three-dimensional globe and a flawlessly beautiful Chinese child in a party-red dress serenaded the Birds' Nest stadium with a hauntingly perfect rendition of the Chinese national anthem.

But just as in the instance of the Chinese astronaut Yang Liwei, things were not always what they appeared. Some of the effects for the ceremony were "embellished" for the TV audience. The government also covered up the fact that Liu Yan, one of the opening ceremony's lead dancers, had fallen from a nine-meter platform during rehearsal and been paralyzed from the waist down. Because of the secrecy surrounding preparations for the performance, Liu Yan lay writhing in pain for almost an hour before being attended to by paramedics.[5] Finally, there was that flawlessly beautiful child whose crystal voice had transfixed audiences. She was not actually singing. Instead she was lip-synching to another child's voice—the actual singer was not deemed pretty enough.

Again, China's electric cars, with their specially trained drivers and Ricardo-engineered systems, gave the impression that the country was charged with unstoppable momentum. But any Western or Japanese auto exec privileged to peek under the hood would have quickly deduced that China's propaganda and its capabilities were wildly out of synch.

Yet, even in the midst of the frantic lead-up to his Olympic debut, Wan Gang was already writing a second and much larger act for domestically built electric vehicles. By October 2008 Wan was discussing a new EV program in addition to the upcoming 2010 World Expo. At a conference in Hunan one strategically positioned Chinese journalist wrote that "Science and Technology Minister Wan Gang was recently heard saying that: 'The Science and Technology Ministry envisions a new program to test electric vehicles in 10 cities.'" Within just two years, reported the mole, the Chinese fleet of "[new energy vehicles] should reach 10,000."[6]

The entire initiative was focused on *xin nengyuan qiche* (新能源汽車) or "new energy vehicles." But the actual definition of new energy vehicles seemed to change with the political and propaganda priorities of the hour. In 2010, Minister Wan explained that "clean" diesels were out, fuel cells would be included, and hybrids would also play a part. But all of these were subservient to the hot technology of the hour: the plug-in electric vehicle. By November, Chinese media confirmed that Chongqing had been chosen as the first test site for the new program, which was called 10 Cities, 1,000 Vehicles (*shi cheng qian liang* 十城千辆).

10 Cities, 1,000 Vehicles had outgrown the 863 Program and the Ministry of Science and Technology. Even though the initial goal of 10,000 vehicles seemed relatively small, the plan pushed aggressively toward bigger numbers over the coming months. It would start with government buses, mail trucks, and other official cars, but then expand to consumer products.

The program would be jointly administered by China's economic planning agency the National Development and Reform Commission (NDRC), the Ministry of Finance (MOF), Wang Gang's Ministry of Science and Technology (MOST), and the technical agency the Ministry of Industry and Information Technology (MIIT). In the two years between 2010 and 2012, the government expected to spend about $3 billion on subsidies for EVs and $15 billion over the following decade. There were also billions in subsidies that didn't show up in the actual budget. These included local subsidies, demonstration projects, land grants, low-interest loans, and other incentives.[7] One of these was the glistening demonstration project at the Shanghai World Expo in 2010.

"A Huge Package"

After the Lehman collapse in America, China's political leadership realized that its economy was facing a potentially dangerous slowdown. Many believed that the implicit deal between China's population and its authoritarian government involved a trade-off between personal freedom and economic growth. In practice, the Chinese had been willing to sacrifice the former for the latter. And so to keep up its end of the bargain, China announced a huge stimulus package.

The People's Republic committed almost $600 billion to expand social welfare programs, promote domestic consumption, and speed infrastructure development. "It's a huge package!" declared a triumphant Dominique Strauss-Kahn—then serving as managing director of the International Monetary Fund. "It will have an influence not only on the world economy in supporting demand, but also a lot of influence on the Chinese economy itself, and I think it is good news for correcting imbalances."[8] The Chinese stimulus was considered one of the most effective in history—far more successful than those in America, Japan, or Europe. Nowhere was this truer than in the automobile sector.

In January 2009, sales for autos were down significantly in comparison with the previous year. The government reacted with a set of policies to incentivize purchases of smaller-sized, fuel-efficient, domestically produced cars. In March it announced that $786 million would be directed toward subsidizing rural farmers to trade in their dirty three-wheel vehicles for cleaner cars and small trucks. Even more important, all small-displacement vehicles would receive a 50 percent cut in taxes—from 10 percent to 5 percent of the vehicle purchase price.[9] Similar "cash for clunkers" programs had been implemented in Japan, the United States, and elsewhere to stimulate automotive demand.

Again, China outperformed. Within a month, China's auto sales skyrocketed. During the same period that automotive sales in America, Japan, and the European Union were tanking, China's rose by 22 percent in a single month, and 49 percent that year. In 2009, China overtook America as the world's largest auto market and never looked back.[10]

Then, in May 2010, the government announced the national subsidies for new energy vehicles. They included up to $7,500 (50,000 renminbi) for plug-in hybrids and up to $9,000 (60,000 renminbi) for pure EVs—both based on battery capacity. Again, there are three core technology components in an electric vehicle: the battery, inverter, and electric motor. In order to qualify for these monies from the Chinese government, the intellectual property for one of these key systems had to be fully owned by a Chinese company.[11] This hinted at something that many industry insiders had suspected all along: China's EV development goals were not actually about cleaning up local air pollution, or reducing greenhouse gas emissions that cause global warming, or even diminishing oil imports. Instead, China was focused on winning the race to develop a new generation of cars. There was a big pot of renminbi at the end of Beijing's policy rainbow and also political rewards for those who got with the program. So local governments and manufacturers eager to please Beijing rushed to develop their own EV.

Journalists and China-watchers observed this dash toward electrification with a mixture of fear, envy, and unbridled enthusiasm. They knew China's auto industry was built on the technology of Western manufacturers, but they also seemed to believe that the technology-lagging Chinese manufacturers could leapfrog past more developed countries—though this had never happened before in the history of the global auto sector. Every country that had gained some degree of technical advantage in the industry had first mastered existing automotive systems before graduating toward the more complex task of innovation. Honda was a world-class engine company before it leapfrogged the rest in emissions, and Toyota was a globally dominant manufacturer by the time it embarked on its effort to build the Prius hybrid. Tesla was perhaps the singular exception, but it still drew heavily upon technologies and even manufacturing facilities that had been purchased directly from incumbent players.

But many thought China's Zen-master technocrats might be able to skip this stage of development. It was the same compelling narrative Wan Gang had sold to China's leadership a decade earlier, and it was a narrative that far outlived any clear-cut evidence to support it. Indeed, as early as 2010 there were warning signs that Beijing had bitten off more than it could chew.

17

China's Crisis of Competence

To MANY, it appeared China could do anything. Seemingly over-night, Shanghai had erupted from the mud flats of Pudong into one of the world's most modern cities. While Europe, Japan, and America struggled through the Great Recession, China was still on an economic tear. The Communist Party was crisscrossing the country with the world's largest network of bullet trains, and China's results always seemed to outstrip Western expectations. For the Chinese themselves, these kinds of results had started to seem rather pedestrian—they were expected. When China entered the World Trade Organization, it also entered what the chief engineer of the Chinese Automotive Technology Research Center, Huang Yonghe, called its "Golden Decade." During these years, China's auto industry regularly experienced 40 percent year-on-year growth. "We thought it was normal," said Huang. Surely, thought many, if Wan Gang and China's band of economic wizards wanted to leapfrog the West in automotive technology, they could.[1]

But even sophisticated observers failed to appreciate the sheer complexity of building a new transportation system based on the electric car, and the fact that Beijing had not really developed an integrated strategy to accomplish this feat. Many of the international financiers who invested billions of dollars for hedge funds, private equity groups, and banks didn't understand much about China, and even less about China's EV market. All they understood was that they didn't want to miss out on this world-leading EV transformation that

China's government—as well as the Western news media—was talking so much about.

They had heard that the sponsorship for China's EV program came right from the top. "[China's president] Hu [Jintao] personally inserted the private subsidy into the program," recalled one Chinese automotive industry insider. Industrial transformations of this magnitude didn't just pop up every day, and the potential for growth was mindboggling. The global auto industry represented an economy as big as India. And the transformation of that sector meant that that market was up for grabs. Nowhere was the potential more spectacular than in China.

It was easy to overlook Japanese and American efforts in the face of China's booming auto market. After a decade of anemic growth, Japan just wasn't as sexy as China. It was seen as the "sick man of Asia." America's industry was also out of favor. Its largest automaker was now derided as "Government Motors."

But Japan and America were the real driving forces of this transformation. In California, CARB was meticulously creating the policy incentives that would force automakers from around the world to build electric cars. In Japan, bureaucrats were coordinating with industry to fine-tune the mechanisms to launch their EV sector on a sustainable path of growth. Not least, Japan was investing prodigiously in an extensive network of fast chargers around the country. Nothing as concrete or strategic was taking place in China.

Ironically, many of the same American capitalists who turned up their nose at Washington's meddling with GM and Chrysler were quite enchanted by China's corporatism. In China's authoritarian economy, everything was so *efficient*. Government could just make things happen. Why should EVs be any different?

A steady drumbeat of media sensationalism reinforced this narrative. But on the ground in China, it was hard to shake the feeling that none of the major players really understood how to meet these expectations. No one was in charge, and no one really knew what they were doing. The Communist Party wanted China's companies to build

EVs, and believed that they were going to be, somehow, easier to perfect than vehicles powered by an internal combustion engine. They figured that the necessary motors, inverters, and lithium-ion batteries had all reached a sufficient degree of maturity. Where necessary, they thought, they could force foreign companies to yield up valuable technology in exchange for access to the Chinese market. In order to curry favor with Beijing, Chinese auto companies made sure they looked busy on the research, development, and deployment side of things.

But where was the charging infrastructure? What if foreigners decided not to barter their technology endowment for access to China's market? Where would the technology come from? And who would buy these indigenous Chinese EVs? All these questions were left unanswered.

In an ideal world, the infrastructure to charge EVs would have been sponsored or mandated by the government. And theoretically, these facilities could be installed quite cheaply. China was already building massive amounts of new housing, parking, and roads. With some smart regulation, the ducting and wires for EV charging could have been integrated into this expanding stock of capital.

If China wanted low-cost, high-quality EVs, companies should have been free to procure technology abroad without risking access to lucrative subsidies—just as they were in California. Indeed, had China followed California's lead, foreign automakers would have been encouraged—no, required—to compete with China's local companies to produce the best, most attractive EVs possible for the Chinese market. All this foreign competition would have likely generated business models to entice China's wealthy buyers, a social class already enamored with foreign automobiles, to purchase high-quality electric cars. Indeed, there might well have been a Chinese Tesla.

But instead of running a race for the car of the future, China was on its own domestic circuit. With so little exposure to international markets, they were never going to emerge as a true contender in the global EV space.

In fact, Chinese EV makers rarely had to contend domestically with one another either. On the contrary, it was the provincial and municipal mayors and governors who were fiercely competitive. Local officials believed that the best means to ensure the survival of a local EV manufacturer was to put up walls against competition both foreign and domestic. And so companies regularly enjoyed city, provincial, or regional monopolies on EV sales. While some domestic companies were genuinely excited about the prospects for EVs, others were more tentative. But for largely political reasons, they all charged wildly ahead—many of them without the most elementary understanding of how to build a quality car, never mind an electric car.

The Mountains Are Tall and the Emperor Is Far Away

For Beijing, channeling the forces of this industrial stampede was not easy. China is a country of about 1.3 billion people. For thousands of years its sheer size has made it difficult to control. The country's greatest rulers have been those who imposed organization and peace over China's vast population, economy, and landscape. However, chaotic forces have always lurked just below the surface, threatening to tear China apart, or at least subvert the intentions of its national leaders. One Chinese proverb states that "the mountains are tall and the emperor is far away," meaning that, most of the time, the day-to-day balance of power lies with local officials. This still rings true.

While the central government controls many key policies, local governments often have control of implementation. "The basic structure is decentralization," said Shomik Mehndiratta, who oversaw a World Bank program on EVs in China. "And the instruments they have are very blunt."[2]

Sometimes decentralization has been a magical tool for China. When the country created its Special Economic Zones in the 1970s, decentralization allowed coastal cities to test-drive Chinese capitalism. However, those economic gains were all about international trade, farming, and very low-end manufacturing. For developing a basically new transportation paradigm and for promoting competition in markets that were fundamentally determined by governmental decree, this decentralization, bordering on fragmentation had serious drawbacks.

Put bluntly: if China wanted EVs to succeed quickly, its intense focus on localization of content was a huge mistake. Developing a consumer EV is a systemic challenge. It could not be done in the same way that a company might develop a modular, stand-alone product. Industrial technology clusters and supply chains needed to be nurtured, or components needed to be imported.

Even in the United States, the most sophisticated EV manufacturers were planning to import significant swaths of technology from Japan and Korea. Tesla's battery cells were made by Panasonic, a Japanese company, and the Chevy Volt's battery pack was going to be supplied by LG Chem, a Korean company.[3] Components such as batteries needed to be built in special clean facilities that differed markedly from a traditional automotive factory floor. And GM and Tesla knew that they weren't up to that particular challenge—at least not yet. Neither was any other American company, which was one reason America witnessed a string of bankruptcies among government-sponsored battery producers after the stimulus.

Building the car was just the first of many obstacles. Infrastructure for charging needed to be installed and standards for electronics needed to be agreed upon to avoid a patchwork of mismatched plugs and vehicles. Each company was likely to have its own set of preferences regarding these critical decisions. If every city, state, or company was allowed to pursue its own solution, there was a distinct risk that diffusion of these new fueling stations and vehicles would never reach critical mass.

In a more developed, less protected market, many of these elements balance naturally through the economics of supply and demand, or by virtue of established regulations. However, in an emerging sector like electric vehicles, some aspects of the market simply must be aggressively managed by the state—and risks must be taken. There are huge gaps in data because products and technologies are brand-new. But that is the utility of the state and the essence of state leadership. Battery makers, car manufacturers, service providers (such as charging stations), electrical distribution, and regulatory actors need to be organized so that buyers of electric vehicles can use them seamlessly across city, state, and provincial boundaries and thus integrate them into their daily lives.

In theory, this should not have been difficult for China. After all, the foundation of China's EV effort was government purchases and subsidies. By 2012, the various ministries involved were supposed to purchase at least 30,000 EVs for the "10 Cities, 1,000 Vehicles" program. Dozens of local governments also promised to buy hundreds, thousands, or tens of thousands of Chinese-built EVs. "There will be 20,000 electric vehicles in Beijing by 2012 and all of them will be produced by Beijing Electric Vehicle Company," flatly declared that company's chief technology officer in 2010.

But when cities or provinces or huge state-owned enterprises sought to build their own EVs, they generally tried to exclude outsiders. That didn't just mean GM, Toyota, and other multinational auto companies. Carmakers from other Chinese provinces or cities were just as big a threat. China's EV development and deployment efforts began to be driven by dozens of distinct political and corporate fiefdoms.

Each wanted its own local champion. But China scarcely had the technology to design, assemble, and produce one viable EV model, not to speak of dozens. Unsurprisingly, the resulting products were so poorly made and the infrastructure so spare that China had little chance of generating a private market for EVs. Without sales beyond the government, China's EV market would be stunted. Beijing's subsidies were supposed to deal with this challenge. In many cities and provinces, national subsidies were supplemented by additional funding. In five major cities, cumulative incentives added up to more than $19,000 per car—much higher than anywhere in the United States.[4] But it wasn't enough.

The biggest and most powerful of China's EV fiefdoms included the China National Offshore Oil Company (CNOOC), China's massive State Grid, the China National Petroleum Corporation, and two dozen other gargantuan "state-owned enterprises." Collectively they were called the State-owned Assets Supervision and Administration Commission Electric Vehicles Industry Alliance (SEVIA). But even the companies of the SEVIA did not really have a good handle on how to make EVs a success.

Drilling Down into the SEVIA: The Case of CNOOC

The China National Offshore Oil Company (CNOOC) took an intense interest in EVs around the time of the Beijing Olympics. CNOOC was the muscular remnant of one of China's massive state oil giants. Established in 1982 as a vehicle for Chinese offshore oil exploration, in 2001 CNOOC became a semiprivate company when it launched its initial public offering on the Hong Kong Stock Exchange.[5] Although CNOOC was one of only three Chinese oil producers, at that time of low oil prices the company was only valued at $6 billion. To put that number in context, $6 billion was less than about a fifth the market capitalization that Tesla Motors commanded in August 2014. And CNOOC was a company that was going to be responsible for supplying a significant proportion of China's oil demands over the coming century. CNOOC's leadership knew they were poised for growth and fully intended to disabuse stock traders of their lowball valuation.

Not long after CNOOC stock started trading in 2001, the company's CEO, Fu Chengyu, had breakfast with BP's CEO John Browne, who wanted to know just how large Fu intended to grow his company. "Chevron level," said Fu. Surprised, Browne told Fu that this was very, very aggressive. But, Browne politely added, he would give Fu "the benefit of the doubt."[6] In ten short years, its value had climbed from $6 billion to $95 billion—about 1.5 times larger than the Chevron of 2001.[7] Like so many other things in China, it was hard not to be impressed.

So in 2010, when a CNOOC-affiliated startup called CODA went to Wall Street to raise funds to build electric cars in China, Western execs and money managers were all ears. Ten years earlier, the idea would have seemed preposterous. But in 2010, America's hardboiled capitalists couldn't get enough of CNOOC, electric cars, or China. CODA was a trifecta.

Sitting in on these meetings one could see the power of the "China first" narrative that had engulfed America's chattering classes and financial community. "I've seen it! Everything's going electric in China—everything. It's going to go much faster than here in the U.S. Much faster than any of us expect! It's already happening," said one banker during a CODA pitch.

China's push to leapfrog the West was an attractive investment thesis. And in the context of China, anything connected to CNOOC seemed like a particularly good bet. It had staked out a position as the most progressive and forward-looking of China's oil giants. It installed wind turbines on offshore oil platforms to power those facilities and worked to cut carbon emissions. In 2010 CNOOC announced a 1,000-megawatt offshore wind project—about as much energy as a large nuclear reactor produces—in Bohai Bay, three hours from Beijing.[8] This was at a time when the United States was still bickering over permitting offshore wind turbines near Cape Cod. With companies like CNOOC buying into China's EV project, the possibilities seemed endless.

In 2008, CNOOC started to place its own bets—very large bets—on EVs. The company began buying up pieces of what might eventually become an integrated EV system.

Divine Power: Lishen

CNOOC's binge started in a big way in 2009 when it made a surprise announcement: it planned to invest almost $1 billion in the Tianjin Lishen Battery Joint Stock Corporation (aka, Lishen). That year, Lishen lagged just behind the well-known private company BYD as China's second-largest producer of lithium-ion batteries. "We found a good company with very good technology, working for the space program, and good management, but no one willing to invest," said CNOOC's CEO in the fall of 2010. CNOOC stepped up to the challenge.

With the financial heft of one of CNOOC behind it, Lishen was soon on a fast track to growth. CNOOC's massive profits allowed it to make generous investments to expand production capacity and technological capabilities. There was zero mystery to reading these tea leaves. Good batteries were the heart of a competitive EV, and Lishen was at the heart of CNOOC's EV plan.

Lishen had deep roots in the Chinese R&D edifice. In the mid-1990s, Lishen was spun out of the 18th Battery Research Institute as a commercial entity owned by the city of Tianjin.[9] In Chinese, the name Lishen (力神) means "divine power," and this company's patron saint was Qin Xingcai, who successfully propelled its expansion over more than a decade.[10]

One reason for the name Lishen is that the company's early customers included China's space program and military. In fact, Lishen sat right around the corner from a massive 863 Program research lab where a thousand Chinese scientists were building new kinds of batteries for submarines, satellites, and guided missiles. But the company's clients were not solely domestic. Lishen was also one of the largest battery suppliers to the American electronics giant Apple.[11] Like most large companies in China, Lishen also benefited from a murky system of subsidies for land, taxes, cost of capital, etc. In sectors like solar cell manufacturing, Western companies and governments often complained that these supports made it all but impossible to compete with the Chinese producers.

In EVs, Lishen's major effort was its joint venture with the Chinese-

American startup CODA. That partnership inhabited a new factory on the opposite side of the city of Tianjin. The project started as a $100 million 60/40 split between the American and Chinese company, and for Lishen technology transfer from the U.S. side was one of the major attractions. After CNOOC's investment in 2009, Lishen's lithium-ion manufacturing capacity rocketed past BYD's.[12] In 2010, CNOOC's decision to invest an additional $200 million in the joint venture forced CODA to go to private equity investors in New York to match the capital call.

By the end of 2010, it planned to install sufficient capacity to produce 20,000 hundred-mile EV battery packs a year. The sky was the limit. "The next year that will rise to 50,000, and the third year to 100,000," explained CNOOC's CEO in 2011.[13]

Lishen had little to lose, and much to gain. CNOOC would invest capital in new facilities, and Lishen would build the batteries for China's expanding EV fleet. But there was a hitch. For this plan to actually work, many other components of a much more complex machine would also have to function.

Keyi Power

If people were going to buy EVs in China, they would also need access to charging infrastructure. But many Chinese lived in large apartment buildings without dedicated parking. Without a dedicated charging point, how could someone possibly use an EV? CNOOC's notional solution to this question came from another one of its investments: Keyi Power.

As CNOOC had surveyed the technology landscape in 2008, something called "battery swapping" had caught its fancy. Battery swapping allowed an EV driver to change a used battery for a new battery—like you would change the battery in a flashlight. In the West, battery swapping was almost exclusively the province of the luminary clean-tech startup Better Place, which was founded by former SAP executive Shai Agassi.

The history of Better Place, as told by Agassi, is that since the mid-2000s he had been wrestling with the problem of "how do you run a whole country without oil." Then "on a random visit to Tesla . . . . [he] suddenly found out that the answer comes in separating between car ownership and battery ownership."[14]

Agassi's big idea was that by creating a system where electric vehicles could swap out spent batteries easily, he could surmount many of the cost and range issues inherent to EV technology. All cars needed was access to a battery swap station. In some senses, it was a typical American corporate conceit: success was all about the business model, and none about the fundamental technology. But the idea was not in itself new; in fact, it was a century old.

Agassi showcased his idea at a Davos Forum for Young Leaders, where he met Shimon Peres, the former president of Israel. There Peres suggested that Agassi do something about his plan, and out of that conversation emerged the management and fund-raising team that would create Better Place. Peres's network supplied them with a champion, much capital, and even the technology for the battery's plug-in device. The startup used clips adapted from the missile-release systems for Israeli fighter jets. Now, instead of dropping bombs, these clips were adapted to swapping batteries.[15]

With Peres's backing, Better Place plugged into a voluminous stream of cash and by 2010 had raised more than $700 million. Much of that came from players like Morgan Stanley, HSBC, Vantage Point Venture Partners, and other top-tier American and Israeli investment groups. "Shai was this messianic evangelist," remembered one early investor. "His mission was to end reliance on oil, and I totally got it. . . . I met Elon Musk around the same time and to me there was no contest, Shai was just much more compelling."[16] Based on a funding round in 2011, the market valuation for the company was $1.25 billion—making it one of the highest-valued productless companies of all time. [17]

In general, the Japanese did not like the idea of battery swapping. METI had funded a small Better Place demonstration, but TEPCO decided that battery swapping accentuated one of the EV's biggest problems. "Batteries are expensive, and that is the biggest problem with EVs," said Anegawa's deputy, Hiroyuki Aoki. In other words, Better Place doubled the size of the EV's battery cost problem to deal with the subordinate and lesser problem of recharging times. "The solution is quick charging, not Better Place."

But CNOOC disagreed. So it approached Ouyang Mingao—who had run the Beijing Olympics fete for Qinghua University—for ideas on how to get into the battery swapping game.

Like Wan Gang, Ouyang had also traveled abroad for his graduate education. When he returned, he was eventually put in charge of the New Energy Vehicle center for Tsinghua, China's most prestigious engineering university. Another similarity was that Ouyang was not a member of China's Communist Party. In fact, he was vice chairman of the central committee for a political party called the Democratic League.

As a young man, Ouyang had studied locomotive engineering under an American professor named Spencer C. Sorenson at the Technical University of Denmark. Together with Sorenson, Ouyang was researching the massive diesel/electric powertrain systems that drove locomotives—or "hybrid electric vehicles," as Ouyang jokingly called them years later. In fact, it was good preparation for one of the future leaders of China's electric vehicles program. To understand the complex electric hybrid systems in diesel locomotives, one needed detailed knowledge of "electrical motors, engines, electrodynamics, and also transmissions and power electronics"—all the components critical to EVs.[18] Ouyang's professor Sorenson had happened to work for the Ford Motor Company and was very active in the Society of Automotive Engineers.[19]

Years later, as the director of Qinghua University's State Key Laboratory of Automotive Safety and Energy, Ouyang had a variety of tools at his disposal he could use to assist CNOOC in its bid for battery swapping—political connections, school budgets, and a coterie of China's best engineers, who were his students. There was currently no battery swapping technology in China, but that didn't mean that it couldn't be done. Ouyang approached some of his pet grad students to see if they were interested.

One of these was Tian Shou. Like Ouyang and Wan Gang, he had experience in the international auto sector. Tian had spent years working for GM, and held three degrees in automotive engineering—a B.S. from Qing-hua and an M.A. and Ph.D. from Germany's University of Aachen.

At twenty-eight, Tian had left GM with a group of friends to open a startup that was chasing the hybrid and electric technology wave. "We didn't have a specific project," said Tian. "But we all had a strong technical background."[20] Ouyang Mingao, Tian, and the others thought they were up to the job.[21] So, at Ouyang's request and with CNOOC's sponsorship, they assembled a response to Better Place.

In a dark warehouse on the Qinghua University campus, behind a cluttered desk, a team of graduate students and some recently minted Ph.D.s fussed over a computer screen. In front of them sat what looked like a metal box filled with rollers. The sides were latticed by accordion metal arms that seemed like they should allow the box to rise and fall. Around the corner from that, hidden behind another fence of temporary partitions, was a surprisingly sophisticated automotive bay with a full-size sedan on top, and that same accordion box underneath. In demonstration, the box rose swiftly, raising the car four inches on its shocks and unplugging the car's battery. A conveyor belt of metal rollers then rolled the battery away and plugged in a new power pack in similar fashion. The entire process took about three minutes—Keyi Power was in business.

More impressive than the swapping station itself was the fact that Keyi Power's small team was able to complete the prototype in about four and a half months for about 1 million renminbi—less than $200,000.[22] In no small part, that was because of the support structure provided to them by their partner company, CNOOC, and other members of the SEVIA. This was the model of centralized state capitalism that the Americans and Japanese both admired and feared. It seemed to be the embodiment of China's corporatist advantage.

They were heady times. CNOOC and the startup settled on a formula that would allow both companies access to the intellectual property and give Keyi Power a position as a supplier for CNOOC. It also allowed the startup to sell their swapping systems elsewhere. Keyi used SEVIA as a technology resource. It contacted Changan, one of China's largest automotive groups, and asked it to customize a vehicle for them, and Changan was instantly responsive.[23] After all, they were both members of the SEVIA. The cars were delivered by the time the new battery swap system was ready for demonstration.[24]

"[We want to be] one of the best equipment suppliers for EVs internationally," explained Tian. He was confident that his little startup, with its big supporters, would play an important role in the electrification of China's fleet. He had reason to be. CNOOC owned service stations throughout the country, and had the ambition to expand these into EV battery swapping stations. All this provided a big potential leg up in the policy-driven Chinese EV market.

Of course, the broader opportunity was global. "In 2010 Better Place was the largest single clean-tech investment for Morgan Stanley," Tian opined. "They are crazy for electrification."[25]

But Tian's professor, Ouyang Mingao, was more circumspect. He was happy to help Keyi Power, CNOOC, SEVIA, the 863 Project, and others to build China's EV program, but this whole concept of "leapfrogging" didn't sit well with him. In fact, he had been engaged in a relatively public policy dispute with Wan Gang over China's EV future. China, thought Ouyang, should start by promoting the lowest-end EVs, and move up the value chain as it gained competence. This would be a very long-term prospect, but Ouyang thought it had a better chance of success.

State Grid

By 2010, another critically important member of the SEVIA was also starting to recoil from the leapfrog narrative. Lai Xiaokang, head of advanced technology for State Grid, had helped plan the expansion of China's grid from a backward, run-down communist relic into the largest—and one of the most sophisticated—transmission systems in the world. Lai understood the importance of strategic planning and had two persistent worries about China's EV initiative: not enough planning and not enough data.

China's electricity market has scores of publicly and privately-owned generation companies—the companies that actually produce electricity. But its transmission was a firm duopoly. The smaller of the two grid companies is South Grid, which covers the Guangdong area (including BYD's home turf of Shenzhen) and a few other provinces. In 2010 South Grid supplied about 235 million people with electricity. In other parts of the world, South Grid would be considered a giant. But in China, it is a junior partner to State Grid, which covers about 88 percent of the country geographically, and supplies almost a billion Chinese with power. It was the third-largest corporate employer in the world—right behind Wal-Mart and CNPC.[26]

Every day, State Grid was responsible for providing electricity to almost a billion people, and its entire operation lived and breathed on data. The previous year, China had added 90 gigawatts of generation capacity—more than existed in the entire United Kingdom, where the electrical system had taken more than a century to build. State Grid had to integrate this new juice into China's transmission system and get it where it needed to go. Clearly, no company would be more important to EV infrastructure in China than State Grid. "We are happy to work with them . . . but they cannot do it without us. They focus on the cars a lot, but the grid is a vital component," explained Lai.[27] And to make that EV infrastructure work on a massive scale, State Grid would need more data—much more data.

And State Grid, which was intimately familiar with the process of building out new infrastructure for China, just wasn't as hot and heavy for EVs as China's Communist Party leadership. The technical problems of charging EVs were basically surmountable. They had shown that at the Olympics and again at the Shanghai Expo. But massive deployment in a city like Beijing was different.[28] There simply hadn't been enough planning and there wasn't enough information to propel the kind of expansion China's policy makers were talking about.

In his own way, Lai did what he could to be helpful. Lai had State Grid purchase some of those famous electric buses as company shuttles, and installed charging stations in front of his headquarters. And Lai himself even drove a BYD-brand electric vehicle to work every day—all in the name of data collection.[29]

But China, thought Lai, was going too fast. He understood that the government wanted to deploy EVs in massive numbers over the next few years. He just didn't see how it was going to happen.[30] And neither, it seemed, did the leadership of the SEVIA.

A "Team" of Rivals

Driving from State Grid to the headquarters of the SEVIA in Beijing, one sees gleaming towers that are the corporate palaces of China's state-owned enterprises. Each has its own cavernous lobby, and the edifices are emblazoned with corporate logos across their façades. But in 2011, the SEVIA—where China's electric vehicles revolution was supposedly taking shape—inhabited a much more modest wing of C-class office space in a dusty, somewhat remote corner of the city.

At SEVIA headquarters, two or three dozen staff from constituent companies ran the show. CNOOC, which had about 100,000 employees in 2011, only spared a few. One employee from the SEVIA who preferred to remain anonymous explained that after eighteen months of collective effort, most of the group's progress consisted of writing various reports and white papers. There was not much progress on deployment of cars or charging infrastructure, and China was certainly not in the midst of a technology revolution. Something was clearly not clicking.

The Beijing Electric Vehicle Company

China's cities were scarcely more organized. They were under intense political pressure to deploy EVs, but if they were going to spend their money on buying electric cars, they wanted these cars to be bought and built locally—regardless of whether their local car company actually had the skills to build a competitive EV. One example of this phenomenon was the Beijing Automotive Industrial Holding Company (BAIC).

For years Chinese economic planners tried to "rationalize" BAIC out of existence. But in the 2000s, that started to change. "The Beijing government finally came to the realization that a big city like Beijing needs a big corporation as a pillar of economic growth," explained Frank Liao, chief technology officer of BAIC's subsidiary, the Beijing Electric Vehicle Company (BEVC). "Before it was not like that. Before they were trying to get rid of us," Liao chuckled.[31]

Frank Liao had led Chery's Olympic collaboration with the British engineering firm Ricardo before he was poached to lead BAIC's EV program. A husky man with a hearty laugh, Liao had gone to the United States and learned fluent English, obtained a Ph.D. from the University of Wisconsin, and worked in some high-profile American startup companies. Liao was even a consultant on GM's famous EV1 program. Liao also held the distinction of being perhaps the only person in Beijing who stopped his car at crosswalks, where pedestrians regarded him with deep bewilderment, even suspicion, as if he were simply waiting to mow them down. He had returned to China as a "sea turtle" to work in the automotive industry.

Liao was not the only sea turtle recruited by BAIC. His boss, Wang Dazhong, president of the BAIC group, studied for his Ph.D. at Cornell and then worked at GM for almost two decades. Later he became managing director of greater China operations for the tier-one automotive supplier Delphi, thereafter serving as a vice president for GM's partner, the Shanghai Automotive Industrial Corporation. In 2010, BAIC recruited Dazhong as its new president.[32]

"BAIC is really attracting the cream of the crop," boasted Liao. "We are backed by the central government through a lot of resources, land grants, and most importantly subsidies and support in the marketing area."[33] But the Beijing Electric Vehicle Company (BEVC) was at best an improvisation. It was hastily incorporated in June 2010 in direct response to the announcement of EV subsidies from China's central government. Despite the fact that it had literally no experience in building EVs, the city of Beijing decided to order EVs almost exclusively through the BEVC and its sister company Foton.[34] BEVC was asked to produce 25,000–35,000 electric vehicles for the Beijing government between 2010 and 2012—which would have made its output of plug-in electrics somewhere in the neighborhood of Nissan's 2013 LEAF sales in the United States.[35] Filling this order was supposed to be Frank Liao's consuming mission.

One thing the company had going for it was that city support was allowing it to spend liberally on technology from abroad. In 2009, the company paid about $200 million for three automotive platforms from GM's ailing subsidiary Saab. The deal went through relatively easily, as Saab was verging on bankruptcy and BAIC had a multibillion-dollar line of credit courtesy of the city of Beijing.[36] This strategic asset was supposed to help BAIC surmount technology hurdles. "That kind of bought us three to five years of development time," explained Liao.[37] But this was not EV-specific technology; it was merely a set of better designs for chassis, steering columns, and other industry standard components—things that any international company would have already worked out long before.

But the Beijing Electric Vehicle Company had an answer for the problem of EV know-how. It intended to work with international automotive consulting companies like Ricardo or its German and Austrian counterparts FEV and AVL in order to design their electric vehicles. Liao stressed that these partnerships would not follow the same turnkey formula that his previous company, Chery, used with Ricardo leading up to the Olympics—BEVC would play a more active role in technology development.[38] But this path forward seemed to ignore the complexity of the supply chains needed to support the production of tens of thousands of EVs in such a short time.

Indeed, things seemed completely turned upside down in China. In America, one of the greatest challenges to a startup company was finding a customer. But the Beijing Electric Vehicle Company already had a customer lined up. What it lacked was a product.[39]

Before long, these seemingly self-evident problems began to manifest themselves in ways that were increasingly hard to ignore. BAIC's initial goal was to deploy 5,000 EVs for the city of Beijing in 2011, but by November 2011 the BEVC had yet to deliver its first. A car had been prototyped, but it had not yet been approved by Chinese regulators. Liao was hoping that the approval would come in the next two to three months and that BEVC could start manufacturing and delivering products in 2012.

By that time, Liao had decided that he had better hedge his own bets. He announced plans to found a new company with a British inventor based not on electric vehicles, but on flywheel energy recovery in automobiles. A flywheel is like a spinning top. When the car slows, a heavy disk captures the energy and returns it to the driveshaft upon acceleration.[40] The technology was interesting, but not new. And Liao's retreat was not a good sign for China's electric car of the future.

Shenzhen's "Edison": The Case of BYD

Things were not looking much better for China's private sector. If an American knows anything about China's EV market—or even its automotive sector—they likely know the name BYD. The company catapulted to prominence in 2009 after Warren Buffett's storied financial empire, Berkshire Hathaway, purchased a 10 percent share in the concern.

BYD's rise was explosive, improbable, and cloaked in mystery. One version of the story goes something like this: BYD's founder, Wang Chuanfu, was the son of poor farmers who died when he was a child. As a result, Wang was raised by an older brother (and perhaps a sister, too). Receiving his bachelor's degree from the Central South Institute of Technology, Wang gained acceptance to the Beijing Non-Ferrous Research Institute, which had a strong program in battery science, and obtained his master's degree there. Like the director of CNOOC's battery company, Lishen, Wang was asked to start a state-owned battery company, in this case to be spun off from its parent research center and established in Shenzhen—China's supercharged southern Special Economic Zone.

But Wang did not stay long. He led the government venture for only about a year before abruptly exiting. Shenzhen is a frenetically capitalistic environment and you might say that Wang got bitten by the entrepreneurial bug. Wang saw an underserved market that could be used as a catapult into the global economy, and he wanted to profit from it.

BYD's early years are filled with contradictions. Today BYD is known as "build your dreams" but some Chinese media reports claim that the company's initials originally stood for "Bring You Dollars."[41] This makes sense, as BYD was actually founded as a sort of "get rich quick" manufacturing scheme that derived its competitive advantage through flaunting Japanese environmental regulations. Tokyo had suddenly banned the manufacture of nickel-cadmium batteries for environmental reasons, but Wang knew that there was residual demand. So he scraped together some money—from a putative "cousin" in Hong Kong—and set up a factory that was all but certain to "Bring You Dollars"—while simultaneously poisoning the environment.[42]

BYD grew rapidly and established a reputation for respectable quality. A major breakthrough came when Motorola gave BYD a contract to compete with Sony and Sanyo as a lithium-ion cell supplier. These batteries were environmentally benign and based on lithium-iron phosphate chemistry—the same chemistry as Tianjin's Lishen and one that runs many of today's laptops and cell phones.[43]

By the mid-2000s, BYD had abandoned its nasty nickel-cadmium cells and embraced the "clean-tech" label with gusto. BYD started to market itself as a company that was highly concentrated on delivering sustainable technologies like solar panels, power storage systems, and electric bikes.

In July 2002, the company's founder took BYD public on the Shenzhen Stock Exchange and ended up with more than $200 million of cash on hand.[44] BYD had already been dabbling in electric bicycles, which were set to flood the streets of China's cities. And cars were also of great interest to Wang. So within six months of the IPO, BYD announced its acquisition of the Tsinchuan Automotive Company Ltd.—a flagging state-owned auto manufacturer.

They worked to improve and refine the company's models, and before long had a rapidly expanding national network of dealers. Though they were not the highest-quality cars, BYD's vehicles were attractive and roomy—characteristics that other companies, including GM, had found were important to Chinese consumers. They were also sold at just the right price point for China's rising middle class. By 2009, BYD's F3 sedan was the number-one-selling car in China.[45]

By 2010, BYD had 180,000 employees who worked, dined, and lived together in massive compounds. The company claimed that 11,000 employees were directly involved in research and development activities, which is more than ten times the number that inhabited Bell Labs at its peak. "I was there when it started," recalled Christina Lampe-Onnerud, the former CEO and founder of an erstwhile BYD competitor named Boston-Power. "I remember these huge [dining] halls filled with chopsticks . . . it was just amazing."[46]

In two large halls off the headquarters' entryway, the company showcased the prodigious number of technologies BYD could build in-house. These ranged from LCD screens, to internal combustion engines, to laptop computers and automobiles. It seemed BYD could build almost anything. In this light it is easy to see why Buffett's partner Charlie Munger fell in love with the company—calling its founder "a combination of Thomas Edison and Jack Welch." Munger eventually led Berkshire Hathaway's BYD investment.[47] This was BYD's biggest coup yet.

But while BYD was omnivorous, it was also very young in terms of management and technology. In 2010, the company's director of technology and strategy was Aaron Miao, a youthful Ph.D. with mussed-up hair and generally seen wearing a blue auto mechanic look-alike shirt. He looked like an assistant or even an intern. The average age of a BYD employee was reputed to be twenty-three years old. Miao himself was thirty, with a freshly minted degree from Virginia Tech. The job at BYD was his first position out of graduate school.[48]

Both Miao and the company took pride in the fact that their efforts proceeded the Chinese rush into EV development. "We founded the electric car research institute in 2005 and had a plug-in hybrid electric on the market by December of 2008," explained Miao.[49] Despite their youth, they were not some Johnny-come-lately. Indeed, by 2009, BYD had also developed a pure electric vehicle in addition to its plug-in hybrid. But then electric vehicles were still a footnote from a business perspective; that year they sold fewer than fifty of their electric hybrids.[50]

But in the West a powerful narrative grew up around BYD in the popular media. The company was hailed as an emerging technology giant.

Automotive industry insiders were not as impressed. Many believed BYD's success was based on working around patents from other countries, disaggregating complex production processes into more menial tasks that could be done by hand, and sometimes illegally arrogating international intellectual property (IP) for domestic consumption. *Car and Driver* magazine called one of BYD's models "essentially knock-offs of a previous-generation Toyota Corolla and a turn-of-the-century Honda Accord."[51] The company was even accused of plagiarizing its logo from BMW.

"BYD has a huge team of people studying other companies' intellectual property," commented an industry analyst at a luncheon. "And BYD never tries to hide that." But Aaron Miao took exception to this assessment. "We don't steal technologies from other companies," he said, adding, "whether other companies developed similar technologies before we do, I'm not sure about that."[52]

In the spring of 2012, the city of Shenzhen took delivery of 1,500 battery electric vehicles, but BYD was having trouble expanding past its own local government-sponsored market.[53] "It's good at the start," asserted Miao, "[if] local, or regional, powers provide you with support and an assured market."[54] But it was also a problem. If Chinese companies didn't need to compete with each other, how would they ever be able to compete with anyone else?

In addition to the national production subsidies for electric cars (60,000 renminbi, or $9,000), Shenzhen's local subsidy was as large again. This meant that the combined subsidy was almost four times as large as China's 2009 per capita income.[55] But even with these wild subsidies there was no real market for BYD's electric vehicles.

Its EVs suffered two fatal flaws: high price and low quality. One well-placed industry expert put it this way: "They see themselves as a technology startup, not a nitty gritty assembly company like Toyota . . . quality is not improving."

Soon there were malfunctions, fires, and a host of other problems with the BYD product line. Local authorities tried to keep these issues away from prying eyes, but eventually this cordon sanitaire broke down. From 2010 to 2012, BYD's stock plummeted almost 90 percent before rebounding slightly.[56] In Berkshire Hathaway's 2008 annual report, BYD was described as an "amazing Chinese company in which we have a 10% interest," but by 2012, some analysts were fingering BYD as Buffett's "rare mistake."[57]

Beyond the steady trickle of reports of BYD's cars catching fire and blowing up, there was an even greater problem. Consumers just didn't want to buy them.[58]

Foreigners

But even as China's EV efforts foundered, it continued to shut out the one group that could potentially save its national ambitions. Foreign companies were, by far, the most likely bet to produce capable, attractive, competitive electric vehicles for the Chinese market. But China's government had worked assiduously to undermine them. They could not receive EV subsidies unless they worked with a Chinese partner that owned full IP rights to at least one of three key systems for electric vehicles—the battery, electric motor, or inverter. And foreign companies didn't want to give away their cutting-edge technology. It's easy to see why: China's EV market was small, growth was anemic, and many Chinese companies—as well as the Chinese government itself—had a history of copying, stealing, and selling IP from foreign partners whenever and wherever they could.

In 2012, the head of America's National Security Agency called China's ongoing theft of U.S. industrial knowledge and intellectual property "the greatest transfer of wealth in history." Annual U.S. losses were estimated by one study to be between $250 billion and $338 billion.[59] In a story describing one particularly egregious incident of IP theft from an American wind power technology company called American Superconductor Corporation, Bloomberg News spoke of China's government-sponsored IP theft in the following terms:

This campaign has been in the works for years and targets a swath of industries: biotechnology, telecommunications, and nanotechnology, as well as clean energy. One U.S. metallurgical company lost technology to China's hackers that cost $1 billion and 20 years to develop, U.S. officials said last year. An Apple Inc. (AAPL) global supply manager pled guilty in 2011 to funneling designs and pricing information to China and other countries; a Ford Motor Co. (F) engineer was sentenced to six years in prison in 2010 for trying to smuggle 4,000 documents, including design specs, to China. Earlier this month, the National Aeronautics and Space Administration told Congress that China-based hackers had gained access to sensitive files stored on computers at the Jet Propulsion Laboratory.[60]

But despite all this, some foreign companies were still interested in the Chinese EV market. GM was selling more cars in China than in the United States—and so was Nissan. Enormous walls were put in their path, but foreigners remained interested in the idea of China's EV market. Even as China's government pressured GM to give Chinese companies the technology for its plug-in Volt, GM cautiously planned to begin exporting small numbers of Chevy Volts to China.

"They have a different market requirement than we do and their different market requirements place them closer to a commercially viable [electric] vehicle than we are in the US," said Keith Cole, the head of government relations for GM International.[61] He explained that GM planned to develop EVs focused on Chinese consumer needs and preferences. "I don't see us jumping into that the way Nissan has, but it's something we want to look at. In China we're looking at the market with open eyes, and there are lots of possibilities."[62]

Once Again, Behind the Times

By early 2012, China's leadership was beginning to understand just how badly their initial foray into the Great Race had gone. Communist leaders started talking about building hybrids instead of EVs. But Chinese hybrids were also a stretch. Putting battery issues aside, producing high-quality hybrids—without simply copying Toyota's technology—was probably more challenging than producing a decent EV.

Wan Gang still hoped for China to produce one million New Energy Vehicles by 2015. But another ministry thought China could build only 500,000 EVs on that timeline. Many industry observers thought even that number was a stretch.

"Chinese companies need time," said Xiao Chengwei, a battery scientist from the 863 Program and one of the planners of China's national EV initiative.[63] And by late 2011, Xiao himself had come to the conclusion that—as politically fraught as the endeavor might seem—China ought to collaborate more with Japan.

Xiao's office sat in a brand-new technology park on the outskirts of Tianjin—one of China's traditional hubs for automotive, and now battery, manufacturing. His building was flanked by construction zones heaped with corrugated metal, fiberglass panels, and partitions—signs of progress in China's booming economy. Countless Chinese "princelings" and government officials had mined such construction projects for personal gain—using *guanxi* (關係), or personal relationships, to get rich. For the prosperous and powerful in China, perhaps no symbol of wealth was more omnipresent than a German or Italian luxury car. But such creature comforts were out of reached for Xiao, as he spent his days toiling away on China's strategic road map for the industrial future. Cars were his life, but his personal ride was a bare-bones domestic model.

Still, Xiao believed China could do better. On a sunny winter day, he answered his phone. "They're here," said a voice on the line. Xiao raced downstairs and into the sunlight, where a Toyota rep deferentially handed him the key to a short-term loaner. It was a glistening, new plug-in hybrid Toyota Prius. Next to the Audis and Porsches favored by Chinese elites, it didn't look like much. But Xiao understood the significance of the moment: Toyota was literally handing him the keys to their cutting-edge EV technology. In a sense, the implication was clear: China could have all the technology it wanted and needed; it simply had to play by internationally accepted rules, and perhaps collaborate a bit more with Japanese partners.

Xiao gently pulled on the handle. As he settled in, the door closed with an exquisitely engineered "thunk." His eyes gleamed wide as his hands traced the instrument panels of the shiny Japanese make for the first time. Xiao floored the accelerator, and the car slid silently to 40 mph on the deserted Tianjin campus. "This is really nice," he said almost wistfully.[64] It was nice. Unfortunately, it was also made in Japan.

18

The Great Race

I N 2012 the American media continued to weave tales about China's looming technology threat. However, close observers of China's economy—including the Chinese themselves—understood that the wheels were coming off its bold EV initiative. One China watcher went so far as to write a piece called "Who Killed China's Electric Car?"[1] The "dream," he said, had "mutated into something of a nightmare ensnared in interest group politics and lack of clear strategies."[2] And even if China's fiefdoms had worked together seamlessly, there is a question as to whether they had the technical know-how to produce a high-quality EV on their own. After all the hype, all the money, and all the political capital spent, it was a failure of epic proportions. As the United States and Japan broke away from the pack in yet another round of the Great Race, China was trailing far behind.

At the same time, it was quite clear that Washington was not dominating the competition, either. In America, the real victor—the force behind America's EV program—was California. The state's dogged regulators and politicians had spent years battling automakers, then the Bush administration—all in order to realize their goal of cleaner air, and eventually zero-emission cars. It had been a long journey, but California was on the cusp of a transformation. They had finally cajoled most major automakers in the world to start developing electric cars. Thanks to Elon Musk, the state also had Tesla—an electric car company of its very own.

But America was not alone. Across the Pacific, Japan was also

streaking into the future. There, a well-lubricated machine for industrial policy and state-corporate collaboration was allowing EVs to
slowly erode oil's monopoly over its personal transportation sector.

So while Washington and China controlled the largest automotive
industries in the world, it was California and Japan that dominated
the technology agenda. California was succeeding despite its diminu-
tive resources, and Japan was doing so in the face of enormous national challenges.

The Money Factor

How was this possible? Money, it turned out, was not the most important factor. China, the United States, and Japan all promised to inject
similar funding into EV development and deployment between 2010
and 2020—that number was probably the lowest in Japan. By comparison, California's expenditures didn't even figure.[3] On the other
hand, China certainly had some of the richest subsidies for EVs, but
that didn't seem to matter. So what then was the secret to success?

A House Divided

In both California and Japan, EVs were overwhelmingly considered a long-term investment in clean air, lower oil imports, and reduced carbon pollution. They might not pay dividends immediately,
but eventually they would make a big difference. However, EVs
turned into a lightning rod for controversy among a certain class of
Washingtonians—mostly those who were more interested in the in-
stant gratification of political controversy and scandal than the long-
term success of America's manufacturing economy.

The politicization of electric vehicles came as a shock to some in the
American auto industry. An enormous number of executives at GM,
Ford, and Chrysler were Republicans—Republicans who had built
good trucks, championed a generation of SUV drivers, and fought

Democratic unions and environmental priorities for decades. When they were attacked by fellow Republicans it was like being turned on by a friend. "Your natural ally is convinced you're the devil," said one high-level GM exec about Republican lawmakers in Congress. "The Republicans decided that our success would be Obama's success, and that was a bad thing."

This strange American tribalism came to a head during the 2012 presidential election as Republicans set their sights on Obama's efforts to promote clean energy. Presidential candidate Newt Gingrich captured the spirit of the times when he hollered to a raucous crowd of supporters that "you cannot put a gun rack in a Chevy Volt!" and received thundering hoots and applause. America's right also cheered GM's distress during a spate of undeserved bad publicity resulting from NHTSA's investigation of postcollision fires in the Volt's battery pack.[4] (In the end, NHTSA found that neither the Volt, nor any other BEV sold in the United States posed a greater threat than gasoline-powered autos.) These attacks reached a crescendo when Mitt Romney took time out during a presidential debate to bash an American champion. Romney railed against Obama, saying that he had put billions "into solar and wind, to Solyndra and Fisker and Tesla and Ener1. . . . You don't just pick the winners and losers," he jibed, "you pick the losers."

Bad Karma

The politicization of the U.S. EV program was strange. What's worse, it made it even more difficult to have a reasonable discussion regarding some very real problems that had cropped up in America's EV industry and clean energy policy. Some of the funding dispensed by Washington over the years had gone to questionable ventures. Even Chelsea Sexton, an avowed champion of electric cars (and the de facto spokesperson for much of the industry), was critical of the federal government's role in funding the Finnish EV startup Fisker Automotive. "Who does [Kleiner Perkins] have naked pics of?" she said she asked herself. "Because there wasn't any other way."

Perhaps no two companies better demonstrated both the perils and promise of the federal government putting its money behind the clean energy economy than Fisker and Tesla. They were both recipients of Advanced Vehicles Technology Manufacturing Program loans, they were both producing $100,000+ sports cars, and they were both newcomers to an entrenched domestic automotive industry. Yet despite these similarities, their fates diverged sharply in 2011.

For Fisker, the year was a steady drumbeat of negative news. Sales were slow and the Karma, Fisker's flagship vehicle, was something of an enigma. With solar panels on its roof, a battery, and electric drive, it was supposed to be the eco-friendly sportster of the future. But its cramped interior barely seated four and traveled only thirty-five miles before running out of batteries and switching to a 20-mpg internal combustion engine. The performance was fine, but not fantastic. It was a hard sell.

Then, in the spring of 2012, Fisker's image problems solidified when their car "bricked" during a test drive by *Consumer Reports*. "It looks awesome. It is low, it is sleek, it is sensuous," crooned the reviewer. But, he added, "it's also broken."

Consumer Reports had purchased the $100,000 vehicle from a dealer and it traveled less than two hundred miles before the car fritzed out. Eventually, this particular Fisker Karma had to be hauled away on a flatbed truck. Later that year DOE froze payments of Fisker's government-backed loans, and in April 2013, Fisker filed for bankruptcy.[5]

Tesla's Compulsive Visionary

Like Fisker, Tesla would have almost certainly gone bust without Washington's backing—or some other unexpected lifeline. But unlike Fisker, Tesla made good on its transformational promises. This was partly due to government financing, but also to the obsessive drive and brilliance of company founder Elon Musk.

Five children and two marriages after starting his quest, Musk had succeeded in building what former U.S. Secretary of Energy Steven Chu proudly called "the most innovative company in America."

For a long time, there was something joyless about Musk's journey. When asked by a young fan how he buoyed his spirits as the going got tough, Musk bluntly responded that he did not. "My drive," he said, "is sort of disconnected from hope, enthusiasm, or anything else. I just . . . I actually don't care about hope or enthusiasm. . . . I just give it everything I've got—irrespective of what the circumstances may be. Yeah," he said, pausing, "you just keep going and get it done."

But Tesla's compulsive visionary had set the company on course for a remarkable rise. It had succeeded in establishing some high-profile partnerships with Toyota and Daimler over the preceding years—both companies had invested in the EV startup—and its own Model S sedan development was going so well that Tesla accelerated its launch from July up to June 2012. The car had neck-snapping acceleration and it had an electric range approaching three hundred miles. It also had the best crash test ratings of any vehicle ever tested by the NHTSA. The interior was minimalist but remarkably functional. To boot, the car seated up to seven passengers—five adults in the main cabin and two children in the rear-facing child jump seats. It was quite a package: acceleration and handling of a supercar, safety of a Volvo, seating of a minivan, wicked curves, and a powertrain that was a blissful playground for performance enthusiasts and technologists alike.

Consumer Reports, which had trashed the Fisker Karma, called the Tesla Model S the best car it had ever driven. Period. The *Wall Street Journal* called it "the most impressive feat of American industrial engineering since . . . Mr. Musk's SpaceX successfully launched and recovered a spacecraft that rendezvoused with the international space station."[6] Although SpaceX had achieved that goal only a few months earlier, it was a sincere compliment.

Indeed, Musk was perhaps the only person in history to found both a rocket and car company and had frequently opined that building Tesla was "much harder." Musk was tightly wound, and more than a bit manic, but it was hard not to admire his single-minded drive to remake the industrial world. "I'm working about a hundred hours a week," he said opening a Tesla dealership in London. "People often ask: 'Are you having fun?' I say I should be, but it wouldn't be true to say that I am. But I'm not asking people to feel sorry for me."[7]

In 2012 all that work started to pay off. Momentum was building and Musk was beginning to loosen up. First, the company piqued investor interest by introducing another aggressively styled all-electric prototype, called the Model X, an SUV that boasted the acceleration of a Porsche 911, the energy efficiency of an EV, and a very cool entry and egress design that Tesla called "falcon-wing doors"—they swung upward like a set of wings when they opened.[8] As more and more Model S sedans flowed off of Tesla's assembly lines, the company powered up its network of free "superchargers" across the United States, Europe, and even China. Later they introduced a battery swapping system as well.

For Tesla's luxury competitors, the company had emerged as an unexpected terror. It was the bestselling car in eight of the twenty-five richest zip codes in America—more than any other vehicle.[9] For Tesla short sellers it was even worse. Indeed, 2013 was the perfect storm.

Each new innovation was launched as a media extravaganza reminiscent of Steve Jobs's famous Apple events—only Tesla's products often debuted with a soundtrack of house music thumping in the background. Style, substance, technology, and sizzle—Tesla had it all.

Many on Wall Street kept waiting for Musk to fumble the ball. But by the second quarter of 2013, Tesla was beginning to beat back market skepticism. In May, Elon Musk's confidence was building, and he warned short sellers—those betting against Tesla stock—of an impending "tsunami of pain."

When Tesla sold 4,900 Model S sedans in the first quarter—about 400 more than expected—the company eked out its first ever profit: $11 million. It wasn't much—only about 12 cents per share—but it beat every analyst's expectation, and this triggered a feeding frenzy for Tesla stock. Those holding Tesla didn't want to sell, but those shorting Tesla—which accounted for about 40 percent of the company's outstanding float—simply had to buy to cover their positions. It was a "short squeeze."

Prices marched higher and higher. From $37 at the beginning of April, past $40, then $50. By mid-May, Tesla shares were flirting with $90, and by June they had blasted past $100. And even as the short squeeze subsided, Tesla's stock continued to soar. Its dramatic rise brought the company new prominence and notoriety in the world of fund managers and day traders. Its shares continued to scream north toward $200. By 2014 Tesla was trading in the $250 range with a market capitalization around $30 billion and it was exporting its flagship Model S to Europe, Japan, and China.

Starting in early 2013, rumors began to circulate that Tesla would take the plunge and start manufacturing lithium-ion batteries in-house. In cooperation with its Japanese partner Panasonic, it planned to build a $5 billion "Gigafactory" that by 2020 would pump out enough battery packs for 500,000 long-range EVs every year. That volume represented more than the entire global production of lithium-ion batteries in 2013 and was projected to reduce battery costs by about 30 percent in time for the launch of Tesla's low-cost third generation vehicle. And as if that wasn't enough, Tesla planned to power the whole factory on renewable energy.

New Mexico, Arizona, and Nevada all jockeyed aggressively for Tesla's big investment. And so did Texas—which was more than a bit ironic considering the state's ongoing love affair with fossil fuels and the fact that it had banned Tesla sales within its borders (supposedly because they transgressed its dealer franchise rules). The decision came on September 3, 2014: Nevada took the prize. For an estimated $1.3 billion in tax incentives, it had purchased the 50 gigawatt facility. Governor Brian Sandoval proclaimed the investment would "change Nevada forever" and estimated that over its twenty year life span, the Gigafactory would bring $100 billion in economic benefits to the state. To put that number in context, Nevada's 2013 GDP was less than $125 billion. The Gigafactory was a potential game changer—not just for Nevada, but for the world.

So Tesla was the example of what Washington could do right. While Fisker, A123, and a number of other battery and EV investments crashed, Washington had helped Silicon Valley give birth to a new American car company—and one of the greatest cars the world had ever known.

California's Dream Comes True

Part of CARB's dream had been that someday electric car makers would build factories and R&D centers in the state. But California's major aspiration had been for clean vehicles to fill its roads and highways. That was exactly what was happening and Sacramento's reach was about to lengthen significantly.

In late 2013, on a crisp fall morning in Sacramento, there was not a cloud, nor puff of smog in sight. A brilliant sunrise peeked out from behind the state's darkened, deserted capitol building. Just a few blocks away, the California Environmental Protection Agency was a hive of activity. TV crews frenetically laid cables, and set their camera angles. Executives from Honda, Hyundai, Ford, BMW, and GM all clustered around—and so did leaders from the American Lung Association and Consumer Federation. CARB chairman Mary Nichols was about to speak.

So much had come full circle since Nichols had first joined CARB in 1974. Jerry Brown was, once again, California's governor. Nichols was running the Air Resource Board. America and the world had just come through a nasty energy crisis and globally the problems of air pollution and greenhouse gas emissions seemed more urgent than ever.

But a lot of progress had also been made. Some of that progress could be seen through a bank of windows behind her: nestled between the building's granite walls and local grasses, a 2014 Chevy Volt and 2014 Nissan LEAF bestrode the CalEPA's plaza. Across the street, CARB's parking garage was packed with EV charging stations, and dozens—if not hundreds—of EVs were crammed inside. More than a dozen EV models were on the market, with more on the way. In 1974, clean air had been a dream for California, and a decade later EVs were a wild ambition. But in 2013 both were very real.

Mary Nichols's big announcement was that California and eight other states were setting a floor for EV deployment over the next decade: 3.3 million vehicles by 2025.

The announcement was a formalization of something carmakers had expected, feared, and fought against for decades. California was driving into the future, and it was not going alone. Now others were officially along for the ride. And that meant that the global automakers were coming, too. "This agreement is a continuation of an extraordinary legacy," Nichols told her audience from a modestly apportioned room on the CalEPA's ground floor.

California provided consumer rebates and other incentives to coax people into purchasing EVs. Some of these were remarkably effective and remarkably cheap. For instance, the state allowed EVs to use high-occupancy vehicle lanes regardless of how many people were inside. This made a huge difference in EV sales. When the Chevy Volt was first released it hadn't qualified for this special privilege—its engine wasn't clean enough for California's strict standards. So while LEAF sales took off, the Volt's sales were relatively tepid. Californians purchased about three times as many LEAFs as Chevy Volts. GM worked overtime to address the problem and when it introduced a version of the Volt with an internal combustion engine that did qualify for high-occupancy lanes, sales surged.

In 2012, little California deployed more electric vehicles than mighty China. In 2013, Tesla's Fremont factory outpaced China's entire EV production.[10]

California wanted to keep its hard-won air quality, but it also wanted to address the issue of climate change. And so it instituted a number of regulations to reduce greenhouse gas emissions. But California's cuts in greenhouse gas emissions would be for naught if other countries did not learn from the state's experiences and mistakes.

And there was a lot to learn. The state's regulators had discovered just how powerful and imperfect markets could be. Sometimes they didn't work on their own and needed to be fixed. Sometimes regulation was required to promote public goods that seemed utterly self-evident.

Dan Sperling, the head of the Institute for Transportation Studies at the University of California, Davis and member of CARB opined on this seemingly inexplicable fact: "Why did we need new regulations to tell people to save money on fuel economy?" he said. The answer? Markets frequently fail and consumers don't always think rationally.[11]

On the other hand, California's regulators realized that markets could be an extraordinarily effective tool to achieve public goods. They had created their own markets for ZEV credits—designed to incentivize EV deployment and reduce emissions. For every sale of an EV, an automaker was awarded a certain number of ZEV credits. And by requiring automakers to obtain EV credits in proportion to their California sales, CARB provided an incentive for innovation that would not have otherwise existed. The critical thing that eased compliance was that this system was a market. Producers could buy, sell, and trade credits between themselves at will. It worked beautifully. The trading system richly rewarded market leaders like Nissan and Tesla—turning zero-emissions vehicle sales into credits that were good as gold. They could be bartered with other manufacturers for cold, hard cash and that windfall helped make Tesla profitable.

All this is why one begrudgingly respectful former auto executive called California the "center of the world" for automotive regulation.[12]

Later, away from the crowds of that morning's announcement, Nichols reflected on California's place in the global economy. With a twinkle in her eye, she paraphrased something her old friend Jerry Brown had just told a high-level delegation from India. "He said, 'People around the world look to California and they see what we did— what it looked like in the forties—and they see what it is today. And they say to themselves, if we do what they did, we can be just like California: beautiful, rich and diverse.'" She paused for a moment, reflecting on both the truth and the irony of that statement. "Isn't that fabulous!" she blurted—breaking into mirthful giggles.

A King Without a Kingdom

In Japan, however, the situation was significantly more complex. Just as Anegawa's vision of an electric car was gaining force, his hope for a "nuclearized" automobile was fading. During the spring of 2012, every single one of Japan's nuclear plants sat idle—making the country "nuclear-free" for the first time in forty years. It was a major blow. Anegawa had built Japan's EV program with the intent of promoting nuclear power—even as the entire automotive world told him that EVs were a hopeless quest. But what now?

EVs were doing fine, and so was Anegawa. Plug-in vehicles were on a steady upward growth trend and "Crazy Anegawa" was world-renowned for kick-starting a global technology revolution. But TEPCO was in serious trouble. Anegawa's friends and colleagues in TEPCO's nuclear section—the same ones who had chided Anegawa's reckless decision to abandon his nuclear engineering career—were reviled in the wake of the Fukushima meltdown.

TEPCO had made grievous sins of commission and omission, before, during, and after the Fukushima nuclear crisis. And now TEPCO was responsible for trying to restart one of the world's largest fleets of nuclear reactors—a fleet worth many tens of billions of dollars. But Japan's nuclear allergy was worse than ever. The country's Nuclear Industrial Safety Agency had been dismantled because no one trusted them. It was being replaced with a Nuclear Regulatory Agency—which was still a work in progress.

Still Anegawa believed that Japan *needed* nuclear energy. The cost of fueling natural gas, coal-, and oil-fired generation to replace Japan's mothballed nuclear fleet was bleeding the country's foreign exchange, and putting Japan's manufacturers at a structural disadvantage against foreign competitors. Restarting Japan's bedeviled nuclear fleet would be a huge boon to the country's economy, but so long as twenty-four-hour antinuclear vigils haunted METI's main office in Kasumigaseki and TEPCO's headquarters in Shimbashi, it seemed an impossible dream.

To do so, TEPCO would need someone with diplomatic finesse, managerial competence, technical know-how, and an entrepreneurial moxie that was, to say the least, uncommon. They would have to be a true believer in the goodness of Japan's nuclear genie, but could not be tainted by the stench of TEPCO or METI's recent failures. In so many ways, it was bound to be a thankless job. For whoever was chosen would be a king without a kingdom—and fighting enormous odds. Nonetheless, the position would be a fulcrum of vast power and influence—not just for TEPCO, but for Japan and the global economy.

It came as something of a shock when TEPCO's board tapped Taka-fumi Anegawa for this herculean task. Anegawa was made the managing executive officer of TEPCO and chief of the secretariat for the Nuclear Reform Special Task Force—charged with remaking TEPCO's nuclear culture. "He was surprised," Anegawa said with a laugh, pointing at his former deputy Aoki—who was now in charge of TEPCO's much-streamlined EV program. "He said, 'Why do they want the EV guy to lead TEPCO's nuclear program?'" Anegawa smiled and Aoki roared.

Anegawa's candidacy was likely boosted by the success of Japan's EV effort. By 2011 Japanese companies were producing the vast majority of the world's EVs. Japanese companies also provided the batteries, motors, corporate backing, and technological foundation for many—if not most—of the EVs produced and sold by foreign companies elsewhere. In terms of developing and commercializing new EV technologies, Japan was clearly a pacesetter.

But coming off the heels of such a success, why would Anegawa accept the thankless task of promoting TEPCO's nuclear program? "Fukushima Daiichi is ruined. We have to settle it down and clean it up," he said. "That is a very tough job. Restarting the remaining nuclear power plants, that is another tough job," he mused. "But that is my characteristic. I am a very strange guy. If something seems very difficult, I want to do it." None of this seemed to bother Anegawa. "You know," he said, "JFK said we should go to the moon because it is difficult, not because it's easy."

Aoki chimed in: "I remember one time when we rented a car in the United States. When I'm not sure about directions, I will slow down and ask. But [Anegawa], he just says, 'Go!' . . .When he feels curious about it, he just goes. That's Anegawa's style."

And so Japan's perennial Don Quixote, Takafumi Anegawa, set out to write a new chapter in his lifelong love affair with nuclear energy.*

China's "Great Leap" Lands Flat

But what about Wan Gang's bold vision? Between its dozens of EV programs across the country, China only produced six thousand plug-in electric vehicles in 2012—and hardly more than that in 2013. China had neither the technology nor the skills to build a world-class electric car on its own, and Beijing's policies made things worse. It forced China's automakers to go without the benefit of international technology—or the challenge of international competition. It became increasingly clear that the reasons for building electric cars in China were mostly political. In the words of one executive who preferred to remain anonymous, "companies do not want to build these cars, and consumers do not want to buy them."

Unlike California, which allowed automakers to buy EV credits, pay fines, or otherwise opt out of the state's EV program, the political pressures inherent in China's EV development propelled every major Chinese automaker to build its own EV. It made little sense. The confluence of national strategy and local interests generated a spiral of increasingly perverse results. Ultimately, the market for these new EVs was the government (not private consumers) and sales were ensured by each

---

*Anegawa had laid a sturdy foundation and the support for Japan's EV program now extended to the very top of Japan's ruling hierarchy. Eighty years earlier, Nobusuke Kishi—who later served as Japan's postwar prime minister—had put in place laws to eject Ford and GM from Japan's young automotive market and ensure the survival of Toyota and Nissan. In 2012, Kishi's grandson Shinzo Abe was elected prime minister, and he was absolutely intent on maintaining Japan's industrial leadership. Abe wanted to lead a resurgence in Japan's transportation and advanced manufacturing sector—not just domestically, but worldwide. Traveling to America, he offered to provide the technology and financing for a new maglev bullet train between Washington, D.C., and Baltimore, and back home Abe promised to invest more than a billion dollars in EV infrastructure over the coming years.

manufacturer's local "policy market"—in other words, government procurement. This eliminated competition and chipped away at quality.

However, along the way China did succeed in vacuuming up valuable technology from a number of distressed American brands—just as it had done with Jeep and Saab. For ten years, Volvo had been owned by Ford. Its reputation for safety and quality had made it the car of the sensible urban intelligentsia. But in 2010, Ford sold Volvo to Geely—a Chinese auto company. The stimulus-funded companies A123 and Fisker also went to Chinese buyers. A Chinese bidder even made a run at acquiring Arnold's once-beloved Hummer—which after 2007 had lost its luster in the American market.

By the summer of 2013, Wan Gang had started discussing the phaseout of China's EV subsidies, and a refocusing on R&D.

"We Can't Compete with Tesla"

It would be a mistake to think that this was the end of electric vehicles in China. In fact, it was only the beginning. One perspective on this aborted revolution came from Huang Yonghe, the chief engineer at the massive China Automotive Technology Research Center. Huang was a young man before he had the chance to ride in a car, but by 2014 he was part of an elite priesthood of Chinese automotive technology. His massive research facility in Tianjin was responsible for everything from crash testing to certifying advanced battery packs.

"Look," said Huang through heavy blue rings of cigarette smoke in his Tianjin office. "We may have the biggest automotive market in the world, but we don't have the best technology. We can't compete with Tesla."

But that did not mean China was out of the race. "We can still have the largest EV sector if we start simple, and just keep moving in the right direction." In Huang's view, it was time for China to refocus and to pursue a strategy more in line with its social needs and technological capacity. It was a plan that looked remarkably similar to the vision of Tsinghua professor Ouyang Mingao who had run China's 2008 Olympic EV showcase.

Electrifying China's transportation system would be critical to overcoming its long-term energy and environmental challenges. But Huang and Ouyang had both grown weary of promises to "leapfrog" the West. In some senses, this attitude mirrored China's embrace of capitalism three decades earlier. Unwilling to officially distance itself from communist ideology, China's leadership had called the new system "socialism with Chinese characteristics." Perhaps EVs could be pursued with the same kind of pragmatism. Huang and Ouyang each believed that China had the technological capabilities and social incentives to build a very different kind of transportation system—call it, electrification with Chinese characteristics.

Ouyang referred to his concept as the "point-line system." Major Chinese cities represented the points, and they were connected by "lines" of high-speed rail networks—electric rail networks. In a decade, China had built 7,500 miles of high-speed rail—the largest network in the world, and more than half of the world's total. Within Chinese cities (the "points"), commuters could travel by electric bicycle, electric bus, low-speed electric vehicle, or even hybrid and plug-in electric cars. In the context of this network, low-speed, low-tech electric vehicles could service the demand for transportation from local commuters.

This was not the vision Wan Gang had propounded to China's leaders more than a decade earlier; it was not a short-term prescription for dominating the international market for EVs; and it was not the futuristic fantasyland of the 2010 GM-SAIC pavilion. But it was a vision that just might work.

"Chinese don't need a car that travels a thousand miles," explained Ouyang. Neither did they need a Tesla. China needed an electric transportation system that worked for a billion people.

And in some parts of China, something like Ouyang's vision was already starting to happen. A few hours outside Beijing, local companies had overinvested in battery manufacturing and they needed to find an outlet for that industrial potential. And so they started to build small, snub-nosed EVs for rural residents and farmers in the areas surrounding the city. The countryside adjacent to the provincial city of Jinan was already doing a brisk business in cheap, low-speed electric cars.

They didn't go fast, and they didn't go far, but they could be fueled by the grid—which was more efficient and convenient than installing gas stations across rural China. And electricity off the grid was much cheaper than petroleum. In the city of Hangzhou, low-tech EVs were also on the move. A company named Kandi was deploying a vending machine–style electric car–share system. Its cars could barely top 50 mph. But in an urban setting, this was just fine and its deployment numbers were surging.

Huang also figured out that China had something to learn from California. In the spring of 2014 he invited Dan Sperling of the California Air Resource Board to a special conference in Tianjin at the China Automotive Technology Research Center. The conference was called the "Seminar on California Zero-Emission Vehicle (ZEV) Plan and New Energy Vehicle Promotion in Chinese Cities."

In fact, in 2014 there were many signs that China had not let go of its electric dream. A bevvy of new EV models—many built by Sino-foreign joint ventures—were set to launch in China over the coming years. In October 2014 Volkswagen's CE Jochem Heizmann announced that his company would soon offer more than twenty EV models in China. And China's air pollution and foreign oil dependency were still intensifying. Rather than leapfrog, perhaps China's destiny was to be a fast follower.

And the Winner Is . . .

In some senses, China, Japan, and the United States were all contenders to win this first stage of the final season of the Great Race. Clearly the personalities, political systems, and environmental considerations that propelled each of these teams forward were different. In Japan, the enterprising Anegawa convinced the techno-political establishment that EVs were bound to be a critical component of the global auto industry's future. By doing so he built a coalition of pioneers that was much stronger than TEPCO alone. America's preeminent laboratory of democracy, the state of California, rose above the dysfunction of Washington and kept the United States squarely in contention. The

Obama administration gave the industry a boost at a critical juncture, but it was California's Darwinian, mandate-driven EV market that ensured there were rich rewards for those who adapted to its EV policies.

But what of China? In so many ways, it had the resources and institutional capacity to build something new—a commuter system centered around EVs. But at the end of the day, the goals, strategy, and incentives underlying China's policy market were ill-conceived. The bombast of the Olympics in 2008 or the World Expo in 2010 did not bear any lasting advantage; the single-minded focus on indigenous innovation, protectionism, heavy-handed efforts to wrest technology from unwilling foreign companies, and its focus on political, rather than economic, benefits were all wrong.

Less focus on propaganda, greater openness to foreign competition, greater protection for foreign intellectual property, and greater willingness to learn from policy experiments already under way in other parts of the world—such as California—might well have yielded different results.

Indeed, the ingredients to success are relatively clear: strong policies that encourage competition and aggressively reward innovators; securing genuine buy-in from large, technologically sophisticated coalitions; having the gumption to lead and humility to course-correct; and maintaining that delicate balance between strategic clarity and tactical flexibility.

If China's leadership can absorb these lessons and takes advantage of its early failures to engage in self-reflection and ask hard questions, China's failure might yet prove a blessing. But there are conflicting signals from the country's new rulers as to whether that is likely, or even conceivable. On the one hand, in the winter of 2013–14 China confronted a crisis of air pollution that was too damaging and painful to ignore. Researchers estimated that China's people were losing about five years off their lives to air pollution.[13] Although megacities throttled back car sales, many of the problems were already baked into the fiber of the Chinese economy. New policies were implemented to promote EV sales and these policies started to address some of the structural problems with the country's prior EV effort. But steps were tentative.

Indeed, they seemed to reflect China's preference for slow, evolutionary reform—or as Deng Xiaoping called it, "crossing the river by touching the stones." Indeed, as a society, China's ability to confront its recent history, introspect, innovate, and reform is still an open question.

And political leadership is essential to these kinds of sweeping structural, social, and technological transformations. Without leadership from Washington, rural America would have never been electrified, nuclear power would still be a pipe dream, the Internet and semiconductor might not exist, and the roads we drive on would likely end at a figurative city wall—with no highways or rail to unite America's vast interior.

Leadership matters. And in the last twenty years, Japan and California have been much more effective than Washington in their efforts to steer the future of the global automotive industry. They have used smart strategic policies to punch above their weight in the global economy and shape the future of personal transportation.

In his seventeenth-century thesis, *Leviathan*, Thomas Hobbes wrote that the "strength" of the leviathan, or state, derives from its "wealth and riches." In the future, that strength will be more inextricably intertwined with knowledge, innovation, clean energy, and technology than ever before.

To thrive in a field of twenty-first-century leviathans, America will have to formulate a more coherent national mission; we will have to renew and reengineer the building blocks of our economy and politics; we will have to evolve into a new industrial species; but we will also have to trade, cooperate, and work with others.

The world is on the cusp of a physical revolution that could make our roads safe, clean, fast, and efficient—and could free our society from the shackles of oil. We simply need to reach out and grasp it. These changes are part of a broader transformation and decarbonization of the global economy in the twenty-first century that is in fact quite urgent. In this sense, victory in the Great Race, and in the $70 trillion global economy, is not a zero-sum game—at least not necessarily. At the end of the day, this sprint to build the car of the future is a race we all run together. That "we" is not only Americans, Japanese, and Chinese, but all of humanity and life on earth itself. And the sooner we cross the finish line, the better.

19

Afterword

The Last Lap

C ARS ARE SO integral to our lives that it is easy to overlook their trans-formative potential for human society. The changes we will see in coming decades are anything but cosmetic. They will do more than simply improve our fuel economy, emissions, or safety. They will alter our lives in much more fundamental ways.

Indeed, the lines between automotive engineering and automotive fantasy are beginning to blur. Breakthroughs in sensor technology, computer processing power, batteries, chemistry, and elsewhere have laid the groundwork for a future of cars that are smaller, faster, safer, cleaner, and dramatically more efficient; a future not only of electric vehicles, but one that is strikingly reminiscent of the GM-SAIC vision of 2030 at the Shanghai Expo in 2010 (see chapter 1). Clean, smart cities will be navigated by autonomous electric vehicles that zip to and fro while occupants spend their time as they please. It is a future where the blind will drive, mobile offices will become a part of our daily lives, and the concept of a commute will change fundamentally.

There are a number of key technological and social signposts that provide clues to how this system is likely to evolve. Most important among these are changes in fuel economy regulations, electrification, new car ownership models, and the rise of autonomous vehicles. For cities, companies, and countries that embrace these tectonic shifts there is enormous upside potential—tantalizing potential.

Go Farther

The first policy signpost toward the future is important economically and technologically, but somewhat mundane: increased fuel efficiency. The U.S. Environmental Protection Agency has mandated that cars achieve an average of 54.5 mpg by 2025. There are a number of paths to achieving this goal, but they will all stretch the limits of conventional engineering. To some extent, all automakers will migrate toward new, lightweight construction based on aluminum, carbon fiber, or other materials. Honda believes it can do the rest through improvements to the internal combustion engine alone, whereas Toyota, and much of the rest of the industry, are firmly committed to hybrid or EV technology. A shakier prospect—though one that Japanese industrial planners, many auto manufacturers, and the state of California are aggressively pursuing—is fuel cells.

But even if fuel cell costs fall precipitously—as it appears they may be poised to do—infrastructure remains a very significant obstacle. Hydrogen is not a readily available fuel and building out the infrastructure for hydrogen vehicles would be enormously expensive. Hydrogen would have to be produced in massive quantities, and it would have to be delivered and then dispensed at custom-built hydrogen refueling stations. In the near term, the reductions in greenhouse gas emissions are modest and the fuel is bound to be expensive. And what is the ultimate consumer benefit? EVs promise cheap fuel delivered directly to the consumer's home. Hydrogen is less disruptive.

The hydrogen model is one in which oil companies have a future both refining hydrogen and running refueling stations. Car companies like the fact that fuel cells provide long range—just like traditional internal combustion engines. They also like the fact that they can manufacture fuel cells in-house—again like traditional internal combustion engines. "For automakers fuel cells are more of a technology fix," said one CARB board member. "They don't have to start messing with other consumer preferences, so it's easier for them to imagine fitting it into a market—it fits more closely to the way that vehicles are used now. Almost all of them have their own proprietary fuel cell technology. Whereas buying a battery is 10K out the door."[1]

In 2014, one surprising voice of dissent against hydrogen was Fiat and Chrysler's CEO, Sergio Marchionne. In 2014 he lambasted fuel cells. "Somebody needs to prove to me that if you are going to use fossil fuels to produce hydrogen then you are going to end up with a carbon footprint that's more beneficial than combustion," he said. "Prove that to me and then I'll listen to you."

Many thoughtful advocates see hydrogen as a critical component of the transportation future—especially for heavier vehicles, or long-distance travel. But the road to a hydrogen future is long indeed—and paved with massive government subsidies. For with hydrogen there are potential long-term benefits, but few near-term upsides.

Beyond Petroleum?

In comparison, things look auspicious for EVs. In 2010, when the first mass-consumer EVs were sold commercially in the United States, America's transportation system was fundamentally linked to oil. Now drivers have a choice regarding how, when, where, and with what to fuel their cars. Companies that not long ago scoffed at plug-in vehicles (and even hybrids) are putting billions of dollars into developing the future of electrification. For instance, BMW is building a new generation of cars based on batteries and carbon fiber bodies. One of these, the i3, has already won considerable praise from critics. In April of 2014, BMW announced that it was increasing its production of the i3 by 40 percent because of unexpectedly strong European demand. Its sportier cousin, the i8, is an attempt to fill the niche that the Fisker Karma failed to exploit—a sensuous Tesla-like range-extended electric sports car. Soon both the i3 and the i8 will be vying for market share in a fairly crowded field of electric and range-extended electric cars.

Although the capital costs of electric vehicles will continue to be higher than for comparable gasoline-powered cars for some time to come—perhaps decades—prices are already low enough that based on a total cost-of-ownership calculation, EVs are beginning to look attractive for some consumers.[2] Today, the fuel to drive an EV a given distance costs about a third the price of the gasoline that would be required to take you the same distance. What's more, electricity prices are relatively stable. So while combustion engines will continue to rely on volatile world oil markets, EV owners can fill up at home on predictably priced (and low-cost) "eGallons."

Secure Energy

Ever since the transition from horses to Model T's, Americans have had to rely on a delicate supply chain of oil wells, tankers, pipelines, and refineries for fuel. In recent years, disasters such as Hurricane Katrina or Japan's tsunami have exposed the fragility of this finely balanced bucket line.

Today, solar power provides the prospect of personal "energy independence" from oil—or anything else. Solar panels cost about 1 percent what they did thirty years ago, and they are still dropping in price. Tesla's founder, Elon Musk, sits on the board of a company called SolarCity, which will finance the installation of solar panels for free and then pay them off by selling the electricity to homeowners for rates that are significantly lower than what they would pay the local utility. For about $4,000, Nissan offers a system that allows a home to be powered by an EV for up to two days in case of power outage or other emergency. And in Japan, about 10 percent of Nissan LEAF drivers are already opting for this "Vehicle to Home" adaptor.[3]

Even without solar panels, electric power tends to be restored much sooner than liquid fuel supplies—in part because gasoline cannot be transported or dispensed without the electricity needed to operate the network of pipelines, pumps, and control rooms used in liquid fuel distribution. In this sense, EVs have the potential to increase the speed of recovery from a man-made or natural disaster and thus the resilience of our energy and transportation system.

A Force Multiplier for Renewables

Perhaps an even bigger impact stems from the possibility of integrating EVs into a much broader renewable energy system. In the future, EV batteries will likely be used as storage and management assets for large-scale renewables in at least two ways.

First, EVs could be useful for something called frequency balancing. The electrical grid is like a finely tuned guitar: any mismatch between supply and demand has the potential to impair its functionality, or even break its components. Thousands of tiny adjustments a minute help keep this guitar strumming in tune—at a frequency very close to 60 hertz. What that means is that the massive generators producing electricity for the grid rotate exactly sixty times a minute. If the draw on the grid becomes too strong, it will create resistance that slows down these generators—which could theoretically have catastrophic consequences.

"Frequency balancing" employs power plants that are not baseload generators to periodically add electricity to the grid and thus ensure that small changes in electricity draw do not perturb this mechanism. EVs connected to the grid could employ their batteries to accomplish this same task, adding or subtracting power depending on the needs of the system—potentially eliminating the power plants that serve this function today.

However, the much bigger opportunity is to use batteries for storing renewable energy. Most renewable power supply is intermittent. This simply means that it does not produce power all the time—and sometimes produces power unpredictably. Wind power is only available when the wind blows and solar panels only produce electricity when the sun shines. Electric utilities in places like Colorado and California with high proportions of renewable energy are becoming increasingly sophisticated in their ability to predict and manage the power output from these intermittent energy sources, but the one thing that would really be a game changer for renewable energy would be a cheap and abundant source of energy storage—in other words, a massive bank of low-cost batteries.

Electric vehicles connected to the grid may someday provide this. When the wind is blasting at full tilt, or the sun is blazing, EV batteries could soak up excess energy from the grid. And when there is a shortfall, an EV with an 18- or 24-kilowatt-hour battery (like the Volt or the LEAF) or a larger battery (like Tesla's 80-kilowatt-hour unit) could feed a few kilowatt-hours back into the system. A less ambitious approach is for electrical utilities to use EVs as a "demand response" mechanism—allowing them to charge EVs when demand is low, and dial back EV charging when demand is high. This could help deal with the cyclical nature of daily electricity demand as well as spikes in renewable generation.

For practical purposes, large amounts of EV battery storage connected to renewable energy resources could transform intermittent renewables into so-called baseload capacity—that is, generation that can dispatch electricity consistently, all the time, throughout the day.

No Strings

Other technological breakthroughs have the potential to make this system relatively seamless. For example, wireless charging systems—currently under development by numerous companies, including Qualcomm—could allow EVs to be charged without plugging in, through inductive charging. That is something that would be simply impossible for a gasoline, diesel, natural gas, or hydrogen-fueled vehicle. These systems could even be integrated directly into roadways. Cars stopped at stoplights or driving along special wireless charging lanes could freely charge up their batteries, or give energy back to the grid, without even stopping. This would both solve intermittency problems associated with renewable energy and create a system in which EVs had essentially unlimited range. At Korea's Advanced Institute of Science and Technology, such a system is already being piloted in public buses.[4]

A Better Mousetrap

Of course, a less infrastructure-intensive solution to short EV ranges is easier to implement. And that is why the number-one goal in EV research and development is the pursuit of a cheaper and more power-dense battery. Since the time of the Sunraycer, EVs have graduated from lead-acid batteries, to nickel metal hydride batteries, to lithium-ion batteries. Today much of the focus within the field of battery research is on tweaking and improving various lithium-ion-based chemistries. But today's advanced batteries only have a small fraction of the energy potential of gasoline—perhaps 1–2 percent.

For the future, two of the most promising chemistries are lithium silicon and metal air. Companies like Amprius are working on improving the durability of lithium silicon batteries—which have a dramatically higher energy potential than lithium-ion chemistries.[5] But metal air batteries are seen as the holy grail of energy storage. Extraordinarily light and amazingly power dense, metal air batteries actually have the theoretical potential to compete with the energy density of gasoline and diesel, though they are currently far from commercial viability.[6]

A Bright, Bumpy Road

The global EV market will progress in leaps and bounds over the coming decades, but there will also be growing pains and setbacks. There will be bankruptcies, and battery fires. And, as is usually the case with new technologies and business models, negative headlines will often be far out of proportion to the actual significance of the underlying news. We have already seen this in NHTSA investigations of the GM Volt and Tesla Model S—and also some of the negative political rhetoric directed at the sector from the American right wing.

And in addition to technological issues, there are also significant regulatory issues to address. One outstanding problem is the charging standard underlying the fast-charging infrastructure for EVs. At a very basic level, this issue has to do with the shape of the plug used to connect to an EV fast charger. (Of course, that is just one superficial manifestation of other technical differences underlying the different fast-charging standards.) Fast charging can add 50 or 60 miles of range to an EV battery in 15 to 20 minutes, and in many ways it is a more economical way to increase the range of current EVs than simply build cars with bigger batteries. But there is a simmering conflict in the international auto industry regarding what kind of fast chargers to use as the global standard.

The earliest (and as of 2015 the most widely deployed) fast-charging standard was TEPCO's CHAdeMO system—developed by Anegawa's team and an international consortium of electronics and auto manufacturers. However, early on many U.S. and European auto companies decided not to support TEPCO's CHAdeMO standard and instead opted to develop their own. Together they designed and lobbied for the Society of Automotive Engineers J1772 combo-plug standard. Technically, there was nothing wrong with the new device, but the Japanese were far more nimble and aggressive in their efforts to deploy CHAdeMO infrastructure. While BMW, GM, and Daimler worked their political connections in Washington to build a coalition behind the J1772 standard, Nissan and TEPCO deployed thousands of fast chargers in Japan and around the world to complement their expanding fleet of EVs. Whether Nissan's aggressive infrastructure deployment efforts will be enough to tip the market in favor of CHAdeMO is yet to be seen. CHAdeMO may coexist with the J1772 plug, or it might eventually be squeezed out of U.S. and European markets. But considering the scale of investment already made in CHAdeMO chargers, that outcome seems unlikely.

China is also developing its own, and there is one other standard that may prove to be quite important for the EV ecosystem: the Tesla Supercharger. Tesla is building a global network of "superchargers" powered by solar panels, much to the annoyance of many EV advocates in Sacramento—who would rather see Tesla adopt one of the other standards. But for Tesla, it is a strategy that makes eminent sense. They don't need to wait for anyone else, and by adding a few hundred dollars to the cost of each $100,000 car, the company can easily offset the capital cost of building out a relatively ubiquitous charging infrastructure. With this, Tesla can provide its drivers with free fast-charging and essentially unlimited driving range for the life of the vehicle. To demonstrate the end of range limitations for Tesla's Model S, Elon Musk has promised to take his sons on a coast-to-coast road trip across the United States.

To Each According to His Needs?

But electrification isn't the only trend that is going to change the way we think about cars. Today there are shifting ideas in the United States about the nature or even the desirability of car ownership. Over the coming decades we are likely to see a dramatic increase in the utilization of so-called car sharing arrangements. New business models like Zipcar or Car2Go are allowing consumers most of the perks of automotive ownership with dramatically reduced overhead, risk, and hassle. Both of the aforementioned services strategically park their vehicles in high-density residential neighborhoods and operate off automated radio frequency identification based (RFID) rental and entry systems.

In the case of Zipcar, members can use their computer or smartphone to reserve a car for an hour or a day according to their needs. When a customer is done, he or she simply returns the car to its designated spot for the next user.

Daimler's Car2Go is a slightly more radical concept. It uses the company's pint-size Smart cars plus a GPS tracking system to execute a minute-by-minute, point-to-point rental system. Using a smartphone application users can see a map of hundreds of vehicles available for use in their city and can locate the vehicle that is closest to their current position. They enter the car using an individualized RFID-embedded swipe card. When they arrive at their desired location, they simply end the reservation—making the car available for another user. Car2Go is widely deployed in many major cities across Europe and the United States.

Of course, these sharing models are not without downsides. Customers might have to reserve a vehicle hours or days in advance—or walk half a mile to get to where the car they want to drive is parked. And sometimes cars are not available when users want them. But for many urbanites, these systems are a reasonable alternative to car ownership.

Car sharing systems have the potential to solve a host of car-related problems. For instance, today most cars spend about 95 percent of their time parked—in other words they are used for only about 5 percent of the day, and the rest of the time are simply taking up valuable real estate. Maintenance is extraordinarily inefficient for single-owner cars. Although most car owners do not want to spend their days thinking about windshield wiper fluid and oil changes, they inevitably do. By moving toward models like car sharing, where vehicles are utilized by more than one person and a professional fleet manager oversees upkeep and maintenance, this busywork is dramatically reduced and made much more efficient.

With car sharing it is also easier to justify the cost of higher-quality vehicles. This includes systems that could make cars safer, more comfortable, more efficient and give them better performance. For instance, today cars are designed to last a couple of hundred thousand miles. The business model underlying this planned obsolescence means that there's no good reason to invest in materials that would increase that life span. At a recent press conference the head of Nissan R&D explained that the company would not use carbon fiber because it was "too durable."[7] And in the context of individual vehicle ownership, it is hard to justify the cost or durability of carbon fiber. But with car sharing, capital costs can be spread out over a much larger base of users, and savings on things like increased fuel economy can translate directly into corporate profits. In that context, it is much easier to imagine companies and people willing to embrace higher capital costs in exchange for lower operating costs in the form of energy savings and extended life span.

These new models of vehicle ownership may accelerate the day when our cars are no longer made of steel, but of advanced composites. It is even conceivable that car services like Zipcar and Car2Go—which provide a service rather than a product—could become leading profit centers for auto manufacturers.

Why Drive, When You Can Surf?

Another trend that promises to change the character of the car of the future is an overall decline in driver's license registrations among Americans. In 1983 almost 90 percent of American nineteen-year-olds held a driver's license. In 2010, Americans were richer and owned more cars than in 1983, but the proportion of nineteen-year-olds with driver's licenses was less than 70 percent. With improved access to mass transit, the Internet, and other forms of communication, fewer young Americans are making the decision to get licensed.[8]

Overall, people are driving less. More than half of New York City households (56 percent) don't have a car. This may seem unsurprising in the cramped quarters of Manhattan, but plenty of other cities are also trending the same way. In Washington, D.C., Boston, Philadelphia, San Francisco, and Baltimore more than 30 percent of households are car-free.[9]

The New Race: The Pizza Man Cometh

But perhaps nothing harbors more potential to effect a fundamental paradigm shift in transportation than autonomous vehicles. The concept of a car that drives itself begins to blur the lines between cars and robots in potentially profound ways. And while it sounds like something out of a science fiction movie, that reality is already here today. If the modern era of electric cars started with the Sunraycer's epic

race across the Australian Outback (see chapter 5), one might argue
that the modern era of autonomous vehicles started with a much more
humble pizza delivery in San Francisco.

In 2008, the Discovery Channel show *Prototype This!* decided to
explore different ways of delivering a pizza to their research hangar
on Treasure Island in San Francisco Bay. It was an admittedly imbecilic
spectacle—and entirely "made for TV." But the prototypers put their
all into it. They investigated various techniques, including slingshots,
parachutes, and blimps. They tested the g-forces a pizza could withstand before its deliciousness and edibility were compromised. They
even tried to post a flying pie with a twenty-foot helium-filled diri-
gible.

Each of these efforts was invested with an almost mystical aura of
importance. But the climax of the episode was heralded by the appearance of a gangly six-foot-six University of California, Berkeley
grad named Anthony Levandowski.

Levandowski was a bona fide whiz kid. In his mid-twenties he was
already a veteran businessman, technologist, and entrepreneur. By
2008, he was serving as the front man for a talented group of Bay Area
technophiles working to transform a humble Toyota Prius into something much more compelling.

From certain camera angles, Levandowski's Prius betrayed telltale
scars of collisions past. But those nicks were barely noticeable underneath the garb of sensors that hugged the car. These instruments fed
data to sophisticated onboard computers and eventually the steering
system and drivetrain. Levandowski's team had tapped into the car's
control systems—which generally transmit signals from the steering
wheel, gas pedal, and brakes—and established direct access to the vehicle's driving components.

The hope was that these sensors and controls, in concert with
some mapping accomplished the day earlier, would be able to pilot
a pizza across San Francisco's Bay Bridge, onto Treasure Island, and
into the Discovery Channel's research hangar—completely autonomously.

At go-time Levandowski and the TV hosts stood on a flatbed chase truck holding a remote kill switch—just in case something went wrong. A ghostly steering wheel jittered back and forth—appearing to literally drive itself. The inventor and the TV hosts chortled nervously as the car made disconcertingly wide turns and stuttering stops. They winced through a few near misses with motorcycles and pedestrians.

San Francisco police shut down an entire span of the Bay Bridge to allow the experiment to go all the way to Treasure Island. But as the car crept onto the lower level of the bridge, its GPS failed—the steel and concrete structure above it had blocked the signal. Now the robot was solely dependent on its onboard sensors. It soldiered on. But as it approached the sharp off-ramp toward Treasure Island, Levandowski's autonomous car slowly smooshed into a concrete barrier. The car ground to a halt, unable to move.

Levandowski jumped into the car, disengaged the twitching steering column, and set it back on course for delivery. There were high-fives all around, but in reality it was a mixed success.

Driving Blind

But five years later, the awkward robot had transformed into a sleek, formidable, and truly autonomous driving machine. In the interim, Google had acquired the autonomous vehicles company, and management at the cash-flush Silicon Valley giant had been so impressed by the team's results that they eventually gave them a virtually unlimited development budget.

Google helped them step up the processing power, user interface, and publicity surrounding the vehicle. Once the car was ready to go, the mother ship also engineered a much more impressive and profound media sensation than a simple pizza delivery.

On March 28, 2012, Google posted a YouTube video of a handsome and nattily dressed man named Steve Mahan rolling into traffic in a visibly modified Prius. What made this particular hybrid excursion special was that Mahan was 95 percent blind. Soon he was zooming down the streets in the "Google Car." As the Google Car ably piloted Mahan about his daily routine he ruminated about how such a vehicle could change his life. Mahan picked up his dry cleaning and pulled through the drive-through at a neighborhood taqueria—eating lunch on the road thereafter. It was quite a spectacle and soon the Google Car was an Internet sensation.

By 2012, Google claimed it had logged 600,000 miles, with the only accident occurring when one of its employees was manually driving and rear-ended another Prius—something that is actually quite believable for anyone who has witnessed Levandowski's automotive multitasking.

By 2013, the Prius had been swapped for a fleet of sleek Lexus SUVs—emblazoned with the Google logo. On top of each Lexus sat a lidar system—which looked a bit like a spinning Christmas tree stand. Other than that, all of the sensory and control elements unique to the Google Car—GPS, control interfaces, computer modules, etc.—had been integrated into the vehicle.

The cars had been exhaustively tested and much of the angst regarding their performance was gone. On highways, one fleet of Google Cars was robust and truly autonomous. Another fleet of vehicles was becoming a common sight on the streets around the tech giant's Mountain View, California, campus.

While early demonstrations were like crack cocaine for the media, none of the auto companies paid the Google Car much attention until 2011. That was when the Nevada Legislature shocked the industry by passing Assembly Bill (AB) 511—which explicitly laid out the regulations for testing and practicing autonomous driving in the state. Soon other states followed, including California, Florida, and Michigan, as well as the District of Columbia.[10]

Automakers were used to being closely involved in the drafting of any new legislation related to the industry. But now, as lawmakers began to consider bills on autonomous driving, it was the industry that was driving blind. Google's technical/regulatory push lit a fire under the rest, and soon every major automaker had instituted a crash program to develop automated cars. Many—including Nissan and

Daimler—announced commercialization goals in the 2020 time frame. Google was shooting for 2017.

The legal and regulatory issues surrounding automation were sure to be tricky (for example, if no one was driving, who was financially liable in the case of a crash?). But it was also an enormous opportunity. An autonomous vehicle could be worth a lot to the consumer and there was palpable public excitement surrounding the issue. Automakers wanted to harness that power.

There was no turning back. For academics and policy makers it was suddenly legitimate, reasonable, and even necessary to start pondering the implications of a future with cars that drove themselves and what this might mean for automakers, cities, and countries around the world. Different people used different terminologies with various meanings to describe these robotic cars—self-driving cars, robot cars, automated vehicles, and autonomous vehicles, to name a few. However, the ultimate goal was generally understood to be a car that could drive itself.

Although theirs was not the first autonomous car, Google broke the logjam. And that is why one might say that automation is not simply the next frontier, but the finishing line in the Great Race. For in some profound sense, automated cars cease to be cars. They are, instead, robots. And these robots have the potential to address social problems ranging from time management, to emissions, to vehicle safety.

In the United States alone, thirty thousand people die annually as a result of car crashes. One study by NHTSA showed that human error caused or contributed to 99 percent of incidents.[11] This means that automation could potentially save tens of thousands of lives a year in America and millions globally. Done properly, automation could allow for cars that are smaller, swifter, more efficient, and less resource intensive than the cars we drive today.

In the spring of 2014, Google revealed a new set of autonomous vehicles that the company had built from scratch. They had a distinctive, buglike shape and a roomy interior. But more interestingly, they had no steering wheel.

Sit Back, Relax, Enjoy the Ride

The implications are manifold—almost too many to imagine. They start with simple things like traffic. One early application of fully autonomous driving is likely to be autonomous parking. This is likely to help ease urban congestion and traffic flows. Drivers have a nasty habit of circling around as they look for parking that is close to their destination and this mass of poorly coordinated drivers and distracted motorists looking for a piece of real estate clogs up city roads.[12] But within a decade, some Americans may be able to exit their vehicles, send them off to park, then summon them back at will with the flick of a smartphone. (In October 2014, Tesla released a new version of the model S with automated features including self-adjusting cruise control, lane keeping, and self-parking.) Vehicles will likely be digitally connected to—or at least be able to communicate with—each other. This should allow for more seamless integration of our enormously complex transportation system.

Of course, there will be cybersecurity and other concerns. Inevitably people will worry about the safety of these robots. But it seems quite likely that autonomous vehicles will in fact be fundamentally safer. Unlike humans, they won't get distracted by their kids fighting, or vacation plans, or a pretty face on the corner, or job stress. That's because the car's full-time job will be to get you to where you are going and to keep you safe. Insurance companies have already expressed interest in lowering their rates for autonomous vehicles.

In fact, autonomous vehicles may end up being the most significant safety innovation since seat belts. How many uneasy teenagers have found themselves in a vehicle with an unsettlingly intoxicated classmate or friend? How many partygoers have unsuccessfully implored an impaired driver not to get behind the wheel? How many lives have been lost to mindless texting, distraction, or drunk driving? With autonomous vehicles, such concerns may disappear within decades.

On a day-to-day level, autonomous vehicles will ease the stress and monotony of commuting in heavy traffic. Perhaps they will prove to be the ultimate cure for "road rage." Rather than wasting countless hours steering cars around town as the herd lurches from place to place, autonomous vehicle passengers will be able to surf the Web, watch TV, read the newspaper, or just sit back, relax and enjoy the ride as their car safely and smoothly delivers them to their desired destination.

Cars that don't crash could also be much smaller and lighter, with fewer safety features. Rather than merely cushion the impact of a crash, autonomous vehicles should be able to avoid them altogether in all but the most extreme circumstances. Airbags probably won't disappear, but they will be increasingly superfluous.

Greater precision and awareness will allow cars to travel in long, dense lines on highways. In industry parlance, this is called "platooning." Platooning will cut aerodynamic resistance and save 15–20 percent on energy use. Volvo has already shown how such "road trains" can allow drivers to disengage from the task of highway driving and rely on a lead vehicle to guide them along safely and at high speeds. Someday autonomous vehicles might drive on roads that look more like tracks—with just enough width for precisely calibrated vehicles to glide along.

When 2+2=10

The intersection between car sharing, electrification, and autonomous vehicles is where things get truly exciting.

Today most people drive large cars capable of seating four or five people, even when there is only one person inside. This is incredibly inefficient. But if we instead drove cars that were autonomous, electrified, and shared—rather than individually owned—that might all change. Fleet managers could match the capabilities of the vehicle to the needs of the passenger. Instead of driving around in huge, gasoline-filled metal boxes with the seating capacity and fuel sufficient to haul a family across a state, car shares may be able to use small, sleek, carbon-fiber, electric pods with just enough charge necessary to get consumers to their destination—rotating this fleet to make sure each car always has enough juice to fulfill its mission. A trip for a single individual across town would require only a small, single-passenger car.

This confluence of technologies could also address many problems of the developing world. For instance, in 2013 the United States had 786 cars per 1,000 people, and China had only about 100.[13] It is hard to imagine China ever attaining rates of car ownership as high as the United States—such a society would simply be too resource intensive. But a sophisticated car-sharing system could provide most of the benefits of car ownership for China with few of the associated costs and a much more efficient utilization of capital.

Conceptually, car services like Uber—which allow you to order a ride on demand from a personal driver with greater comfort and efficiency than most taxi services—are already halfway there. With automated vehicles, these systems will be even more convenient, efficient, safe, and comfortable than they are today.

With cars moving seamlessly from customer to customer, or parking themselves outside urban centers, cityscapes could be transformed. Parking strips could be replaced by actual parks; traffic congestion would disappear; vehicles could choose to store themselves at whichever depot offered the best deal on charging, or paid the highest fee for using the car's battery to balance the grid. Electrification would clean up urban air quality and the unsightly oil slicks that wash off our roads into ponds, streams, rivers, and bays. Indeed, burning oil could be a thing of the past. Today Americans spend about fifty minutes a day commuting.[14] That's about three hundred hours a year. With autonomous vehicles this time could be put to use for work, family, or leisure.

Someday in the not too distant future, Levandowski's humble pizza delivery Prius may be seen as the Elijah to a new, better era of human mobility.

Transformation

We cannot yet predict but we can readily imagine some of the consequences of this transformation. The vehicle technologies developed and deployed over the coming two decades will fundamentally transform our lives.

Not long ago, people kept large rolodexes of index cards alphabetically organized with the names and addresses of friends, family, and colleagues. People memorized phone numbers and communicated via pay phone. Today our smartphones can tap into troves of information that are, for practical purposes, limitless. This information is what lubricates the gears of the twenty-first-century economy. Just like rolodexes, driver's licenses may soon be seen as an antiquated relic of the twentieth century.

Electric and autonomous vehicles are bound to enable an entirely new culture and energy system. Cars will pick us up at the airport and fetch our dry cleaning, chauffeur our kids to school, and retrieve our groceries from the store. Batteries from our cars will likely be used to absorb excess power from wind turbines and solar and nuclear energy—day and night—and then feed that energy back into the grid as needed. Cities will become quieter and cleaner as communities embrace electrification. Death rates from lung conditions caused by automotive pollution will decrease and fatal car accidents will no longer be viewed as the macabre cost of doing business in a motorized society.

Endgame

Once upon a time, automakers were bound to a specific nation or geography. But today they are much more free to follow the market and economics of production. For just this reason, Honda, Toyota, and other Japanese companies have invested billions in R&D operations in California and built factories across the United States and China. But jobs and corporate influence can also flow the other way. The Shanghai Automotive Industrial Corporation is already a partial owner of GM, and today GM sells more cars in China than in the United States.

Like the railroads, Internet, or nuclear energy, the success of emerging automotive technologies will be highly dependent on enabling government policies. If we do not pursue them in America, others will pursue them in Shanghai, Stuttgart, or Tokyo. Industry and innovation are bound to follow the markets generated through strategic economic planning. It is easy to imagine American automakers—petrified of lawsuits and stymied by unclear or unfavorable laws, rules, and regulations—falling behind. And that should be a serious concern. Autonomous and electric vehicles will provide an economic edge for the societies that embrace them that may even outstrip the importance of the jobs in the automotive manufacturing economy. To compete in the twenty-first century, America will need to capture those efficiencies.

We have seen remarkable transformations over the past hundred years—wondrous transformations—and there will be more to come. But it would be a mistake to think that America's technological dominance is somehow ensured by the innovative capacity of Silicon Valley, or the excellence of our research universities, or the leadership of California's government. Indeed, political dysfunction in Washington poses a serious threat to our competitive position. Nonetheless, America is still very much in the running. Today, General Motors, Chrysler, Tesla, and even Henry Ford's motor company are all contenders. To enable their success, America will have to support new research, business models, laws, and regulations. And America cannot rest, for the competitive field is fierce, and the global race to build the car of the future, or shall we say robot of tomorrow, is on.

SELECT BIBLIOGRAPHY

Agassi, Shai. "TED 2009: Shai Agassi's Bold Plan for Electric Cars." TED, accessed January 15, 2012, http://www.ted.com/talks/shai_agassi_on_electric_cars.html.

Ainsworth, Ed, and Louis C. McCabe. 1949. "Cause of Smog's Eye Smarting Told: Dr. McCabe Declares Organic Peroxide found in Air 'in Surprisingly Large Quantities.'" *Los Angeles Times,* February 26.

Amsden, Alice H. 1989. *Asia's Next Giant: South Korea and Late Industrialization.* New York: Oxford University Press.

Anderson, G. E. 2012. *Designated Drivers: How China Plans to Dominate the Global Auto Industry.* Singapore: Wiley.

Anegawa, Takafumi. 2011. Interview.

———. 2013. Interview.

Annual Report of the Top Ten Electric Power Companies of Japan. 2011. FEPC.

Aoki, Hiroyuki. 2011. Interview.

———. 2013. Interview.

A123 Systems Stock Information. A123 Systems Inc. accessed February 8, 2012, http://ir.a123systems.com/stockquote.cfm.

Aquinos, Steve. 2009. "Misremembering John Dingle." *Mother Jones.*

Associated Press. 2011. "Onagawa: Japanese Tsunami Town Where Nuclear Plant Is the Safest Place," http://www.guardian.co.uk/world/2011/mar/30/onagawa-tsunami-refugees-nuclear-plant.

Automotive News. 1990. "A Defeat for 40 MPG, but Car Industry must Lead in Conservation." *Automotive News,* October 1.

Background on Alternative Fuel CAFE Rulings. "Background on Alternative Fuel CAFE Rulings." National Highway Traffic Safety Administration, accessed February 8, 2012, http://stnw.nhtsa.gov/cars/rules/rulings/cafe/alternativefuels/background.htm.

Bank of Japan. 2012. *BOJ Time-Series Data Search.*

Barboza, David. 2009. "Still Dancing in Her Dreams." *New York Times,* April 17.

BBC. 2009. "Profile: Geely Automobile." BBC News, December 23.

Bell, Larry. 2012. "Obamacar: Bad Karma for Taxpayers." *Forbes,* September 25.

Berkshire Hathaway. 2008. *Berkshire Hathaway 2008 Annual Report.*

Block, Fred, and Matthew R. Keller. 2009. "Where Do Innovations Come From? Transformations in the US Economy, 1970–2006." *Socio-Economic Review* 7:3: 459–83.

Bloomberg TV. 2012. "BYD May be Warren Buffett's 'Rare Mistake.'" June 30.

Boekestyn, Alex, Brian Knibb, Stewart Pedder, and Alex Woodrow. 2011. *Advanced Energy Storage and Distribution*. IHS Supplier Business.

Boffey, Philip. 1982. "National Labs Reel Under Criticism and Investigation." *New York Times*, August 24.

Boyer, Robert. 1998. *Between Imitation and Innovation: The Transfer and Hybridization of Productive Models in the International Automobile Industry*. Oxford and New York: Oxford University Press.

BP. 2011. *BP Statistical Review of World Energy June 2011*.

Branigan, Tania, and Justin McCurry. 2011. "Fukushima 50 Battle Radiation Risks as Japan Nuclear Crisis Deepens." *Guardian*.

Brown, Edmund G. 2008. "Governor Delivers Remarks at Orange County Coastkeepers & Inland Empire Waterkeeper Dinner."

Brown, Warren. 1985a. "Ford Threatens U.S. Over Fuel Economy Rules." *Washington Post*, November 2, A1.

———. 1985b. "Lowered Auto Fuel Economy Gets Boost." *Washington Post*, May 16, E1.

Bureau of the Environment. 2009. "Tokyo Metropolitan Government Starts the Project to Promote Widespread Use of EVs and PHVs."

Burkhard, Jim. 2011. Interview.

Burns, Matt. 2012. "Tesla Unveils the Model X, an Electric CUV with Futuristic Gullwing-Like Doors." *Tech Crunch*.

BYD Auto. "About BYD." Accessed March 22, 2012, http://www.byd.com/about .html.

CAFE Overview. "CAFE Overview: Frequently Asked Questions." U.S. Department of Transportation, accessed February 6, 2012, http://www.nhtsa.gov/cars /rules/cafe/overview.htm.

Calder, Kent E. 1988. *Crisis and Compensation: Public Policy and Political Stability in Japan, 1949–1986*. Princeton, NJ: Princeton University Press.

———. 1993. *Strategic Capitalism: Private Business and Public Purpose in Japanese Industrial Finance*. Princeton, NJ: Princeton University Press.

Caldwell, Jessica. 2013. "Drive by Numbers—Tesla Model S is the vehicle of choice in many of America's wealthiest zip codes." Edmunds.com, October 10, 2013, http://www.edmunds.com/industry-center/analysis/drive-by-numbers-tesla -model-s-is-the-vehicle-of-choice-in-many-of-americas-wealthiest-zip-codes .html.

California Air Resources Board. 2009. "California Exhaust Emission Standards and Test Procedures for 2009 and Subsequent Model Zero-Emission Vehicles and Hybrid Electric Vehicles, in the Passenger Car, Light-Duty Truck and Medium-Duty Vehicle Classes."

California Air Resources Board Mobile Source Division. 1996. "Low-Emission Vehicle and Zero-Emission Vehicle Program Review." California Environmental Protection Agency.

California Environmental Protection Agency. 2010. "2010 Zero Emission Vehicle Credits." Accessed December 16, 2011, http://www.arb.ca.gov/msprog/zevprog /zevcredits/2010zevcredits.htm.

Callon, Scott. 1995. *Divided Sun: MITI and the Breakdown of Japanese High-Tech Industrial Policy, 1975–1993*. Stanford, CA: Stanford University Press.

CARB. 2012. "California's Advanced Clean Cars Program." CARB, accessed March 23, 2012, http://www.arb.ca.gov/msprog/consumer_info/advanced_clean_cars /consumer_acc.htm.

————. 1990. Resolution 90–58, September 28.

————. 2009. "White Paper: Summary of Staff's Preliminary Assessment of the Need for Revisions to the Zero Emission Vehicle Regulation."

————. "CARB Mission Statement." Accessed March 23, 2012, http://www.calepa .ca.gov/About/mission.htm.

————. "Key Events in the History of Air Quality in California." California Air Resources Board, accessed February 9, 2012, http://www.arb.ca.gov/html/brochure /history.htm.

CarStations.com. "Electric Car Stations," accessed February 8, 2012, http://car stations.com/.

Carter, Jimmy. 1982. *Keeping Faith: Memoirs of a President*. New York: Bantam Books.

Carter, Kelley. 2003. " 'Hybrid' Cars Were the Oscars' Politically Correct Ride." *USA Today*, March 30, http://usatoday30.usatoday.com/life/2003-03-30-hybrids_x .htm.

Cattaneo, Oliver et al. eds. 2010. *Global Value Chains in a Postcrisis World: A Developmental Perspective*. The World Bank.

CBS Detroit. 2012. "A123 Recalling $55M in EV Batteries Made in Livonia." March 26, 2012.

Center for Biological Diversity v. NHTSA, 1, 14831 (United States Court of Appeals for the Ninth Circuit 2007).

Center for Internet and Society, Stanford Law School. 2014, "Automated Driving: Legislative and Regulatory Action." Accessed January 13, 2014, http:// cyberlaw.stanford.edu/wiki/index.php/Automated_Driving:_Legislative _and_Regulatory_Action.

Central Valley v. Goldstone, Order on Motions and Counter-Motions for Summary Judgement on Plaintiffs' Claims for Relief on EPCA Preemption and Foreign Policy Preemption. United States District Court for the Eastern District of California, 2006.

Cha, Ariana E., and Maureen Fan. 2008. "China Unveils $586 Billion Stimulus Plan; Amid Unrest, Package Would Address Social, Political and Economic Concerns." *Washington Post*, November 10, 1.

Challen, John. 2008. *Great Call from China*. Q4, Ricardo Quarterly Review.

Chalupsky, Mary. 1979. "Electric Car Outlook Is Modest." *Washington Post*, July 1, G6.

Chapman, Emmett A. 1923. "Japan Faces Terrific Housing Problem." *Washington Post*, October 7, 48.

Chapman, Margaret L., Arun P. Elhance, and John D. Wenum. 1995. *Mitsubishi Motors in Illinois: Global Strategies, Local Impacts*. Westport, CT: Quorum Books.

Chen, Yuyu et al. 2013. *Evidence on the impact of sustained exposure to air pollution on life expectancy from China's Huai River policy*. Proceedings of the National Academy of Sciences.

Chengyu, Fu. 2011. Interview.

Chicago Tribune. 1981. "We're Miles Away from '74." *Chicago Tribune,* February 22, 2.

Child, Charles. 1996. "EV1 Serves as GM Halo Car with an Attitude." *Automotive News,* February 12.

China Daily. 2010. "Are SOEs the Economy's Friends Or Foes?" *China Daily,* September 2.

China Monitor. 2012. "No. 13: Alternative Energy Vehicles Industry: Hybrid Gets Fast-Tracked, as Electric Loses Power." *China Monitor.*

China National Offshore Oil Company. 2007. Company Chronology. http://en .cnooc.com.cn/data/html/news/2007-07-02/english/228531.html.

China State Grid. "Welcome to State Grid Company of China." State Grid Corporation of China, accessed March 21, 2012, http://www.sgcc.com.cn/ywlm/gsgk-e /gsgk-e/gsgk-e1.shtml.

Christian Science Monitor. 1928. "Is China to Jump the Motor Age?" *Christian Science Monitor,* November 21, p. 18.

———. 1930. "Ford Executive Analyzing China." *Christian Science Monitor,* October 28, 7.

Chrysler, Mack. 2011. "Japanese Auto Industry Faces Somber Market." Wards Auto.

Clenfield, Jason, and Norie Kuboyama. 2011. "Tokyo Electric Slumps Most on Record After Bankruptcy Concerns Resurface." June 6, 2011, Bloomberg.

Coast Guard, Japan. 2011. "Japan Tsunami Strikes at Sea." http://www.bbc.co.uk /news/world-asia-pacific-12797471.

Coifman, Jon. 2002. "California Gov. Gray Davis Signs Landmark CO2 Pollution Measure; New Law Uses Power of American Know-how to Tackle Global Warming." Natural Resources Defense Council.

Cole, Keith. 2010. Interview.

Collantes, Gustavo Oscar. 2006. "The California Zero-Emission Vehicle Mandate: A Study of the Policy Process, 1990–2004." Ph.D. diss., University of California, Davis.

Collantes, Gustavo, and Daniel Sperling. 2008. "The Origin of California's Zero Emission Vehicle Mandate." *Transportation Research Part A: Policy & Practice* 42 (10): 1302–13.

Crain, Keith. 1993. "Wave a Magic Wand." *Automotive News,* April 26, 1993.

Crawley, John. 2011. "Fuel Economy Standards: Obama Administration Proposes Doubling Fuel Efficiency by 2025." Thomson Reuters, November 16.

Currie, David P. 1979. "The Mobile-Source Provisions of the Clean Air Act." *University of Chicago Law Review* 46 (4): 811–909.

Davidson, Jonathan M., and Joseph M. Norbeck. 2011. *An Interactive History of the Clean Air Act.* Burlington, MA: Elsevier Science.

Davis, Pat. 2012. Interview.

Demont-Heinrich, Christof. 2011. "An EV Tax Rebate Simpler, More Fair than Tax Credit." *SolarCharged,* January 27.

Diamond, Robbie. 2010. Interview.

"DOE Nobel Laureates." U.S. Department of Energy, accessed February 6, 2012, http://science.energy.gov/about/honors-and-awards/doe-nobel-laureates/.

Doerr, John, and Bill Joy. 2007. "The Blue Sky Project." *Fortune,* May 7.

Downs, Erica. 2008. "China's 'New' Energy Administration." *Brookings*, November–December.

Downs, Erica Strecker, and Project Air Force. 2000. *China's Quest for Energy Security*. Santa Monica, CA: Rand.

Dredge, Bill. 1959. "Auto Makers Will Study UCLA Anti-Smog Discovery: Use of Copper Oxide Catalyst Stirs Interest." *Los Angeles Times*, August 23.

———. 1961. "Anti-Smog Devices for 1963 Cars Scheduled: Positive Crankcase Ventilating System Will Be Used." *Los Angeles Times*, December 7, B1.

Duce, John. 2009. "Cnooc Group may Set Up Electric-Car Battery Network." *Bloomberg*, November 2.

Economist Intelligence Unit. 2012. *Economist Intelligence Unit Automotive Database*.

Economist. 2009. "Banzai! A Landslide Victory for the DPJ in Japan." *Economist*, August 31.

———. 2010. "Floundering in the Foggy Fortress." *Economist*, February 27, http://www.economist.com/node/15579893.

———. 2011. "How Long Are American Commutes?" October 16, http://www.economist.com/blogs/freeexchange/2011/10/surveys.

ECOtality Inc. "Blink Network Locator." Blink, accessed February 8, 2012, http://www.blinknetwork.com/locator.html.

Edgarton, Jerry. 2012. "Yes You Can Put a Gun Rack in a Volt." CBS News, February 23.

Edmunds. 2012. "2012 Fisker Karma." February 28.

Eizenstat, Stu, Daniel Yergin, and Levi Tillemann-Dick. 2009. Interview.

Electric Power Research Institute. 2013. *Total Cost of Ownership Model for Current Plug-in Electric Vehicles*. Electric Power Research Institute 2013 Technical Report, June, http://www.epri.com/abstracts/Pages/ProductAbstract.aspx?ProductId=000000003002001728&Mode=download.

Electrification Coalition. 2009. *Electrification Roadmap: Revolutionizing Transportation and Achieving Energy Security*.

Elkind, Ethan N. 2012. "Electric Drive by '25: How California Can Catalyze Mass Adoption of Electric Vehicles by 2025."

Elsey, George M. 1950. *Secretary Acheson and the Defense of Korea*. Remarks by Dean Acheson Before the National Press Club, ca. 1950. Harry S. Truman Administration, Elsey Papers. Memorandum available at http://www.trumanlibrary.org/whistlestop/study_collections/korea/large/documents/pdfs/kr-3-13.pdf.

Emch, Adrian. 2009. "PRC Mergers: MOFCOM Takes Control." Sidley Austin LLP, http://www.sidley.com/files/Publication/9d254420-2511-49c8-ab6f-197ad58d5fbd/Presentation/PublicationAttachment/3a3abd76-d1f1-44c1-a8b0-1a3f77bdfd31/Nov09%20CS%20Merger%20control.pdf.

Emission Standards for New Motor Vehicles or New Motor Vehicle Engines. Public Law, US Code Title 42, Chapter 85, Subchapter II, Part A, § 7521.

Environmental Defense Fund. "California's Clean Cars Law." Accessed February 14, 2012, http://www.edf.org/transportation/policy/california-clean-cars-law.

Environmental Protection Agency. 2012. "The Guardian: Origins of the EPA." Accessed February 12, 2012, http://www.epa.gov/aboutepa/history/publications/print/origins.html.

Environmental Protection Agency, Office of Mobile Sources. 2012. "Milestones in Auto Emissions Control Fact Sheet." http://www.epa.gov/otaq/consumer/12 -miles.pdf.

Evans, Peter B. 1995. *Embedded Autonomy: States and Industrial Transformation.* Princeton, NJ: Princeton University Press.

EV Project. 2012. "The EV Project Webpage." ECOtality, accessed February 8, 2012, http://www.theevproject.com/overview.php.

Fa, Guo B. "The Issuance of the Primary Duties of the Internal Organs of the Ministry of Industry and Information Technology and Staffing." Ministry of Industry and Information Technology, accessed March, 19, 2012, http://www.miit.gov .cn/n11293472/n11459606/11606790.html.

Fackler, Martin. 2012a. "Declining as a Manufacturer, Japan Weighs Reinvention." *New York Times,* April 15.

———. 2012b. "Japan Weighed Evacuating Tokyo in Nuclear Crisis." *New York Times,* February 27, 2012.

Fisher, Dan, and Robert Fairbanks. 1973. "Reagan Replaces 4 on State Air Board." *Los Angeles Times,* December 15, A1.

Fletcher, Seth. 2011. *Bottled Lightning: Superbatteries, Electric Cars, and the New Lithium Economy.* New York: Hill & Wang.

Flink, James J. 1988. *The Automobile Age.* Cambridge, MA: MIT Press.

Ford, Gerald R. "Remarks on Taking the Oath of Office." Miller Center, accessed February 6, 2012, http://millercenter.org/president/speeches/detail/3390.

Ford, Peter. 2008. "China Aims to End Pessimism with $586 Billion Economic Stimulus Package." *Christian Science Monitor,* November 12, 7.

Fortune. "GLOBAL 500: *Fortune* Magazine's Annual Ranking of the World's Largest Corporations." CNN.com, accessed March 19, 2012, http://money.cnn.com /magazines/fortune/global500/2010/snapshots/2255.html.

Foster, Peter. 2008. "Beijing Olympics: Chinese Dancer Injured in Opening Ceremony Rehearsal 'Paralysed.'" *Telegraph,* August 13, http://www.telegraph.co .uk/sport/olympics/2551869/Beijing-Olympics-Chinese-dancer-injured-in -opening-ceremony-rehearsal-paralysed.html.

Frank, F. 2012. "BYD Signs Over Another 1500 Vehicles to Shenzhen, Making the world's Largest Electric Vehicle Fleet." *China Car Times.*

Freedom Car and Fuel Partnership. "Freedom CAR and Fuel Partnership 2009 Highlights of Technical Accomplishments," http://www1.eere.energy.gov /vehiclesandfuels/pdfs/program/2009_fcfp_accomplishments_rpt.pdf.

FuelEconomy.gov. "What Is FuelEconomy.Gov?" U.S. Environmental Protection Agency and Department of Energy, accessed February 6, 2012, http://www .fueleconomy.gov/feg/FE_Fact_Sheet.pdf.

Fujii, Kiyotaka. 2011. Interview.

Fukushima Nuclear Accident Independent Investigation Commission. 2012 Executive Summary of the Official Report of the Fukushima Nuclear Accident Independent Investigation Commission.

Gallagher, Kelly Sims. 2006. *China Shifts Gears: Automakers, Oil, Pollution, and Development.* Cambridge, MA: MIT Press.

GAO Highlights. 2009. United States Government Accountability Office, http:// gao.gov.

Gates, Max. 1993a. "Big 3 Tighten Federal Lab Ties." *Automotive News,* October 25.
———. 1993b. "U.S. Makes a 'Decent Proposal'; Offers $ 1 Billion for Hyper-Clean Car." *Automotive News,* May 10.
General Motors. 1967. "General Motors Proudly Announces the Production of its 100 Millionth Vehicle in the United States."
———. 1990. Press conference with Roger B. Smith.
———. 2009. "Chevrolet Volt Battery: An Introduction." Available at https://media.gm.com/content/dam/Media/microsites/product/volt/docs/battery_101.pdf.
Gergen, David. 2008. "Gergen: Bush Punted Automotive Problem to Obama-Rollins: Bush Is Going to Be Hoover." CNN December 21, 2008.
Gerschenkron, Alexander. 1966. *Economic Backwardness in Historical Perspective: A Book of Essays.* Cambridge, MA: Belknap Press.
Ghosn, Carlos. 2005. "Carlos Ghosn: Nissan's Turnaround Artist." CNN, http://edition.cnn.com/2005/BUSINESS/04/20/boardroom.ghosn/.
———. 2010. Interview of Carlos Ghosn by Daniel Yergin.
Global Times. "2009 Top Ten Best-Selling Cars in China." Accessed March 22, 2012, http://autos.globaltimes.cn/photo/2010-01/500394.html.
Goeller, David. 1988. "Congress Passes Plan to Spur Development of New Vehicles; Incentives Offered for Use of Alternative Fuels." *Washington Post,* September 25, a04.
Goff, Tom. 1968. "Toughest Smog Bill Signed by Reagan." *Los Angeles Times,* July 26, 3.
Gold, Jenny. 2008. "Cutting Worker Costs Key to Automakers' Survival." National Public Radio, December 23.
Goodwin, Craufurd D. W. 1981. *Energy Policy in Perspective: Today's Problems, Yesterday's Solutions.* Washington, D.C.: Brookings Institution.
Google Finance. 2012. "CNOOC Limited (ADR) (NYSE:CEO)."
Gordon, Deborah et al. 2012. *A Policy Framework for Electric Vehicles.* Carnegie Foundation, Washington D.C.
Gordon-Bloomfield, Nikki. 2011. "How Much has Nissan Spent on Electric Cars? $5.6 Billion . . . and Counting." *Green Car Reports.*
Granoff, Michael. 2014. Interview.
Green Car Congress. 2010. *Nikkei Editorial Urges Japan to Match US, China EV Moves.* http://www.greencarcongress.com/2010/07/nikkei-editorial-urges-japan-to-match-us-china-ev-moves-.html.
Grey, Tony. 1979. "The Drive to More Miles Per Gallon." *Christian Science Monitor,* October 22, 1.
GS Yuasa Corporation. 2011. "Lithium Energy Japan to Commence Work on Rittoll Plant."
Hakim, Danny. 2004. "Automakers Sue to Block Emissions Law in California." *New York Times,* December 8.
Halberstam, David. 1986. *The Reckoning.* 1st ed. New York: William Morrow.
Halvorson, Bengt. 2013. "Nissan R&D Chief: Carbon Fiber Is Good For Planes, Not Cars." *Green Car Reports,* November 27, http://www.greencarreports.com/news/1088723_nissan-rd-chief-carbon-fiber-is-good-for-planes-not-cars.
Hammond, P. Brett, Rob Coppock, and National Research Council. 1990. *Valuing*

Health Risks, Costs, and Benefits for Environmental Decision Making: Report of a Conference. Washington, DC: National Academy Press.

Harwit, Eric. 1995. *China's Automobile Industry: Policies, Problems, and Prospects.* Armonk, NY: M. E. Sharpe.

———. 2001. "The Impact of WTO Membership on the Automobile Industry in China." *China Quarterly* 167: 655–70.

Haxthausen, Eric. 2011. Interview.

Hayasaka, Akito. 2013. Interview.

Hayes, Denis. 1977. *Rays of Hope: The Transition to a Post-Petroleum World.* 1st ed. New York: Norton.

Hedrick, James B. 2010. *Global Rare-Earth Production: History and Outlook.* U.S. Rare Earths, Inc.

Heller, Steven "Mac." 2010. Interview.

Hendricks, D. L. et al. 2001. "The Relative Frequency of Unsafe Driving Acts in Serious Traffic Crashes." Summary Technical Report, Prepared for U.S. Department of Transportation, National Highway Traffic Safety Administration, Traffic Safety Programs Office of Research and Traffic Records Under Contract No. DTNH22-94-C-05020. January. http://www.nhtsa.gov/people/injury/research /UDAshortrpt/UDAsummtechrept.pdf.

Hill, Gladwin. 1967. "Reagan Loses Out on Pollution; Legislature Rejects New Board." *New York Times,* August 13, 80.

Hiraoka, Leslie S. 2001. *Global Alliances in the Motor Vehicle Industry.* Westport, CT: Quorum Books.

Hirose, Katsuhiko. 2013. Interview.

Honda Motor Company. "Honda History." Honda Motors, http://world.honda.com /history/ limitlessdreams/manttrace/text03/index.html.

———. 2012a. "Honda: Launch of the AP Lab." Honda Motor Company, http:// world.honda.com/history/ challenge/1972introducingthecvcc/text02/index.html.

———. 2012b. "Honda: Achieving Lean Combustion through Trial and Error." http://world.honda.com/history/challenge/1972introducingthecvcc/text03 /index.html.

Hong Kong Exchanges and Clearing Ltd. "BYD Co Price Movement." Accessed March 22, 2012, http://www.hkex.com.hk/eng/csm/priceMove.asp?LangCode =en&mkt=hk&StockCode=1211.

Hornblower, Margot. 1977. "Mandatory Curbs on Fuel Coming, Schlesinger Says." *Washington Post,* March 27, p. 1.

Hosaka, Shin. 2010. "Views and Policies on Japan's Automotive Industry." February 25.

Huang Yonghe. 2013. Interview.

Huddle, Norie, Michael Reich, and Nahum Stiskin. 1975. *Island of Dreams: Environmental Crisis in Japan.* New York: Autumn Press.

IHS Automotive. *China: Influence of Government Fleet Purchases on Vehicle Sales in China.*

———. 2011. *Engine Trends.*

———. 2012. *IHS Automotive Forecasting* [自動車に関するアンケート].

IHS Emerging Energy Research. 2010. *Global Solar PV Supply Chain Strategies: 2010–2025.*

IHS Supplier Business. 2011. *The Electric and Rang Extended Electric Light-Vehicle Report.*

Immel, A. Richard. 1976. "The Big Stick: California's Air Board Breaks New Ground with Pollution Limits." *Wall Street Journal,* June 9, p. 1.

Ingrassia, Paul. 2010. *Crash Course: The American Automobile Industry's Road from Glory to Disaster.* New York: Random House.

Intergovernmental Panel on Climate Change. 2007. *Climate Change 2007: Working Group III: Mitigation of Climate Change.*

International Energy Agency. 1993. *Electric Vehicles: Technology, Performance and Potential.* Paris and Washington, D.C.: OECD.

International Organization of Motor Vehicle Manufacturers. 2012. "OICA Production Statistics." Accessed March 20, 2012, http://oica.net/category/production -statistics/.

Jacobs, Chip, and William J. Kelly. 2008. *Smogtown: The Lung-Burning History of Pollution in Los Angeles.* Vol. 1. Woodstock, NY: Overlook.

Jameson, Sam. 1981. "Japan to Cut Auto Sales to U.S. by 7.7%." *Los Angeles Times,* May 2.

Japan Automobile Research Institute. 2003. "For the Next Generation: EV, HEV & FCV."

Japan Automobile Research Institute FC-EV Research Division. 2011. *Electric Vehicles in Japan.*

Japan Hydrogen & Fuel Cell Demonstration Project. Accessed December 16, 2011, http://www.jari.or.jp/jhfc/e/jhfc/index.html.

Japan. Tsūshō Sangyōshō and Nihon Bōeki Shinkōkai. 1972; 2001. *White Paper on International Trade* [Tsūshō hakusho. English]. Tokyo: Japan External Trade Organization.

Johnson, Chalmers A. 1982. *MITI and the Japanese Miracle: The Growth of Industrial Policy, 1925–1975.* Stanford, CA: Stanford University Press.

———. 1995. *Japan, Who Governs? The Rise of the Developmental State.* New York: Norton.

———.1999. "The Developmental State: Odyssey of a Concept." In *The Developmental State,* edited by Meredith Woo-Cummings. Ithaca, NY: Cornell University Press.

Johnson, Erik, and Mike Sutton. 2009. "BYD F3DM/F6DM/E6." *Car and Driver,* January.

Johnson, Kelly. 2012. "California Car Dealers See Jump in Sales." *Sacramento Business Journal,* January 20.

Jones, M. Jeffrey. 2007. *Oil Company Greed Seen as Major Reason for High Gas Prices.*

———. *Majority of Americans Expect $4 Gas Prices This Summer.* Gallup, May 30, 2007.

Josephson, Matthew. 1959. *Edison: A Biography.* 1st ed. New York: McGraw-Hill.

Kadota, Ryusho. 2012. 死の淵を見た男 吉田昌郎と福島第一原発の五〇〇日. PHP研究所.

Kamata, Satoshi, and Ronald Philip Dore. 1983; 1982. *Japan in the Passing Lane: An Insider's Account of Life in a Japanese Auto Factory* [Jidōsha zetsubō kōjō. English]. 1st pbk. ed. New York: Pantheon Books.

Katz, Richard. 2013. *Mutual Assured Production.* Foreign Affairs July/August 2013.

Kawahara, Akira. 1998. *The Origin of Competitive Strength: Fifty Years of the Auto Industry in Japan and the U.S.* Tokyo and New York: Springer.

Keebler, Jack. 1991. "Looking at the Pros and Cons of Alternative Fuels." *Automotive News* February 25, 1991.

Khan, Matthew E. 1996. *New Evidence on Trends in Vehicle Emissions. RAND Journal of Economics* 27:1: 183–96.

Kingdon, John W. 1984. *Agendas, Alternatives, and Public Policies.* Boston: Little, Brown.

Kishimoto, Michihiro. "Japanese Rare Metals Policy." Presentation, Japan Oil, Gas and Metals National Corporation.

Knee, Iron. 2010. "Jobs Lost Under Bush v. Obama." Talking Points Memo, accessed April 23, 2012, http://politicalirony.com/2010/02/06/jobs-lost-bush-v-obama/.

Knight, Ben. 2012. Interview.

Kodama, Fumio. 1991. *Analyzing Japanese High Technologies: The Techno-Paradigm Shift.* London and New York: Pinter.

Koh, Yoree. 2011. "The Tracks of Banri Kaieda's Tears." *Wall Street Journal* blog.

Kohli, Atul. 2004. *State-Directed Development: Political Power and Industrialization in the Global Periphery.* Cambridge and New York: Cambridge University Press.

Komiya, Ryūtarō, Masahiro Okuno, and Kōtarō Suzumura. 1988. *Industrial Policy of Japan.* Tokyo and San Diego: Academic Press.

Kōsai, Yutaka. 1986. *The Era of High-Speed Growth : Notes on the Postwar Japanese Economy* [Kōdo seichō jidai. English]. Tokyo: University of Tokyo Press.

Kovacs, Pal, Torsten Eng, and Stan Gordelier. 2010. *Public Attitudes to Nuclear Power.* Nuclear Development: Nuclear Energy Agency, http://www.oecd-nea .org/ndd/reports/2010/nea6859-public-attitudes.pdf.

Kraemer, Susan. 2010. "World's Largest Offshore Wind Farm Begun by China." *Clean Technica,* October 23.

Krebs, Michelle. 2004. "Behind the Wheel/2004 Mitsubishi Galant; another Baby Born in Hard Times." *New York Times,* August 1, http://www.nytimes .com/2004/08/01/automobiles/behind-the-wheel-2004-mitsubishi-galant-another-baby-born-in-hard-times.html.

Kumita, Kunihiko. 2013. Interview.

Kuroda, Haruhiko. "The 'Nixon Shock' and the 'Plaza Agreement': Lessons from Two Seemingly Failed Cases of Japan's Exchange Rate Policy." *China & World Economy* 12, 3.

Kyodo News. 2011. "Iwate Saw Wave Test 38 Meters."

Lai, Xiaokang. 2011. Interview.

Lampe-Onnerud, Christina. 2011. Interview.

Lampton, David M. 2001. *Same Bed, Different Dreams: Managing U.S.–China Relations, 1989–2000.* Berkeley: University of California Press.

Letters and Visits Bureau of Changsha City. Chengsha Petition website, accessed March 20, 2012, http://www.csxfj.gov.cn/.

Levin, Doron P. 1991. "Detroit's Assault on Mileage Bill." *New York Times,* May 11.

Levine, Steve. 2010. "The Great Battery Race." *Foreign Policy,* November.

Levs, Josh. 2008. "Big Three Auto CEOs Flew Private Jets to Ask for Taxpayer Money." CNN, November 19.

Liao, Frank, and Daniel Yergin. 2010. Interview.

Lieberthal, Kenneth, Michel Oksenberg, and David Lampton. 1986. *Bureaucratic Politics and Chinese Energy Development*. Washington, DC: U.S. Dept. of Commerce, International Trade Administration.

Lieberthal, Kenneth. 2004. *Governing China : From Revolution through Reform*. 2nd ed. New York: Norton.

Lindgren, Mattias and Gapminder. "Income Per Person." Accessed March 22, 2012, http://www.gapminder.org/data/.

Liu, Ying. 2011. Interview.

Lone, Stewart, and Christopher Madeley. 2005. *The Automobile in Japan*. LSE STICERD Research Paper No. IS494.

Los Angeles Times. 1933. "China Progress Astounds Hall." *Los Angeles Times*, July 18, A16.

———. 1949. "Methods Developed for Cleansing Air: Los Angeles Group Reports Progress in Eliminating Nuisances in Smog." *Los Angeles Times*, March 29.

———. 1958. "Red China Luxury Car has Silk Rug Carpets." *Los Angeles Times*, August 27, p. 28.

———. 1959. "The Political Drive Against Smog." *Los Angeles Times*, October 29.

———. 1960. "Gov. Brown on Smog." *Los Angeles Times*, February 25, B4.

———. 1973. "Air Board Stacked, GOP Senator Says." *Los Angeles Times*, December 21, A25.

Loveday, Eric. 2011. "Construction of Nissan's Smyrna Battery Plant on Schedule." *Autobloggreen*, January 3.

———. 2014. "2013 Plug-In Electric Vehicles Sales Results for China." *Inside EVs*, January.

Lubetsky, Jessica F. 2011. *History of Fuel Economy: One Decade of Innovation, Two Decades of Inaction*: PEW Environment.

Lun, Jingguang. 2002. "Clean City Vehicles in China." Department of Automotive Engineering, Tsinghua University.

Ma, Damien. 2011. "Who Killed China's Electric Car?" *Atlantic*, November 7.

MacArthur Memorial Foundation. 1990. Symposium, William F. Nimmo, General Douglas MacArthur Foundation, Old Dominion University, and MacArthur Memorial. *The Occupation of Japan: The Impact of the Korean War: The Proceedings of the Seventh Symposium*. Norfolk, VA: The Foundation.

MacArthur, Douglas, Vorin E. Whan, and United States Military Academy. 1965. *A Soldier Speaks: Public Papers and Speeches of General of the Army, Douglas MacArthur*. New York: Praeger.

Macauley, Alvan. 1930. "People Enriched by Automobiles." *New York Times*, January 5, A1.

Madrid, Christopher, Juan Argueta, and John Smith. 1999. "Performance Characterization 1999 Nissan Altra-EV with Lithium-Ion Battery." Southern California Edison.

Mann, Jim. 1989. *Beijing Jeep: The Short, Unhappy Romance of American Business in China*. New York: Simon & Schuster.

Mao Zedong. 1965. *Selected Works of Mao Tse-Tung*. Peking: Foreign Languages Press.

Marchionne, Sergio. 2014. *Recovery Road? An Assessment of the Auto Bailout and the State of U.S. Manufacturing*. The Brookings Institution.

Markey, Ed. 2007. "Bill Takes Aim at 'Hummer Tax Loophole.'" National Public Radio, June 17.

Markus, Frank. 2003. "Keio University Eliica." *Car and Driver*, October. http://www.caranddriver.com/news/keio-university-eliica-auto-shows.

Martineau, Robert J., and David P. Novello. 2004. *The Clean Air Act Handbook*. 2nd ed. Chicago: American Bar Association.

Martinez, Nate. 2011. " Quick Comparison: 2011 Nissan Leaf vs. 2012 Mitsubishi i-MiEV." *Motor Trend*, August 3.

Marx, Karl, and Friedrich Engels. 1947. *Das Kapital: Kritik Der Politischen Ökonomie*. Volksausgabe ed. Berlin: Dietz.

Matthews, Joe. 2010. "The Hummer and Schwarzenegger: They Probably Won't Be Back." *Washington Post*, February 28.

Matsuzawa, Shigefumi. 2006. "将来エコカー電気自動車普及を!," accessed October, 13, 2011, http://matsuzawa.cocolog-nifty.com/blog/2006/10/post_c292.html.

Maxcy, George, and Aubrey Silberston. 1959. *The Motor Industry*. Cambridge Studies in Industry. London: Allen & Unwin.

Mazzucato, Mariana. 2013. *The Entrepreneurial State: Debunking Public vs. Private Sector Myths*. London: Anthem Press.

McCain, John. 2008. Speech in Jacksonville, Florida.

McCarthy, Tom. 2007. *Auto Mania: Cars, Consumers, and the Environment*. New Haven, CT: Yale University Press.

McCombs, Phil. 1980. "Electric Car: A Rapidly Growing Infant." *Washington Post*, June 9.

McLear, Aaron, and Bill Maile. 2008. "Governor Schwarzenegger Announces EPA Suit Filed to Reverse Waiver Denial." Vol. GAAS:001:08. Available at http://gov.ca.gov/news.php?id=8400.

McNamara, Brendan. 2009. "FTC Order Sets Conditions for Panasonic's Acquisition of Sanyo." http://www.ftc.gov/opa/2009/11/sanyo.shtm: Federal Trade Commission; http://www.ftc.gov/opa/2009/11/sanyo.shtm; http://www.ftc.gov/os/caselist/0910050/091124panasanyocmpt.pdf; http://www.ftc.gov/os/caselist/0910050/index.shtm.

Mehndiratta, Shomik. 2010. Interview.

———. 2011. *The China New Energy Vehicles Program: Challenges and Opportunities*. World Bank.

Metcalf, Bob. 2008. Conversation with author at MIT Energy Initiative Business Plan Competition.

METI. 2009. 特許出願技術動向調査報告書:リチウムイオン電池.

Miao, Aaron. 2011. Interview.

Michael, David C. 2009. *China's Stimulus Packages: Opportunities and Roadblocks*. Boston Consulting Group and US-China Business Council.

Michels, Spencer, dir. 2005. *Clearing the Air*. PBS News Hour, 2005.

Ministry of Economy, Trade and Industry, Government of Japan. 2010. "Japan's Manufacturing Industry."

———. 2012a. "History of METI." http://www.meti.go.jp/english/aboutmeti/data/ahistory2009.html.

———. 2009b. Organizational Chart. Accessed January 9, 2012, http://www.meti.go.jp/english/aboutmeti/data/aOrganizatione/pdf/chart2009.pdf.

————. 2010. "Japan's Manufacturing Industry."

————. 2011. "Outline of 'Electricity Supply-Demand Measures in Summer Time.'"

————. 2011. "Japan's Approach and Perspective on Next-Generation Vehicle."

————. 2011. "Follow-Up Results of Electricity Supply–Demand Measures for this Summer."

————. 2006. 新世代自動車の基礎となる次世代電池技術に関する研究会.

Ministry of the Environment, Government of Japan. "Organization of the Ministry of the Environment," accessed January 5, 2012, http://www.env.go.jp/en/aboutus/pamph/html/00pan160.html.

Ministry of Industry and Information Technology, Government of China Website, accessed March, 19, 2012, http://bgt.miit.gov.cn/n11293472/n11294464/index.html.

Ministry of Land, Infrastructure, Transport and Tourism, Government of Japan. 2012. "Organization of the Ministry of Land, Infrastructure, Transport and Tourism, Government of Japan." Accessed January 5, 2012, http://www.mlit.go.jp/common/000026153.pdf.

Ministry of Science and Technology. "The 863 Plan." Accessed March 20, 2012, http://www.863.gov.cn/1/1/index.htm.

————. 2012. "Missions of the Ministry of Science and Technology." Accessed March 19, 2012. http://www.most.gov.cn/eng/organization/Mission/index.htm.

————. "MOST Leadership." Accessed March 20, 2012, http://www.most.gov.cn/eng/organization/leadership/.

Minoru, Shinohara. 2012. Interview.

Mintz, Morton. 1960. "Smog-Killer on All Cars Is Urged by Flemming." *Washington Post*, February 25, A1.

MIT Energy Initiative. 2010. *The Future of Natural Gas*.

Mitchell, Russ. 2009. "The Last Great American Car Guy." *Men's Journal,* http://russmitchell.com/wp-content/uploads/2008/11/MJ_Lutz.pdf.

Mitsubishi. 2003. "Colt EV in-Wheel Test Vehicle."

————. 2009. Mitsubishi Motors Group Environmental Vision 2020. "Leading the EV Era, Towards a Sustainable Future."

Miura, Kenji. 2011. Interview edited by Levi Tillemann-Dick. Ministry of Economics, Trade and Industry.

Moniz, Ernie. 2011. *Interview*, edited by Levi Tillemann-Dick. Former undersecretary of energy for President Clinton.

Mooney, James. 1990. "Where Is Safety in the Fuel Economy Debate?" *Insurance Institute for Highway Safety* 25 (8).

Moorehouse, Ward. 1979. "Oil Pinch, Washington Incentives May Get Electric Rolling in Detroit." *Christian Science Monitor*, May 18, 1.

Mossberg, Walter S. 1980. "The Energy Department Is a Flop." *Wall Street Journal*, August 22.

Motavalli, Jim. 2011a. "The Fisker Karma's 20 M.P.G. Sticker: A Scarlet Letter?" *New York Times*, October 21, http://wheels.blogs.nytimes.com/2011/10/21/the-fisker-karmas-20-m-p-g-conundrum/.

————. 2011b. "Johnson Controls in Divorce Court, with Other EV Companies in the Waiting Room." http://www.plugincars.com/johnson-controls-divorce-court-other-ev-companies-waiting-room-107214.html.

Murray, Charles. 2012. "$100k Fisker Karma 'Bricked' during *Consumer Reports Test*." *Design News*.

Musil, Steven. 2012. "Stanford Ovshinsky, 'Edison of Our Age,' Dies at 89." CNET. October 18, 2012.

Musk, Elon. 2011. Interview conducted by Lincoln P. Bloomfield Jr., chairman, Henry L. Stimson Center, http://www.stimson.org/images/uploads/ElonMusk Transcript.pdf.

Myers, Ramon Hawley, Mark R. Peattie, Qingqi Chen, and Joint Committee on Japanese Studies. 1984. *The Japanese Colonial Empire, 1895-1945*. Princeton, NJ: Princeton University Press.

Naitoh, Masahisa. 2011. Interview.

Naughton, Barry. 1995. *Growing Out of the Plan: Chinese Economic Reform, 1978–1993*. New York: Cambridge University Press.

———. 2008. "SASAC and Rising Corporate Power in China." *China Leadership Monitor*, 24.

Neil, Dan. 2012. "I Am Silent, Hear Me Roar." *Wall Street Journal*, July 6.

Nevins, Allan, and Frank Ernest Hill. 1954. *Ford: The Times, the Man, the Company*. New York: Scribner.

New York Times. 1937. "China Wants Fuel-Oil Cars." *New York Times*, June 10, 41.

———. 1942. "China Turns to Charcoal." *New York Times*, June 19, 9.

———. 1975. "Right on Energy . . ." *New York Times*, December 24.

———. 1979. "Electric Cars: They're Slow, but So Are Gasoline Lines." *New York Times*, July 1.

———. 1980. "Transcript of the Presidential Debate Between Carter and Reagan." *New York Times*, October 29, 26.

津波の様子(宮城県名取市) 撮影 陸上自衛隊東北方面隊. 2011. NHK News.

Nichols, Mary. 2013. Interview.

Nicholson, Tom, James Jones, and Annabell Bentley. 1979. "Small Is Beautiful." *Newsweek*, November 12, 87.

Niedermeyer, Edward. 2009. "Who Got What in the Saab-BAIC Deal?" *The Truth About Cars*.

Nissan Motor Company. 2011. "Zero Emission Leadership." Available at http://www.nissan-global.com/EN/TECHNOLOGY/OVERVIEW/zero_emission.html.

———. 2012. "The Charge Down Electric Avenue Begins." March 24, http://www.nissanpress.co.uk/leaf/html/press-pack.htm.

Obama, Barack. 2011. Remarks by the President on America's Energy Security at Georgetown University.

O'Dell, John. 2002. "Car Companies Team Up to Fight State's ZEV Rule." *Los Angeles Times*, January 23.

Ogino, Norikazu. 2011. Interview. Japan Automobile Research Institute.

Ohnsman, Alan. 2014. "Tesla Rises After Model S Sales in 2013." Bloomberg, January 15.

Okimoto, Daniel I. 1989. *Between MITI and the Market: Japanese Industrial Policy for High Technology*. Stanford, CA: Stanford University Press.

Okuya, Toshikazu. 2010. Interview. Japan External Trade Organization.

Oliver, Ben. 2009. "Mr. Fix It." *Irish Times*, July 6.

Olson, Mancur. 1977; 1971. *The Logic of Collective Action: Public Goods and the*

Theory of Groups. Harvard Economic Studies, vol. 124. Cambridge, MA: Harvard University Press.

Omang, Joanne. 1978. "Despite Energy Worries Electric Cars Aren't Selling." *Washington Post*, February 11, A7.

Orbach, Raymond, Daniel Yergin, and Levi Tillemann-Dick. 2001.

Organisation for Economic Co-operation and Development. 1977. *Environmental Policies in Japan*. Paris: Organisation for Economic Co-operation and Development.

Organizing for America. 2008. "Organizing for America, New Energy for America." https://my.barackobama.com/page/content/newenergy_campaign.

Ozaki, Robert S. 1972a. *The Control of Imports and Foreign Capital in Japan*. Praeger Special Studies in International Economics and Development. New York: Praeger.

Paine, Chris, et al. 2006. *Who Killed the Electric Car?* Sony Pictures Home Entertainment.

Paine, Chris and P. G. Morgan. 2011. *Revenge of the Electric Car*. Independent film.

Patrick, Hugh T. and Henry Rosovsky. 1976. *Asia's New Giant: How the Japanese Economy Works*. Washington, D.C.: Brookings Institution.

Green Mountain Plymouth Dodge Jeep v. Crombie (2007). US District Court for the District of Vermont.

PBS. "Timeline: History of the Electric Car," accessed February 14, 2012, http://www.pbs.org/now/shows/223/electric-car-timeline.html.

Pentland, William. 2013. "Korea Constructs Road That Wirelessly Charges Moving Electric Busses." *Forbes*, August 11, http://www.forbes.com/sites/william pentland/2013/08/11/korea-constructs-road-that-wirelessly-charges-moving -electric-buses.

People's Daily. 2003. "China's First Fuel Cell Car Make Debuts in Shanghai." *People' Daily*, January 16, 2003.

Perkowski, Jack. 2011. Interview.

Phillips, Clay. 2011. Interview.

Pratley, Nils. 2008. "Banking Crisis: Viewpoint: Risk of Paulson Failing Has the Markets Frozen with Fear." *Guardian*, September 25.

Qiu, Lily Lin, Lindsay Turner, and Lindsay Smyrk. 2003. "Proceedings of the 15th Annual Conference of the Association for Chinese Economics Studies Australia (ACESA), Changes in the Chinese Automotive Market Resulting from WTO Entry."

Qiu, Xinping. 2013. Interview.

Rainey, David. 2011. Interview.

Rattner, Steven. 2010. *Overhaul: An Insider's Account of the Obama Administration's Emergency Rescue of the Auto Industry*. Boston: Houghton Mifflin Harcourt.

Rauch, Jonathan. 2008. *Electroshock Therapy*. The Atlantic July/August 2008.

Ray, Julie, and Anita Pugliese. 2010. "World's Top-Emitters No More Aware of Climate Change in 2010." Gallup, http://www.gallup.com/poll/149207/world -top-emitters-no-aware-climate-change-2010.aspx.

Real Clear Politics. 2011. "U.S. Gave $529 Million Loan to Company Now Building Cars in Finland," http://www.realclearpolitics.com/video/2011/10/20/us_gave _529_billion_loan_to_company_now_building_cars_in_finland.html.

Rechtin, Mark. 1994. "CARB Won't Budge on Zero-Emissions Rule." *Automotive News,* January 10, 1994.

———. 1996. "CARB, Makers Agree on ZEVs, 49-State Car." *Automotive News,* February 12, 8.

———. 2001. "ZEV Rule Goes Under the Knife." *Automotive News,* January 22, 3.

Recovery.gov, U.S. government, accessed February 8, 2012, http://www.recovery .gov/.

Redburn, Tom, and Patrick Doyle. 1979. "Regulators Elbowing Detroit Out of Driver's Seat." *Los Angeles Times,* June 17, 1–2.

Reddy, Thomas B., and David Linden. 2011. *Linden's Handbook of Batteries.* 4th ed. New York: McGraw-Hill.

"Reorganization Under Bankruptcy Code." 2012. http://www.uscourts.gov/Federal Courts/Bankruptcy/BankruptcyBasics/Chapter11.aspx.

Ricketts, Camille. 2010. "Better Place Draws Massive $350M to Charge Electric Cars." VentureBeat.Com.

Ridenour, Eric. 2011. Interview.

Riley, Michael A., and Ashlee Vance. 2012. "China Corporate Espionage Boom Knocks Wind Out of U.S. Companies." Bloomberg, March 15.

Riley, Robert Q. 1994. *Alternative Cars in the 21st Century: A New Personal Transportation Paradigm.* Warrendale, PA: Society of Automotive Engineers.

Risen, James. 1985. "Ford Profits Fall 17.5% in Quarter." *Los Angeles Times,* October 26.

———. 1986. "GM Profits Up 42% in Quarter, Off 11% in Year: Firm Cites Investment Costs for Decline in '85." *Los Angeles Times,* February 4.

Risser, Roland. 2012. Interview.

Rogers, Matthew. 2011. Interview.

Rogin, Josh. 2012. "NSA Chief: Cybercrime Constitutes the 'Greatest Transfer of Wealth in History.'" *Foreign Policy,* July 9.

Ronen, Amit. 2014. Interview.

Rusco, Frank. 2012. Interview.

Ryan, Richard A. 2005. "Capitol Hill's Mr. Chairman; for a Record 50 Years, John Dingell has Shaped America." *Detroit News,* October 11, 1.

Ryuchi, Toba. 2011. Interview.

Saad, Lydia. 2003. "Iraq War Triggers Major Rally Effect." Gallup March 25, 2003.

Sadoi, Yuri. 2008. "Technology Transfer in Automotive Parts Firms in China." *Asia Pacific Business Review* 14 (1).

Sakamaki, Sachiko, and Takashi Hirokawa. 2011. "Japan Passes Bill to Back Tepco Compensation for Nuclear Disaster Victims." Bloomberg.

Salisbury, Harrison E. 1956. "No Ford in Future for Soviet Family." *New York Times,* July 17, 1956.

Sandalow, David. 2008. *Freedom from Oil: How the Next President Can End the United States' Oil Addiction.* New York: McGraw-Hill.

Sandalow, David. 2012. Interview.

Schiffer, Michael B., Tamara C. Butts, and Kimberly K. Grimm. 1994. *Taking Charge: The Electric Automobile in America.* Washington: Smithsonian Institution Press.

Schmookler, Jacob. 1962. "Economic Sources of Inventive Activity." *Journal of Economic History* 22 (1): 1–20.

Schumpeter, Joseph Alois. 1950. *Capitalism, Socialism, and Democracy.* 3d ed. New York: Harper.

Schwarzenegger, Arnold, and Jerry Brown. 2007. Speech: California Sues EPA for Stonewalling Landmark Global Warming Law. November 8, 2007. Available at http://oag.ca.gov/news/press-releases/california-sues-epa-stonewalling -landmark-global-warming-law.

Sexton, Chelsea. 2013. Interview.

Shapiro, Ian, Stephen Skowronek, and Daniel Galvin. 2006. *Rethinking Political Institutions: The Art of the State.* New York: New York University Press.

Sharma, Aditya. 2012. "Honda—It Ain't a Dream Without Everyone Being a Part of It." *Autospace,* October 31, http://autospace.co/honda/.

Shimizu, Hiroshi. 2013. Interview.

Shimokawa, Kōichi. 1994. *The Japanese Automobile Industry : A Business History.* London and Atlantic Highlands, NJ: Athlone Press.

———. 2010. *Japan and the Global Automotive Industry.* Cambridge and New York: Cambridge University Press.

Shoup, Donald. 2004. *The High Cost of Free Parking.* Chicago: American Planning Association.

Shnayerson, Michael. 1996. *The Car That Could: The Inside Story of GM's Revolutionary Electric Vehicle.* 1st ed. New York: Random House.

Shogan, Robert. 1976. "Carter Proposes Combining Four Energy Offices." *Los Angeles Times,* September 22, B2.

Simms, James. 2012. "With Incentives, Japan Car Sector Is Spinning Tires." *Wall Street Journal* February 21, 2012.

Sit, Victor F. S., and Weidong Liu. 2000. "Restructuring and Spatial Change of China's Auto Industry Under Institutional Reform and Globalization." *Annals of the Association of American Geographers* 90 (4): 653–73.

Slosson, Mary. 2011. "Berkshire's Munger Stands Behind BYD Investment." Thomson Reuters, July 1.

Smil, Vaclav. 2013. *Made in the USA: The Rise and Retreat of American Manufacturing.* Boston: MIT University Press.

Smith, Adam, and Edwin Cannan. 1994; 2000. *The Wealth of Nations.* New York: Modern Library.

Smith, Sheila A. 2009. "Japan's Moment of Choice." *Council on Foreign Relations.*

Soble, Jonathan, and Leslie Hook. 2010. "Japan Sees Chinese Ban on Mineral Exports." *Financial Times,* September 24, 2010.

Sperling, Daniel. "FreedomCAR and Fuel Cells: Toward the Hydrogen Economy?" Progressive Policy Institute, September 27, 2002.

———. 2002. "Updating Automotive Research." *Issues in S&T.*

———. 2002. *Transitioning from PNGV to FreedomCAR.* Testimony to House Science Committee, US Congress (February 7, 2002).

———. 2011. Interview.

Sperling, Daniel, and James Spencer Cannon. 2007. *Driving Climate Change: Cutting Carbon from Transportation.* Amsterdam and Boston: Academic Press.

Sperling, Daniel, Mark A. Delucchi, Patricia M. Davis, and A. F. Burke. 1995. *Future Drive: Electric Vehicles and Sustainable Transportation.* Washington, D.C.: Island Press.

Sperling, Daniel, and Deborah Gordon. 2009; 2010. *Two Billion Cars: Driving Toward Sustainability.* 1st pbk. ed. Oxford and New York: Oxford University Press.

St. John, Jeff. 2014. "Amprius Gets $30M Boost for Silicon-Based Lithium-Ion Batteries." Greentech Media, http://www.greentechmedia.com/articles/read /amprius-gets-30m-boost-for-silicon-based-li-ion-batteries.

Stammer, Larry B. 1987. "Clean-Burning Fuel for Cars: Arco to Market Methanol in Southland." *Los Angeles Times*, May 22.

Stevenson-Wydler Technology Innovation Act of 1980. Public Law 94, Stat. 2311, 15 U.S.C. 3701, Public Law 96-480.

Stricker, Tom. 2012. Interview.

Subaru. 2008a. "FHI Showcases Its Subaru Plug-in STELLA Concept, a New Prototype Electric Vehicle, at the G8 Hokkaido Toyako Summit." June 27, 2008.

———. 2012. "New York Power Authority Evaluating Subaru R1e Electric Vehicle." Subaru Drive Magazine, Summer 2008. Available at http://drive2.subaru .com/Sum08/Sum08_News_R1e.htm.

Suzuki, Tatsujiro. 2010. "Nuclear Energy Strategy for Sustainable Growth: Aiming at Green Innovation and Life Innovation." Japan Atomic Energy Commission, November 19–20, 2010.

Tam, Pu I-wing. 2009. "Venture-Backed Start-Ups Seek Stimulus." *Wall Street Journal*, July 6.

Tankersley, Jim, and Richard Simon. 2009. "U.S. to Limit Greenhouse Gas Emissions from Autos." *Los Angeles Times*, May 19, 2009.

Taylor, Alex III. 2006. "The Birth of the Prius." *Fortune*, February 24.

TEPCO. TEPCO Corporation Overview. Available at http://www.tepco.co.jp/en /corpinfo/overview/history-e.html.

Tesla Motors. "Facts," accessed March 23, 2012, http://www.teslamotors.com /models/facts.

Thomson, Peter. 2012. *Fukushima Report: Japan Dodged Major Nuclear Disaster.* Anonymous Public Radio International February 28, 2012 http://www.pri.org /stories/2012-02-28/fukushima-report-japan-dodged-major-nuclear-disaster.

Thornton, Emily, and De'Ann Weimer. 1997. "Slow Healing at Mitsubishi." *BusinessWeek* September 22, 1997. Available at http://www.businessweek.com /1997/38/b3545103.htm.

Tian, Shou. 2010. Interview. Keyi Power.

Tillemann-Dick, Levi. 2009a. *BP Solar Plant Tour.*

———. 2009b. "Private Meetings with Korean Officials."

———. 2012. Rebuilding Leviathan: Electric vehicles, Industrial Strategy and the New Energy Economy. Diss. Johns Hopkins University, Baltimore 2012.

Toyota Jidōsha Kabushiki Kaisha. 1988. *Toyota: A History of the First 50 Years.* 1st ed. Toyota City, Aichi Prefecture, Japan: Toyota Motor Corporation.

Troubled Asset Relief Program. 2009. "Troubled Asset Relief Program: Continued Stewardship Needed as Treasury Develops Strategies for Monitoring and Divesting Financial Interests in Chrysler and GM." U.S. Government Accountability Office.

Trudell, Craig. 2012. "A123 Shows Risks as Battery Science Meets Government Cash." Bloomberg, October 18.

Tsuru, Shigeto. 1999. *The Political Economy of the Environment: The Case of Japan*. London: Athlone.

Tsurumi, Yoshi, ed. 1980. *Technology Transfer and Foreign Trade: The Case of Japan, 1950–1966*. New York: Arno Press.

Tyler, Patrick E. 1994. "China Is Planning a People's Car." *New York Times*, September 22.

Ueda, Takayuki. 2008. Interview.

Umeda, Kenji. 2011. Interview.

U.S. Congress, Committee on Oversight and Government Reform. 2011. "How the Obama Administration's Green Energy Gamble Will Impact Small Business & Consumers." Video. Subcommittee on Regulatory Affairs, Stimulus Oversight, and Government Spending. Available at http://oversight.house.gov/hearing /running-on-empty-how-the-obama-administrations-green-energy-gamble -will-impact-small-business-consumers/

U.S. Congress. House. Committee on Science and Technology. Subcommittee on Energy Research, Development, and Demonstration and United States. 1975. *Electric Vehicle Research, Development and Demonstration Act of 1975: Hearings Before the Subcommittee on Energy Research, Development and Demonstration of the Committee on Science and Technology, U.S. House of Representatives, Ninety-Fourth Congress, First Session on H.R. 5470*. Serial no. 94-27. Washington, D.C.: U.S. Government Printing Office.

U.S. Congress. Office of Technology Assessment. 1981. *U.S. Industrial Competitiveness: A Comparison of Steel, Electronics, and Automobiles*. Washington, D.C.: Office of Technology Assessment.

U.S. Congress. 1998. Public Law 105-66, 105th Congress (1998).

U.S. Department of Commerce. Website, accessed February 6, 2012, http://www .commerce.gov/.

U.S. Department of Energy. "About Us," accessed March 23, 2012, http://energy .gov/about-us.

———. ARPA-E website, accessed February 6, 2012, http://arpa-e.energy.gov/.

———. Loan Programs Office, accessed February 8, 2012, http://lpo.energy.gov/.

———. Loan Programs Office, accessed February 8, 2012, https://lpo.energy .gov/?page_id=45.

———. 2004. Office of Energy Efficiency and Renewable Energy. http://www .fueleconomy.gov/feg/bymake/2004MakeList.shtml.

———. 2009. Office of the Chief Financial Officer. DOE FY 2010 Congressional Budget Request: Budget Highlights.

———. 2012. Alternative Fuels Data Center. http://www.afdc.energy.gov/data /10301.

———. 2012. Office of the Chief Financial Officer. 2012. FY 2013 Congressional Budget Request Budget Highlights.

U.S. Department of Transportation. 2011. "Our Nation's Highways: 2011." Federal Highway Administration, Office of Highway Policy Information, Highway Finance Data Collection, http://www.fhwa.dot.gov/policyinformation/pubs/hf /pl11028/chapter4.cfm.

US Department of Transportation, Bureau of Transportation Statistics. 2008. *Omnibus Household Survey*.

U.S. General Accounting Office. 1994. *Electric Vehicles: Likely Consequences of U.S. and Other Nations' Programs and Policies: Report to the Chairman, Committee on Science, Space, and Technology, House of Representatives.* Washington, D.C. U.S. General Accounting Office.

U.S. Government Accountability Office. 1982. *Industrial Policy: Japan's Flexible Approach: Report to the Chairman, Joint Economic Committee, United States Congress.* Washington, DC: U.S. Government Accountability Office.

———. 2009. *Clean Air Act: Historical Information on EPA's Process for Reviewing California Waiver Requests and Making Waiver Determinations.* GAO-09-249R, http://www.gao.gov/assets/100/95941.html.

U.S. Tax Code. Section 179.

Van Biesebroeck, Johannes, and Timothy J. Sturgeon. 2010. *Effects of the Crisis on the Automotive Industry in Developing Countries.* Washington, DC: World Bank.

Vines, Stephen. 1991. "CHINA; Carmaking again on Track, but Experts Scoff at Goals." *Automotive News*, March 4.

Voelcker, John. 2010. "GM Is Building Electric Cars Again, Just Not for Americans (GM)." *San Francisco Chronicle*, November 8, 2010.

W. Edwards Deming Institute. 2012. *Deming the Man—Timeline.* https://www.deming.org/theman/timeline.

Wada, Kenichiro. 2011. Interview.

Wada, Kozuo, and Haruhito Shiomi. 1995. *Fordism Transformed: The Development of Production Methods in the Automobile Industry* Oxford: Oxford University Press.

Wade, Robert, Alice Amsden, Stephan Haggard, and Helen Hughes. 1992. "East Asia's Economic Success: Conflicting Perspectives, Partial Insights, Shaky Evidence." *World Politics* 44 (2): 270.

Wald, Matthew. 1989. "That 'Cleaner Fuel' May Be Gasoline." *New York Times*, August 23.

Wall Street Journal. 1921. "Exporters Claim China Coming Automotive Market." *Wall Street Journal*, July 16, 7.

———. 1931. "China Builds Auto Truck." *Wall Street Journal*, June 16, 1931, 4.

———. 1975. "A Major Presidential Mistake." *Wall Street Journal*, December 26, 4.

Wan, Gang. 2008. Interview by Lisa Margonelli.

Wards Auto. 2012. *U.S. Vehicle Sales, 1931–2011.*

Washington Post. 1923. "First Quake Made Yokosuka Harbor Sea of Blazing Oil." September 10, 1.

Weissman, Jordan. 2012. "The Dramatic 30-Year Decline of Young Drivers (In 1 Chart)." *Atlantic*, July 20, http://www.theatlantic.com/business/archive/2012/07/the-dramatic-30-year-decline-of-young-drivers-in-1-chart/260126/.

White House, Office of the President. 2010. "The Recovery Act: Transforming the American Economy Through Innovation." August.

White House, Office of the Press Secretary. 2012. "Fact Sheet: All-of-the-Above Approach to American Energy." March 7.

Whitney, Lance. 2009. "Panasonic Takes Control of Sanyo." *CNET*, December 9, http://news.cnet.com/8301-1001_3-10413036-92.html.

Williams, Dennis C. "The Guardian: Origins of the EPA." Environmental Protection

Agency, accessed February 10, 2012, http://www.epa.gov/aboutepa/history/publications/print/origins.html.

Womack, James P., Daniel T. Jones, Daniel Roos, and Massachusetts Institute of Technology. 1990. *The Machine That Changed the World: Based on the Massachusetts Institute of Technology 5-Million Dollar 5-Year Study on the Future of the Automobile*. New York: Rawson Associates.

Woo-Cumings, Meredith. 1991. *Race to the Swift: State and Finance in Korean Industrialization*. Studies of the East Asian Institute. New York: Columbia University Press.

Woodford, William H., R. Alan Ransil, and Yet-Ming Chiang. 2012. "Topic Paper # 17—Advanced Batteries: Beyond Li-ion." Working Document of the NPC Future Transportation Fuels Study, August 1, http://www.npc.org/FTF_Topic_papers/17-Advanced_Batteries.pdf.

Woods, Richard, and Sarah Baxter. 2008. "The Great $700 Billion Hold-Up." *Sunday Times* (London), September 28.

World Bank. 2014. *World Development Indicators*, http://data.worldbank.org/indicator/IS.VEH.NVEH.P3

World Nuclear Association. 2012. "Fukushima Accident 2011." Available at http://www.world-nuclear.org/info/safety-and-security/safety-of-plants/fukushima-accident/.

Wren, Christopher S. 1983. "A.M.C. and China Sign Jeep Plant Pact." *New York Times*, May 6, D3.

Wu, Guihui. 2010. Interview. Engineer General, National Energy Administration.

Wu, Yushan. 1994. *Comparative Economic Transformations: Mainland China, Hungary, the Soviet Union, and Taiwan*. Stanford, CA: Stanford University Press.

Xiao Chengwei. 2010a. Interview.

———. 2011. Interview.

———. 2010b. "Overview on Power Batteries for Electric Vehicles in China."

Xing, Yuqing, and Neal Detert. 2010. "How the iPhone Widens the United States Trade Deficit with the People's Republic of China." ADBInstitute.

Xinhua. 2011. "China's Innovation Drive in 'Post-Shanzai' Era." March 11.

Yahoo! Finance. "Summary for CNOOC." Yahoo! Finance, accessed March 21, 2012, http://finance.yahoo.com/q?s=0883.HK.

Yamaguchi, Jack. 2004. "Project G 21." Tech Briefs, http://www.sae.org/automag/techbriefs/03-2004/1-112-3-36.pdf.

Yan, K. F. 2011. Interview.

Yang, Huatang. 2010. Interview.

Yates, Brock. 2003. "A Lot of Acting at the Oscars." *Car and Driver*, July.

Ye, Jianhong. 2011. "New Energy Vehicles Demonstration in China."

Yergin, Daniel. 1991. *The Prize: The Epic Quest for Oil, Money, and Power*. New York: Simon & Schuster.

———. 2011. *The Quest: Energy, Security, and the Remaking of the Modern World*. New York: Penguin Press.

Yomiuri Shimbun. 2008. 自動車に関するアンケート.

Yoney, Domenick. 2008. "UN Agency Donates Electric Buses to the Beijing Olympics," accessed March 20, 2012, http://green.autoblog.com/2008/08/08/un-agency-donates-electric-buses-to-the-beijing-olympics/.

Yoshida, Hiroaki. "All About Electric Vehicles." Mitsubishi Motors, accessed December 21, 2011, http://global.ev-life.com/allofev/vol04/.

Yoshida, Phyllis Genther. 1986. *The Changing Government-Business Relationship: Japan's Passenger Car Industry*. University of California.

———. 2011. Interview.

Zaun, Todd. 2005. "Another Big Bailout for Mitsubishi Motors." *New York Times*, January 29.

Zhang, Benny. 2011. Interview.

NOTES

Introduction

1 Nevins and Hill 1954.
2 Schumpeter 1950.
3 Olson 1977; 1971.
4 Intergovernmental Panel on Climate Change 2007, 5.2.1 Transport Today.

1 The New Emperor and Wan Gang's Eco-Wonderland

1 Smil 2013.
2 Flink 1988.
3 Nevins and Hill 1954.
4 Flink 1988.
5 Wards Auto 2012.
6 Womack et al. 1990.
7 Flink 1988.
8 Yergin 2011.
9 Flink 1988; Wards Auto 2012.
10 Musil 2012.
11 Rainey 2011.
12 Hayes 1977.
13 Sperling 2002.
14 Sperling and Gordon 2010; 2009.
15 Hirose 2013.

2 California Rules: How One State Began a Global Technology Revolution

1 *Washington Post,* Feb. 28, 2010.
2 Matthews 2010.
3 Yergin 2011.
4 Jacobs and Kelly 2008.
5 Ibid.
6 Ibid.

7　Ibid.
8　Ainsworth and McCabe 1949.
9　Jacobs and Kelly 2008.
10　Nichols 2013.
11　Ibid.
12　Yergin 2011.
13　Jacobs and Kelly 2008.
14　Hammond et al. 1990.
15　Martineau and Novello 2004.
16　Jacobs and Kelly 2008.
17　Immel 1976.
18　Ibid.
19　Jacobs and Kelly 2008.
20　Smil 2013, 105.
21　Jacobs and Kelly 2008.
22　Khan 1996, 189.
23　Sperling 2002; Collantes 2006.
24　Davidson and Norbeck 2011.

3　Japan's Strategic Capitalism

1　Smil 2013.
2　Ibid.
3　*Washington Post* 1923.
4　Chapman 1923.
5　Tsurumi 1980.
6　Flink 1988.
7　Tsurumi 1980.
8　Ibid.
9　Toyota Jidōsha Kabushiki Kaisha 1988.
10　Ibid.
11　Ibid.
12　Ibid.
13　Lone and Madeley 2005.
14　Toyota Jidōsha Kabushiki Kaisha 1988.
15　Lone and Madeley 2005.
16　Ibid.
17　Tsurumi 1980.
18　Lone and Madeley 2005.
19　Ibid.
20　Yoshida 1991.
21　Ibid.
22　Calder 1988.
23　Yoshida 1991.
24　Toyota Jidōsha Kabushiki Kaisha 1988.
25　Ibid.

26 Kawahara 1998.
27 Wada and Shiomi 1995.
28 Kawahara 1998.
29 METI 2012a; Ozaki 1972a.
30 Kawahara 1998.
31 Yoshida 1991.
32 Ibid.
33 Elsey 1950.
34 Kawahara 1998.
35 Yoshida 1991; Ozaki 1972a.
36 Yoshida 1991.
37 United States Government Accountability Office 1982.
38 Yoshida 1991.
39 Kawahara 1998.
40 Halberstam 1986; Womack et al. 1990.
41 W. Edwards Deming Institute, 2012.
42 MacArthur Memorial Foundation, 1990.
43 Ibid.
44 Toyota Jidōsha Kabushiki Kaisha 1988; MacArthur Memorial Foundation 1990.
45 Halberstam 1986; Womack et al. 1990.
46 Kōsai 1986.
47 Ibid.
48 Patrick and Rosovsky 1976.
49 United States Congress Office of Technology Assessment 1981.

4 The Audacity of Honda

1 Sharma 2012.
2 Honda Motor Company 2012.
3 Kawahara 1998.
4 Honda Motor Company 2012a.
5 Tsūshō Sangyōshō and Nihon Bōeki Shinkōkai 1972; 2001.
6 Ibid.
7 Yoshida 1991.
8 Toyota Jidōsha Kabushiki Kaisha 1988.
9 United States Congress Office of Technology Assessment 1981.
10 Yoshida 1991; Huddle, Reich, and Stiskin 1975.
11 Kawahara 1998.
12 Honda Motor Company 2012b.
13 Ayrton Senna Memorial Museum 1998.
14 Sakurai 2013.
15 Toyota Jidōsha Kabushiki Kaisha, 1988.
16 Honda Motor Company, 2012b.
17 Organisation for Economic Co-operation and Development, 1977.
18 Honda Motor Company 2012b.

19 Ibid.
20 Ibid.
21 Ibid.
22 Toyota Jidōsha Kabushiki Kaisha 1988.
23 Yoshida 1991.
24 Ibid.
25 Ibid.
26 Tsuru 1999.
27 Tillemann 2012; Tsuru 1999.
28 Toyota Jidōsha Kabushiki Kaisha 1988.
29 Yoshida 1991.
30 Organisation for Economic Co-operation and Development 1977.

5 Sudden Impact

1 Shnayerson 1996.
2 Ibid.
3 Smith 1990.
4 Rainey 2011; Stammer 1987.
5 Phillips 2011.
6 Rainey 2011.

6 CARB's Long Reach

1 Ridenour 2011.
2 Collantes and Sperling 2008.
3 Ibid.
4 Shnayerson 1996.
5 Ibid.
6 Child 1996.
7 Crain 1993.
8 Ridenour 2011.
9 Rechtin 1994.
10 Hirose 2013.
11 Ibid.
12 Taylor 2006.
13 Hirose 2013.
14 Yamaguchi 2004.
15 Knight 2012.
16 Ibid.
17 Ibid.
18 Ibid.
19 Rechtin 1996.
20 Ibid.

7 The Electric Car Is Dead, Long Live the Electric Car

1 Sexton 2013.
2 United States Tax Code Section 179.
3 Paine 2006; Markey 2007.
4 Nichols 2013.

8 Catching China's Eye

1 Yoshida 1991.
2 PBS 2009; Madrid, Argueta, and Smith 1999.
3 Schiffer, Butts, and Grimm 1994; METI 2006.
4 Wada and Shiomi 1995.
5 Gallagher 2006; Salisbury 1956.
6 Vines 1991.
7 Sit and Liu 2000.
8 Perkowski 2011.
9 Economist Intelligence Unit 2012.
10 Qiu, Turner, and Smyrk 2003.
11 Ibid.
12 Cattaneo et al 2010.
13 Yan 2011.
14 Margonelli 2008.
15 Ibid.
16 Margonelli; Liao and Yergin 2010.
17 Lindgren and Gapminder 2011.
18 BP 2011.

9 Sea Turtles, Spaceships, and the Hydrogen Economy

1 CARB 2012.
2 O'Dell 2002.
3 CARB 2012.
4 Freedom Car and Fuel Partnership 2009.
5 Yoshida 2012.
6 Sperling 2009.
7 Lun 2002.
8 Ibid.
9 Ministry of Science and Technology 2012.
10 Ministry of Science and Technology 2009.
11 Ibid.
12 Sperling 2011.
13 *People's Daily* 2003.
14 Liao and Yergin 2010.

10 Crazy Anegawa

1 Anegawa 2011.
2 Kovacs, Eng, and Gordelier 2010.
3 Ibid.
4 Suzuki 2010, The 7th Tsuruga International Energy Forum.
5 Ueda 2008.
6 Reddy 2011.
7 Anegawa 2011.
8 Ibid.
9 Ibid.
10 Ibid.
11 California Air Resources Board 2009.
12 Aoki 2011.
13 Japan Automobile Research Institute 2003.
14 Kawahara 1998.
15 Ibid.
16 Japan Automobile Research Institute FC-EV Research Division 2011.
17 Paine 2011.
18 California Environmental Protection Agency 2010.
19 Yoshida 2009.
20 Ibid.
21 Mitsubishi 2009.
22 Anegawa 2011; Yoshida 2009.
23 Wada 2011.
24 Ibid.
25 Anegawa 2011.
26 Ibid.
27 Krebs 2004; Thornton and Weimer 1997.
28 Department of Energy 2004.
29 Zaun 2005.
30 Mitsubishi 2009.
31 Wada 2011.
32 Anegawa 2011.
33 Mitsubishi 2003.
34 Subaru 2008b.
35 Matsuzawa 2006.
36 Markus 2003.
37 Shimizu 2013.
38 Matsuzawa 2006.
39 Anegawa 2011.
40 Miura 2011; Anegawa 2011.
41 Miura 2011.
42 Japan Automobile Research Institute FC-EV Research Division 2011.
43 Martinez 2011.
44 Subaru 2008a.
45 Ghosn 2005; Ghosn 2010.

46 Economist 1999.
47 Ghosn 2010.
48 Ibid.
49 Ibid.
50 Toba 2011.
51 Nissan Motor Company 2012.
52 Ohga 2013.
53 Nissan Motor Company 2011; Ministry of Economy, Trade and Industry.
54 Paine 2011.

11 I'll Be Back: California Returns

1 Coifman 2002.
2 Sperling 2011.
3 Michels 2005.
4 Michels 2005; Environmental Defense Fund 2009; Hakim 2004.
5 Pawa 2007.
6 United States Government Accountability Office 2009.
7 Schwarzenegger and Brown 2007.
8 Musk 2011.
9 Tesla website.

12 Challenging the Big Green Monster

1 Mitchell 2009.
2 Lutz 2011.
3 Carter 2003.
4 Taylor 2006.
5 Yates 2003.
6 U.S. Department of Energy Alternative Fuels Data Center 2012.
7 Paine 2011.

13 "Scared Shitless": America's Industrial Implosion

1 Knee 2010.
2 McCain 2008.
3 Knee 2010.
4 Pratley 2008.
5 Woods and Baxter 2008.
6 Cole 2010.
7 Gold 2008.
8 Cole 2010.
9 Ibid.
10 Rattner 2010.
11 Levs 2008.
12 Cole 2010.

13 Ibid.
14 Ibid.
15 Mitchell 2009.
16 Rauch 2008.
17 Ibid.
18 Ibid.
19 Ibid.
20 U.S. Department of Transportation 2008.
21 Rauch 2008.

14 Dark Green: Money, Power, and the Stimulus Melee

1   Cole 2010.
2   Rattner 2010.
3   GAO Highlights 2009.
4   Ibid.
5   Gergen 2008.
6   Rattner 2010.
7   Reorganization Under Bankruptcy Code 2012.
8   Cole 2010.
9   Troubled Asset Relief Program 2009.
10 Marchionne 2014.
11 Cole 2010.
12 Yoshida 2012.
13 Stevenson-Wydler Technology Innovation Act of 1980.
14 Cole 2010.
15 Organizing for America 2008.
16 www.Recovery.gov 2012.
17 Doerr and Joy 2007.
18 Rusco 2012.
19 Ibid.
20 Tam 2009.
21 Bell 2012.
22 www.recovery.gov 2012; U.S. Department of Energy Loan Programs Office 2012.
23 Bell 2012; Real Clear Politics 2011.
24 Motavalli 2011b; Edmunds.
25 U.S. Department of Energy Loan Programs Office 2012.
26 White House, Office of the Press Secretary 2012.
27 www.Recovery.gov 2012.
28 Ibid.
29 Trudell 2012.
30 A123 Systems Stock Information 2012.
31 CBS Detroit 2012.
32 Bell 2012.
33 Ibid.

34 Rogers 2011.
35 Rusco 2012.
36 Yoshida 2012.
37 Ibid.
38 Ronen 2014.
39 EV Project Webpage 2012.
40 Ibid.
41 ECOtality 2012.
42 Minoru 2012.
43 Obama 2011.

15 Cataclysm: The Demons of Fukushima

1 Coast Guard, Japan 2011.
2 NHK News 2011.
3 Kadota 2012.
4 Ibid.
5 Ibid.
6 Fukushima Nuclear Accident Independent Investigation Commission 2012.
7 Thomson 2012.
8 Naitoh 2011.
9 Ohga 2013.
10 Nissan 2013.
11 Simms 2012.
12 Green Car Congress 2010.
13 Soble and Hook 2010.
14 Katz 2013.
15 Ibid.
16 Kishimoto 2010.
17 Hedrick 2010.
18 Davis 2012.
19 Risser 2012.

16 Lucky Eights: China's Olympic Scramble and Economic Noncrisis

1 Ministry of Science and Technology 2012.
2 Challen 2008.
3 Ibid.
4 Yoney 2008.
5 Foster 2008; Barboza 2009.
6 Letters and Visits Bureau of Changsha City 2008.
7 Mehndiratta 2011.
8 Cha and Fan 2008.
9 Michael 2009.
10 International Organization of Motor Vehicle Manufacturers 2012.
11 Xiao 2010a.

17 China's Crisis of Competence

1 Wang 2013.
2 Mehndiratta 2010.
3 General Motors 2009.
4 Ye 2011.
5 China National Offshore Oil Company 2007.
6 Chengyu 2011.
7 Google Finance 2012.
8 Kraemer 2010.
9 Chengyu 2011.
10 Tillemann-Dick 2012.
11 Qiu 2013.
12 Xiao 2011.
13 Chengyu 2011.
14 Agassi 2009.
15 Ibid.
16 Granoff 2014.
17 Diamond 2011; Ricketts 2010.
18 Ouyang 2013.
19 Ibid.
20 Tian 2010.
21 Ibid.
22 Ibid.
23 Ibid.
24 Ibid.
25 Ibid.
26 *Fortune* 2011.
27 Lai 2011.
28 Ibid.
29 Ibid.
30 Ibid.
31 Liao and Yergin 2010.
32 Ibid.
33 Ibid.
34 Ibid.
35 Ibid.
36 Niedermeyer 2009.
37 Liao and Yergin 2010.
38 Ibid.
39 Ibid.
40 Ibid.
41 Xinhua 2011.
42 Ibid.
43 Boekestyn et al. 2011.
44 BYD Auto 2011.
45 *Global Times* 2010.

46 Lampe-Onnerud 2011.
47 Slosson 2011.
48 Miao 2011.
49 Ibid.
50 IHS Automotive 2011.
51 Johnson and Sutton 2009.
52 Miao 2011.
53 Frank 2012.
54 Miao 2011.
55 Lindgren and Gapminder 2011.
56 Hong Kong Exchanges and Clearing Ltd. 2012.
57 Berkshire Hathaway 2008; Bloomberg TV 2012.
58 Frank 2012.
59 Rogin 2012.
60 Riley and Vance 2012.
61 Cole 2010.
62 Ibid.
63 Xiao Chengwei 2010a.
64 Ibid.

18 The Great Race

1 Ma 2011.
2 Ibid.
3 Yoshida 2012; Liao and Yergin 2010; Xiao Chengwei 2010a; Sandalow 2012.
4 Edgarton 2012.
5 Murray 2012.
6 Neil 2012.
7 Oliver 2009.
8 Tesla 2012; Burns 2012.
9 Caldwell 2013.
10 Loveday 2014; Ohnsman 2014; *China Monitor* 2012.
11 Gordon et al. 2012.
12 Rainey 2011.
13 Chen et al. 2013.

19 Afterword: The Last Lap

1 Sperling 2014.
2 Electric Power Research Institute 2013.
3 Ohga 2013.
4 Pentland 2013.
5 St. John 2014.
6 Woodford et al. 2012.
7 Halvorson 2013.
8 Weissman 2012.

9 Sivak 2013.
10 Center for Internet and Society 2014.
11 Hendricks et al. 2001.
12 Shoup 2004.
13 World Bank 2014.
14 *Economist* 2011.

ACKNOWLEDGMENTS

THE *GREAT RACE* is a book that was many years in the making and was supported by hundreds. I'm deeply grateful to all of these people and apologize in advance to those whom I have forgotten or did not have space to mention.

First, many thanks to the great team at Simon & Schuster—especially Thomas LeBien, who took a chance on a relatively unknown writer with an unconventional storyline and helped me refine the narrative. Brit Hvide acted as an able sherpa throughout, and Ben Loehnan and Amanda Lang, along with editors, copyeditors, layout artists, and many others, were a great help in getting *The Great Race* over the finish line.

I also want to thank my agent, Gail. I greatly admire her passion for and commitment to bringing big ideas to broad audiences. Almost as soon as we met, she kindly but unsparingly informed me that I needed to punch up my writing if I hoped to engage the public in this important conversation surrounding the future of transportation and energy, and that has made all the difference.

Throughout, there were two other people who put an enormous amount of thought, effort, and goodwill into this project. The first was Dan Yergin. When I took a job working for him a number of years ago as a research assistant, I hit the jackpot. Dan's constant encouragement, feedback, and willingness to share a perspective that was different from my own made this work immeasurably richer and more nuanced. Dan has taught me a great deal, not only about energy, but more importantly about how to *think* about energy, markets, and innovation. He has been a great ally and friend. The second person who has provided editorial and all sorts of other support and feedback is my sister Liberty. She helped me polish my writing and ideas, and generally steered me in the right direction.

The New America Foundation has been a stimulating and supportive home over the past few months. I am particularly grateful to Peter Bergen, who has been a great professor, mentor, and friend throughout the years. I'm also grateful to Anne-Marie Slaughter, Fuzz Hogan, and Andres Martinez for the invitation to join New America. Becky Schafer and Kirsten Berg, along with Amanda Gains, John Williams, Elizabeth Weingarten, Ari Rattner, and others too numerous to mention, have eased the transition from government into the NGO world. Finally, Lisa Margonelli generously shared her interviews with Wan Gang. I now understand why Peter says New America is "the best place he's ever worked in his life."

For two years before coming to New America, I worked for the Obama administration at the Department of Energy. There are dozens of people from that period to whom I'm very grateful. In particular I want to thank David Sandalow, who hired me as an advisor when he was acting as the undersecretary for energy; Secretary Ernest Moniz for his interest in and support of my various undertakings at DOE; Pat Davis, who taught me so much about the technology and policy of the U.S. automotive sector; Sunita Satyapal (who always reminds me that fuels cells are stacked for success!); and Ken Alston, who was a great friend and tutor on clean energy finance.

IHS allowed me access to their data for my Ph.D. dissertation, which served as a foundational document for this book. Ellen Perkins, Freda Amar, Susan Ruth, and Jeff Meyer all helped this process along in diverse ways. The IHS Beijing office (in particular KF Yan and Xiaolu Wang) and the folks at IHS Automotive were helpful in providing everything from human connections to industry insight and office space.

At Johns Hopkins School of Advanced International Studies (SAIS), I would like to thank Kent Calder, who supported my scholarship as both the head of Japan Studies at SAIS and my dissertation advisor at the Reischauer Center. David Lampton provided feedback that was timely and probing and was supportive throughout. I also want to thank Carla Freeman and the SAIS deans.

The California Air Resource Board ends up being one of the heroes of my narrative, and they were also central to my research. In particular, Daniel Sperling—who also serves as head of the Institute for Transportation Studies at UC Davis—has been an anchor and champion. He laid the foundations for this study through his ample scholarship and personal role in promoting EVs through academic analysis, policy, and regulation.

I would be remiss if I did not recognize my collaborators at IRIS Engines, who filled me with respect and admiration for the technological competence, sophistication, and artistry of the American automotive industry. First and foremost among these was my younger brother Corban, who was my sidekick, then partner in crime. Eric Ridenour, who, despite his deep appreciation for the structural rigidities of the automotive world, helped us try to change it. As the former chief operating officer of DaimlerChrysler and current president and CEO of UQM—a company that manufactures electric motor systems for EVs—Eric also provided insight into CARB's close and often cantankerous relationship with Detroit. Simon Pitts, former director of the Ford Focus vehicle line and the Ford-MIT Alliance, whose love of automotive heritage did not interfere with his hunger for shaping the future. Brent Johnson was a source of immense technical competence, business, and emotional support throughout, as was Rob Lachenauer, who has applied his exquisitely organized mind to everything from drivetrains to exhaust aftertreatments to artificial bone grafts.

Dozens of executives from auto companies in China, Japan, and the United States helped shape my understanding of the dance between corporations, nations, and regulators and how they clash and cooperate in what I call The Great Race.

Koji Takebe, a former vice president at Mitsubishi Motors Corporation (MMC) opened up the doors to the groundbreaking work of MMC and its affiliated EV joint ventures in developing the Mitsubishi i—the world's first mass-production electric car. Mr. Takebe arranged dozens of interviews with key actors in the design, development, manufacture, and deployment of the "i"; facilitated factory tours and test drives; and shared his own rich insights into the bureaucratic politics and planning that undergird Japan's mighty automotive industry. At Nissan, Ryuichi Toba and Kiho Ohga met with me on numerous occasions and went out of their way to grant me access to the company's manufacturing facilities and people. Frank Liao, from the Beijing Electric Vehicle Company, shared his textured analysis of the evolution of China's automotive policy and the political forces shaping China's New Energy Vehicles program. At General Motors in Shanghai, Keith Cole, GM's global vice president for governmental affairs, provided insight into the company's relationship with the Chinese government and piercing analysis of the dynamics between General Motors and Washington during critical junctures of the federal government's decision to rescue America's auto industry in 2008 and 2009. In addition to these, dozens of other representatives from industry engaged me in formal and informal interviews. I am especially grateful to the teams at Toyota, GM, Ford, Chrysler, BYD, Mitsubishi, Honda, and CODA—all of whom expended significant time and effort on my behalf.

As for government organizations, in China, Cheng Xiaowei—one of the strategists behind China's 863 Program on EV technology—sat with me for hours, on multiple occasions, to explain his country's goals, processes, and motivations for developing the EV. Many representatives from China's State Owned Enterprises (SOEs), such as the State Grid Corporation and China National Offshore Oil Company—both key players in China's push toward electrification—including individuals from the offices of the state-owned Assets Supervisory and Administration Commission's (SASAC) secretive state-owned Enterprise Electric Vehicle Industry Alliance (SEVIA), took time out of their schedules to be interviewed. A series of interviews was also held with the Beijing Traffic Department, which contends with the realities of a million new cars flooding the streets of China's capital every year.

Current and former representatives of METI and its associated agencies dedicated tens of hours to discussing the evolution and practical points of the ministry's economic planning, its relations with automakers, and its role in the national economy.

Robbie Diamond, Ron Minsk, Sam Ori, and the entire team at the Electrification Coalition were a remarkable font of ideas and introduced me to Shomik Mehndiratta of the World Bank, who willingly shared both his rich insights and expansive network within China's EV world.

Some friends have been particularly helpful and supportive along the way. Martin, Carter, Su, Julie, Michael, Eurry, and Luna have all read my manuscripts and provided feedback that shaped the ultimate work in important ways.

Finally, there is my family. My ten brilliant brothers and sisters were all involved in shaping this narrative and supporting my writing. Charity is a keen analyst of ideas, and time and again she pushed my writing and presentation to the next level. As she has frequently commented, "We make a good team." Charity has been and always will be an inspiration, and I look forward to her forthcoming Simon & Schuster book, which is sure to be a great read. Our family's creative genius, Glorianna, is one of my favorite people and has done a brilliant job on photo sections and graphics. Shiloh, Mercina, Zenith, Kimber (plus Hettie, Willa, and Phin), and Dulcia have all helped out along the way. Our aunt Susie and uncle Eric have been guardian angels over the decades, and that was certainly true over the course of this process.

My grandmother and grandfather Tom and Annette Lantos instilled in all of us a passion for international relations. They taught us that our role in life was public service, and my interest in energy and the environment is really an extension of that drive to better the world. And my grandmother Nancy Dick showed us from a young age that a widowed mother of three could do anything she set her mind to.

Finally, I would like to thank my mother, who blessed us with unconventional life experiences, education, and ten raucous siblings, and my father, Timber Dick, who loved to drive and was ever present with me throughout this project—even after his passing. He was always at the forefront of technology and innovation and inspired in me an appreciation and love for invention that was but a faint echo of the creative symphony that animated his own life. We miss him.

Undoubtedly, I have forgotten or failed to mention others who richly deserve to be recognized. Please pardon the oversight.

Finally, a note on the book's content, any mistakes are the responsibility of the author alone. But much of the credit for *The Great Race* truly goes to the aforementioned network of friends, family, and supporters who helped bring this to fruition.

INDEX

PHOTO CREDITS

1. US Library of Congress. Ford First and Ten Millionth, 1924. http://www.loc
   .gov/pictures/item/det1994022920/PP/.
2. G. T. Sun Co. The devastated urban district immediately following the
   earthquake disaster, 1923. http://www.loc.gov/pictures/collection/pan/item
   /2007664607/.
3. Toyota Motor Co. Three Generations of Toyota.
4. Toyota Motor Co. First Export of Army Truck to China, 1936.
5. Palmer, Alfred T. Tank manufacture (Chrysler). This is the final check, before,
   this 400 horsepower Wright Whirlwind engine is installed, not in a plane but
   in one of the army's huge M-3 tanks. The mechanics are employed at the Chrysler tank arsenal, on the outskirts of Detroit, where 10,000 men are engaged in
   the production of these twenty-eight ton monsters, between 1940–1946.
6. Library and Archives Canada. Propaganda Poster WWII Canada Our Answer
   All-Out Production.
7. Department of Defense. Atomic Bomb (Nagasaki). http://www.af.mil/News
   /Photos.aspx?igphoto=2000446370.
8. Faillace, Lt. Gaetano. Emperor Hirohito and General MacArthur, at their first
   meeting, at the U.S. Embassy, Tokyo, 27 September, 1945. http://memory.loc
   .gov/service/pnp/cph/3c10000/3c11000/3c11000/3c11093v.jpg.
10. Toyota Motor Co. Taichi Ohno.
11. Wikipedia. Chrysler Imperial, 1955. http://en.wikipedia.org/wiki/Imperial
    _(automobile)#mediaviewer/File:Chrysler_Imperial_car-1955.JPG.
12. Los Angeles Times photographic archive, UCLA Library. Highland Park Opti-
    mist Club wearing smog-gas masks at banquet, Los Angeles, Calif., circa 1954.
13. McClanahan, James. Arie Haagen-Smit with lab equipment, 1961.
14. Honda Motor Co. Soichiro Honda with Engine.
15. Honda Motor Co. Isle of Man Champions, 1961.
16. Toyota Motor Co. Eiji Toyoda.
17. Toyota Motor Co. California Headquarters, 1957.
18. Department of Energy. Japan, #1, Mihama. Construction of Kansai Elec. Co.
    345MW Westinghouse Pwr. at Mihama, Japan. c. 1967.
19. Triest, Glenn. Stanford R. Ovishinsky, 2005.
20. Kennerly, David Hume. President and Mrs. Ford, Vice Premier Deng Xiao
    Ping, and Deng's interpreter have a cordial chat during an informal meeting
    in Peking, China, 1975. (http://www.fordlibrarymuseum.gov/images/avproj
    /pop-ups/A7598-20A.html).

21. California Air Resource Board. Governor Jerry Brown, 1975.
22. California Air Resource Board. Mary Nichols, 1975.
23. Unknown. Yoshitoshi Sakurai and Ayrton Senna. With Permission from Yoshitoshi Sakurai.
24. Tschida, Tom. AeroVironment Chairman Paul MacCready shows a cross section of the AeroVironment/NASA Helios Prototype wing spar. Public domain.
25. Dshakes (Wikipedia), GM Sunraycer, 2009.
26. U.S. Department of Defense. Arnold and Bush, 2007.
27. Mario Roberto Duran Ortiz. Prius fleet operated by the New York City Department of Transportation, 2010.
28. Schaeffler AG. Prof. Dr. Wan Gang visited Schaeffler AG, 2011.
29. Plug In America. Piles of crushed GM EV1 electric cars.
30. Tokyo Power Electric Company. Takafumi Anegawa.
31. Mitsubishi. iMieve Water Testing.
32. Tillemann, Levi. Wada and His iMiev, 2010.
33. Mitsubishi. iMieve Cold Testing.
34. Jurvetson, Steve. Elon Musk Taking Questions, 2014.
35. Davd S. Bob Lutz and Donald Trump with the 2006 Cadillac DTS at the New York International Auto Show, 2005 (Flickr, Creative Commons).
36. Nissan. NISSAN GT-R 年モデル / NISSAN GT-R NISMO 表披露会, 2014.
37. C-Span. Government Assistance for U.S. Automakers Hearing, 2008 (screengrab).
38. C-Span. Government Assistance for U.S. Automakers Hearing, 2008 (screengrab).
39. White House Press Office. Barak Obama and Hu Jintao.
40. Tillemann, Levi. Sergio Marchionne at Brookings Institution, 2014.
41. Department of Energy. *Scientist*, 2011. https://www.flickr.com/photos /departmentofenergy/9452926290/.
42. Department of Energy. Secretary Steven Chu.
43. US Navy. SH-60B_helicopter_flies_over_Sendai.jpg, 2011. http://commons .wikimedia.org/wiki/File:SH-60B_helicopter_flies_over_Sendai.j.
44. 保守. Anti-Nuclear Power Plant Rally on 19 September 2011 at Meiji Shrine Outer Garden 03, 2011.
45. Nissan. Nissan Oppama Plant.
46. Ha'Eri, Bobak. Beijing smog comparison August 2005, 2005. http:// en.wikipedia.org/wiki/Pollution_in_China#mediaviewer/File:Beijing_smog _comparison_August_2005.png.
47. Peter23. Beijing national stadium, 2011. (http://en.wikipedia.org/wiki/Beijing _National_Stadium#mediaviewer/File:Beijing_national_stadium.jpg).
48. Voice of America. 2012 Anti-Japan demonstrations3, 2012.
49. Voice of America. 2012 Anti-Japan demonstrations4, 2012.
50. NASA, Elon Musk gives tour for President Barak Obama, 2010. http://www .nasa.gov/multimedia/imagegallery/obama_tour.html.
52. Segway, Inc. EN-V 800px-EN-V_Pride_(Jiao).jpg, 2010. https://www.flickr .com/photos/24641875@N07/4459354228/in/set-72157623526768197/.